# THE FINAL YEARS OF BRITISH HONG KONG

# The Final Years of British Hong Kong

## The Discourse of Colonial Withdrawal

John Flowerdew

*Associate Professor*
*English Department*
*City University of Hong Kong*

Published in Great Britain by
**MACMILLAN PRESS LTD**
Houndmills, Basingstoke, Hampshire RG21 6XS and London
Companies and representatives throughout the world

First edition 1998
Reprinted 1998

A catalogue record for this book is available from the British Library.

ISBN 0–333–68312–9 hardcover
ISBN 0–333–68313–7 paperback

Published in the United States of America by
**ST. MARTIN'S PRESS, INC.,**
Scholarly and Reference Division,
175 Fifth Avenue, New York, N.Y. 10010

ISBN 0–312–17775–5 clothbound

Library of Congress Cataloging-in-Publication Data
Flowerdew, John, 1951–
The final years of British Hong Kong : the discourse of colonial
withdrawal / John Flowerdew.
    p.   cm.
Includes bibliographical references and index.
ISBN 0–312–17775–5
1. Hong Kong—History—Transfer of sovereignty to China, 1997.
2. Hong Kong—Politics and government.   I. Title.
DS796.H757F58 1997
951.2505—dc21                                          97–27124
                                                              CIP

This book is printed on paper suitable for recycling and made from fully managed and
sustained forest sources.

10   9   8   7   6   5   4   3   2   1
07   06   05   04   03   02   01   00   99   98

Printed in Hong Kong

To Lynne, Rupert and Humphrey

# Contents

# Acknowledgements

A lot of people have helped me in the preparation of this book. I would particularly like to record my thanks to the following: Eddie Leung, Clara Mak, Joey Wong, and Jacqueline Young, who worked as research or student assistants at various stages of the project; Barry Lowe, Norman Flynn, and Jonathan Zhu, who took great trouble in reading an earlier draft of the manuscript and giving me very useful feedback; and especially Connie Ng, who worked with me in the last year of what was a five-year project, putting in overtime in helping me with the final stages of the preparation of the manuscript. Thanks also to Daniel Reeves.

I am also very grateful to those people who gave up their valuable time to be interviewed for the book: Hong Kong Governor, Chris Patten, Governor's Spokesperson, Kerry McGlynn, and Governor's Personal Adviser, Edward Llewelyn.

Finally, I would like to thank my family, for putting up with my long hours spent on the book, when we might have been doing other things.

# List of Acronyms

| | |
|---|---|
| ADPL | Association for Democracy and People's Livelihood |
| BPG | Business and Professional Group of the Basic Law Consultative Committee |
| BPF | Business and Professionals Federation |
| BLCC | Basic Law Consultative Committee |
| BLDC | Basic Law Drafting Committee |
| CCP | Chinese Communist Party |
| CFA | Court of Final Appeal |
| CPPCC | Chinese People's Political Consultative Conference |
| CT9 | Container Terminal 9 |
| DAB | Democratic Alliance for the Betterment of Hong Kong |
| Exco | Executive Council |
| GIS | Government Information Services |
| ICAC | Independent Commission Against Corruption |
| ISD | Information Services Department |
| JLG | Joint Liaison Group |
| KCR | Kowloon Canton Railway |
| Legco | Legislative Council |
| MFN | Most Favoured Nation |
| MTR | Mass Transit Railway |
| NCNA | Xinhua (New China News Agency) |
| NPC | National People's Congress |
| OMELCO | Office of the Members of the Legislative and Executive Councils |
| PC | Preparatory Committee |
| PLA | People's Liberation Army |
| PRC | People's Republic of China |
| PWC | Preliminary Working Committee |
| RTHK | Radio Television Hong Kong |
| SAR | Special Administrative Region |
| SEZ | Special Economic Zone |
| UDHK | United Democrats of Hong Kong |

# Introduction

In 1793, the British Government sent an emissary, Lord Macartney, to Beijing, with a view to establishing diplomatic and trade relations with the Middle Kingdom, as China was known at that time. Macartney refused to perform the kow-tow, or ritual prostration, which all emissaries were required to carry out before the Emperor, and the mission ended in failure.

In 1984, Britain and China had a more successful diplomatic encounter in Beijing, and representatives of the two countries entered into an agreement that, in 1997, Britain would return the colony of Hong Kong, 'an accident left over from history', according to the Chinese leader, Deng Xiaoping, to China. This agreement, or Joint Declaration, was widely hailed as a model of international co-operation, peacefully negotiated by two countries with radically different histories, cultures, ideologies and political systems.

In 1992, Britain sent another emissary, Chris Patten, as Hong Kong Governor, to oversee the last five years of British Hong Kong, before it finally became a part of China. Like Macartney, Patten refused to kow-tow to China's rulers, not in the physical sense, but in refusing to co-operate with China's preparations for taking over Hong Kong. Under the terms of the Joint Declaration, Hong Kong had been offered a high degree of autonomy and the continuation of its capitalist way of life for fifty years. This had been negotiated according to Deng's slogan: 'one country two systems'. Patten judged that China was trying to erode Hong Kong's freedom agreed in the Joint Declaration. He also wanted Britain to withdraw with honour and dignity from the last significant colony of what had once been the most powerful empire the world had ever seen. He therefore embarked upon a course of confrontation, a policy which, according to some, was a disastrous failure and, to others, a valiant attempt to preserve those values for which the British Empire was renowned: free trade, freedom of the individual, the rule of law, and democracy.

This book describes the final years of British Hong Kong, with a special emphasis on Patten's attempts to, as he put it, stand up for Hong Kong, and the accompanying clash of cultures and ideologies. Before turning to the Patten era, however, **Part I** of the book describes the development of Hong Kong under British rule from its very beginning. The main focus of the book, nevertheless, is **Part II**, which deals with the final period, the period during which Chris Patten was the last governor.

*  *  *

The most famous view of Hong Kong is its spectacular waterfront skyline of giant gleaming office towers set against the backdrop of the mountain known as The Peak. The view is said to rival, if not surpass, that of Manhattan. The physical parallel is not the only one commonly made with Manhattan. Because of its fabulous wealth, Hong Kong is also regularly touted as the Manhattan of Asia from the economic point of view. It is the gateway to the outside world for China's burgeoning economy, which, since 1979 and Deng Xiaoping's 'open door' policy to the outside world, has become increasingly market- and internationally-oriented. It is also a regional hub for international companies wishing to do business with China and the rest of East Asia.

With its tiny population of only 6.3 million squeezed into an area of just 412 square miles, Hong Kong is the world's eighth largest trading nation, is the world's busiest container port, has the world's sixth largest stock market, is the fifth largest banking centre in terms of the volume of external banking transactions, has an average per capita income among the top ten in the world, and has the world's most expensive real estate. Hong Kong also has the largest number of Rolls Royce cars per capita and the site of its new airport, Chek Lap Kok, is the largest civil engineering project in the world. Over the last two decades, the Hong Kong economy has quadrupled in size. Very low unemployment rates are the envy of the employment and finance ministers of the developed countries. Matching this economic dynamism and sophistication, Hong Kong has 59 daily newspapers and 675 periodicals, it has four terrestrial television channels, is served by the Star satellite television network and has a number of cable television operators. Hong Kong has one of the highest usage rates per capita of population of mobile telephones. Hong Kong is also a healthy society, with a life-expectancy of 81 years for women and 75 for men.[1]

Hong Kong people are very materialistic. They have a reputation for hard work and many of them put in long hours. Saturday is still a half working day for most people. Among the most popular leisure activities are shopping, eating and gambling on horse races. Any Saturday or Sunday sees Hong Kong's plethora of modernistic indoor shopping malls packed with families, couples and individuals jostling each other to get a better look at the goods on display. Popular articles are designer fashions, from the up-market European houses, such as Versace, St Laurent, Chanel, and Gucci, many of which have several outlets in Hong Kong, to the cut-price local chains, such as Giordano, Bossini and Guess. Electronic goods are also very popular. The variety of restaurants in Hong Kong is outstanding, from outdoor noodle stalls and McDonald's to exclusive five star Chinese and European restaurants. Sea-food is particularly popular, but just about any food, from any country, can be found, and Hong Kong people, especially the younger, educated class, love to try other Asian and European cuisines. Hong Kong people also love to gamble. On horse-racing days, the two tracks, one on Hong Kong Island and the other in the New Territories, are packed with punters. Live coverage is provided on radio and television and at off-course betting centres. The sums bet at any one meeting are phenomenal.

* * *

It is difficult for outsiders to understand how Hong Kong, a spectacular testimony to capitalist enterprise, can be reintegrated as a part of the Peoples' Republic of China. In order to start to comprehend how such a state of affairs can come about, it is necessary to look back on Hong Kong's history. A historical perspective explains, on the one hand, why China has never accepted British sovereignty over Hong Kong, although it has suited it, in practice, to tolerate it until 1997. On the other hand, it explains how Hong Kong transformed itself from what British Foreign Secretary Lord Palmerston called 'a barren island with hardly a house on it', at the time of its initial seizure by Britain in 1841, to its present-day status as a sophisticated capitalist metropolis. This historical perspective provides the rationale for Part I of the book.

The following is a brief synopsis.

## PART I

**Chapter 1** describes how Hong Kong came to be a British colony and imperialist activity conducted by Britain and other world powers since the 1840s. China's history since the arrival of the British has been a turbulent one, greatly affected by the intervention of outside forces. It is important to take this into account, in order to understand China's attitude over Hong Kong.

**Chapter 2** describes the period from the establishment of Hong Kong as a British colony, in 1841, until the beginning of Sino-British discussions over the question of sovereignty, in the early 1980s. Hong Kong was acquired by Britain as a place from which to conduct trade with China. The chapter describes the early commercial development of the territory and the sojourner mentality of its residents, most of whom went to the colony on a temporary basis to make their fortunes or as a place of refuge. Following World War II, plans were drawn up to institute constitutional reform and introduce democracy to the territory, but were later dropped. During this period, there were massive influxes of people from China and the emphasis was on social and economic development, both of which, most commentators agree, were successful, the latter spectacularly so. By 1979, concern developed over the 99 year lease which China held over the New Territories, an area which took up 92 per cent of the total area of Hong Kong, and which was due to expire in 1997. The issue was broached by the Hong Kong Governor with the Chinese leader, Deng Xiaoping. Initially the Chinese were unprepared, but, by 1982, they began to reveal their plans for the recovery of the whole of the territory.

Beginning with British Prime Minister Margaret Thatcher's visit to Beijing, in 1982, **Chapter 3** describes the lengthy and difficult negotiations which resulted in the Joint Declaration of 1984, the document which agreed that Britain would return Hong Kong to China, but as a Special Administrative Region (SAR) of that country, with a high degree of autonomy and guarantees concerning the preservation of its way of life as a capitalist entity, governed by the rule of law and enjoying many of the freedoms enjoyed by the capitalist democracies.

**Chapter 4** describes British attempts to introduce an element of democracy into the Hong Kong system, in accordance with provisions in the Joint Declaration, which foresaw gradually developing representative government for the territory under Chinese sovereignty. At the same time, China was drawing up the Basic Law, the mini-constitution which was to flesh out the general principles set out in the Joint Declaration. After initially suggesting fairly rapid development of representative arrangements, under Chinese pressure Britain soon moderated its plans and adopted a policy of converging with the more gradual arrangements which would be set out in the Basic Law being drafted by China.

**Chapter 5** describes how work on the Basic Law and constitutional arrangements was interrupted by events in Beijing, where pro-democracy demonstrations in Tiananmen Square were violently put down by the People's Liberation Army (PLA). Many in Hong Kong had supported the pro-democracy activists and the governments of the

Western world, including Britain, thought that the world's last great remaining Communist government might fall. Order having been re-established, Sino-British relations over Hong Kong resumed in an atmosphere of suspicion on the part of the Chinese of British motives and a concern by Britain to alleviate some of the worries created in the minds of the people of Hong Kong about their future rulers. Britain introduced a number of measures to restore confidence which antag-onised the Chinese side, but soon reverted to her policy of conver-gence with China's plans, and many felt that the colonial government was not doing enough to preserve the autonomy agreed for Hong Kong under the terms of the Joint Declaration.

## PART II

In 1992, the British Government decided to replace the then Gover-nor, Sir David Wilson, a career diplomat with many years experience of Hong Kong and China, with a politician, Chris Patten. There was a consensus in the British and Hong Kong Governments that what Hong Kong needed in the years leading up to the handover of sover-eignty to China, in 1997, was a politician of some standing who could provide leadership and manage a dignified withdrawal for Britain from its last major colony. As Chairman of the Conservative party, Patten had master-minded the election of the Tories, in 1992, to a further period of office under the leadership of his close friend and colleague John Major, as Prime Minister. In doing so, Patten lost his own parliamentary seat, preparing the way for him to accept the Hong Kong governorship, when it was offered to him by Major.

When Patten arrived in Hong Kong, there was a sea change in British policy. Under the previous governor, Wilson, Britain had engaged in what for many was a demeaning retreat, conniving in the erosion of the autonomy that had been negotiated for Hong Kong as a SAR of China, under the terms of the Joint Declaration. Wilson's style was to engage in behind-the-scenes diplomacy with China, con-sistently giving in, according to this view, to Chinese demands on electoral and judicial reform and budgetary matters. He insisted that the most important thing was a smooth transition leading up to the handover and convergence of British administration with China's blueprint for the territory, the Basic Law. Patten, on the other hand, came with a different approach. Where Wilson had stressed that his policies should conform to what China wanted, Patten made his constituency the people of Hong Kong. He acted more like an elected politician who depended on the votes of the people, declaring his openness and accountability. He was not afraid of confrontation with China if he considered this to be in the best interests of Hong Kong and was keen to argue and debate in public.

The second part of the book, which focuses on Patten's tenure as governor, places special emphasis on the rhetorical dimension of his governorship. Where Wilson had conducted behind-the-scenes diplomacy and was concerned with the practical arrangements that would be set in place before Britain's departure, Patten was also concerned with the ideology. He tried to convey to the Hong Kong people the ideological underpinnings of what he promoted as Britain's heritage to the future SAR. In so doing he at the same time prepared the way for an honourable British withdrawal.

By using his rhetorical skills, Patten, who had been closely associated with Margaret Thatcher in his earlier career, attempted to bring about a change in the basic values and assumptions underlying public discourse in Hong Kong. Where Wilson, a sinologist, was willing to accommodate to values held by the Chinese Communist Government and had emphasised the 'one country' dimension of Deng Xiaoping's famous 'one country two systems' formula for Hong Kong's return to Chinese sovereignty, Patten emphasised the 'two systems' dimension of the formula, repeatedly proclaiming what he saw as the particular values which made Hong Kong different from the People's Republic. For Patten, these values were a belief in the free market economy, individual freedom, the rule of law and democracy. While Patten did not stress the fact, these attributes were fundamental to Western liberalism and coincided with his own Conservative party political philosophy. Patten also glossed over the fact that during the colonial era these ideals had only partially been applied to Hong Kong.

**Chapter 6** describes Patten's arrival in Hong Kong, his style, and the effect he had on the community and China.

**Chapter 7** describes the political and social welfare reform programme that Patten proposed at the beginning of his governorship, as a way of taking the initiative away from China in preparing for Hong Kong's future, and the ensuing confrontation with China and the pro-Beijing camp in Hong Kong.

**Chapter 8** describes the continuing confrontation, the abortive 17 rounds of talks to try to reach a compromise with China on the political reform programme, and China's plans to set up a 'second stove', or shadow government, leading up to the handover and beyond.

**Chapter 9** deals with the 1995 elections, which saw victories for the pro-democracy parties; it considers to what extent Patten could be considered a 'one-issue' or 'lame duck' governor; and it describes China's continuing plans for the second stove and a provisional legislature to dismantle Patten's reforms.

**Chapter 10** describes arguments between Britain and China over the handover ceremony in 1997 and Britain's preoccupation with withdrawal with honour. It examines arguments over freedom of speech and China's arrangements for the provisional legislature and appointment of the future Chief Executive.

**Chapter 11**, which is more analytical than the other chapters of the book, examines Patten's rhetoric and how he used it to promote his Western liberal ideology. In his vigorous promotion of this ideology, Patten raises some important questions for those concerned with Asian (and indeed World) affairs. These include the question of Asian versus Western values; the relation between free market economics, the rule of law and democracy; and cross-cultural political communication and negotiating styles.

The final chapter, **Chapter 12**, further details Patten's preoccupation with an honourable withdrawal; it evaluates the pros and cons of Britain's two approaches to the transfer of sovereignty, that of convergence, as espoused by the Foreign Office sinologists, and that of confrontation, as employed by Patten; and it considers the prospects for Hong Kong, following the change of sovereignty. The conclusion is that Patten's governorship was primarily rhetorical; the reforms he introduced will be dismantled by China. But by attempting last-minute democratisation, Britain is able to say that it withdrew with honour. The reforms, which China claims are against what was agreed by Britain and China, provided a pretext for China to introduce a provisional legislature (not provided for in the Joint Declaration or Basic Law) of its own choosing, allowing it to prepare a constitutional system which will permit it to exert considerable control over Hong Kong (as did the British, during the colonial era), within the framework of 'one country two systems'. While it is impossible to predict the future, it is quite possible that Hong Kong will develop a polity similar to those already existing in other Southeast Asian countries, where legitimacy is sought by means of material prosperity provided by a ruling business-oriented elite, rather than by universal suffrage and a high level of 'grass-roots' participation.

\* \* \*

In terms of methodology, the approach of the book is inter-disciplinary, using, in Part I, traditional historical analysis and content analysis of contemporary media reports and commentary, and, in Part II, in addition to media content analysis, analysis of Patten's speeches, interviews, writings, and other public pronouncements, personal interviews with Patten, his spokesperson and his personal adviser, and direct observation of Legislative Council (Legco) sessions, public meetings and other events in which Patten participated.

Something needs to be said about the sub-title, 'The Discourse of Colonial Withdrawal'. By discourse, I mean a domain of language use which is underpinned by a set of common presuppositions. Different social groups create different discourses, or ways of thinking and talking about the same issues. As the French philosopher, Michael Foucault, demonstrated, during one historical period (the middle ages), for example, the mad were thought of and talked about as both threatening and possessing an inner wisdom. During another period (the 20th century), however, madness came to be considered as an illness that needed to be treated.[2]

The British discourse over Hong Kong also developed over time. When Hong Kong was first seized by the British, their action was justified by a discourse which proclaimed the benefits of free trade, what Britain considered to be the universal right of free men to conduct business wherever in the world they saw fit, and the need for business and social behaviour to be regulated according to a rule of law applied equally to all. This discourse was confrontational, as it conflicted with a Chinese discourse which saw trade as a privilege bestowed by the Emperor to his tributary states and a hierarchical conception of law based on the obligations of the elite rather than the rights of the individual.

In modern times, after Britain agreed to return Hong Kong to China, the British discourse was initially conciliatory. Britain adapted its Hong Kong policy and statements about Hong Kong to fit in with China's future plans for the territory. This discourse was not confrontational. It will be referred to in this book as a discourse of 'convergence'. Later, however, with the appointment in 1992 of a new governor, the policy of convergence was reversed and a new discourse, with similarities, as will be seen, to the earlier colonialist one, was adopted. This discourse, because it often ran counter to China's plans for Hong Kong, will be referred to as a discourse of 'confrontation'.

The discourse of colonial withdrawal is therefore actually made up of more than one discourse. It incorporates the discourse of 'convergence' and the discourse of 'confrontation'. Two other discourses within this overall discourse of colonial withdrawal which receive attention in this book are Patten's discourse directed at the people of Hong Kong (as opposed to the Chinese Government), which has a number of characteristic features, and his discourse concerning the British legacy to Hong Kong (which will be dealt with in detail in Chapter 11). In addition, there is also the Chinese discourse on the recovery of Hong Kong. Given China's view that Hong Kong was given up to Britain under duress, this might be referred to as a discourse of 'national retribution'.

Discourses are realised, or instantiated, in language. The discourse of the final years of British Hong Kong, especially the period under Governor Patten, was highly rhetorical. The British Government and Governor Patten wanted Britain's withdrawal from its last significant colony to go down in history as an honourable one. Having agreed with China that Hong Kong would be given back, Britain had very little real power to affect the colony's future under Chinese sovereignty. What real power Britain lacked Patten sought to make up for with words. Considerable attention is paid in this book, especially in Part II, therefore, to Patten's use of language as the means of instantiation of his discourse and the tool for withdrawal with honour. An analysis of Patten's rhetoric is important in a number of ways. Rhetoric has the potential to make a politician's utterances more persuasive, on the one hand, and more memorable and likely to be reported in the media (and the history books), on the other. Patten has been praised for his powerful rhetoric and there is no doubt that he used it as an effective instrument in agenda setting and retaining the attention of the media. At the same time, however, an analysis of Patten's rhetoric may help to explain certain other features of his governorship. His use of metaphor, for example, shows up his ethnocentrism, and his use of humour and sarcasm are important considerations in interpreting his confrontation with China. The way he revelled in engaging in debate is also significant, in his promotion of democracy.

Some colleagues with whom I have discussed this book have been sceptical about the emphasis I place on language, arguing that Cantonese is the mother tongue of most Hong Kong people and therefore Patten's rhetoric will be lost on them, as they will listen to or read a Cantonese translation of his words. In support of my position, I would say, first, that not everything, by any means, is lost in translation. Second, Hong Kong people who do not speak English had the benefit of reports and evaluations of what Patten said through the

Chinese language media. Patten's annual policy speeches, for example, received a tremendous amount of coverage in the Chinese language Hong Kong press, reporting and evaluating his performance. Third, the educated elite group in Hong Kong is English-speaking.[3] As an elitist society, this is the main group to which official discourse is directed. Fourth, and more important, perhaps, from Patten's point of view, the last governor had a number of audiences in mind, not just the average Hong Kong person in the street, when he made any pronouncement. The international press, which would be listening to him or reading him in English, was one of his main audiences. Officials of the Chinese Government, who, if they dealt with Hong Kong, would have been selected on the basis of their command of English, made up another important audience. The writers of history books, who will be English-speaking for the most part, are another important audience. When interviewed for this book, Patten agreed that he had four main audiences: the Hong Kong press, the Chinese Government, the international press, and the British press. He also acknowledged that he was conscious that the history books would be studying what he said during his period as the last Hong Kong Governor.[4]

Colleagues have also questioned my emphasis on Patten's language, on the basis that his speeches might have been written by someone else. Even if this were the case, it is important to bear in mind that Patten was the mouthpiece of the British Government, he was not just speaking for himself, a point he was keen to make, when interviewed for this book.[5] Nevertheless, following interviews with Patten and his advisors, I can confidently say that those speeches (which, of course are only one part of Patten's discourse) cited in this book were written by Patten himself, a politician who takes pride in his rhetorical skill.

* * *

In spite of its theoretical dimension, I have tried to make the book accessible. Those readers who are put off by 'theory' may read the book for the 'story' which it tells, although they might want to omit Chapter 11, with its more theoretical discussion of Patten's discourse and ideology. Those readers who have no knowledge of Hong Kong should have little difficulty in following the book.

On the assumption that more readers would be likely to want to read a book about the final years of British Hong Kong near to the time of the actual handover rather than later, and taking into account the time it takes to edit and produce a book, I took the decision to submit the manuscript in early February 1997. I apologise to readers if subsequent events may have made anything I have said inaccurate. I am reasonably confident, however, that at the time of writing, what I wanted to say in this book will remain the same.

Finally, on Chinese transliteration, I have followed the modern 'pinyin' system, although where well-known historical names are used I have also given the older 'Wade-Giles' version.

# Part I

# 1 The Imperialist Background

During the 18th century, the ancient Chinese civilisation was held in high esteem by educated Britons.[1] Its porcelain, furniture and other artefacts were the source of admiration and widespread imitation. The interior of the Brighton Pavilion, an extravagant essay in *chinoiserie* built by John Nash for the Prince Regent, represents perhaps the most extreme example of such imitation. By the mid-19th century, however, views had changed and China came to be seen as an obstinate nation, refusing to open its doors to trade. By this time, the British Empire was reaching its apogee, its wealth built upon a powerful navy and unrestricted trade with both its official and unofficial empires. Only China, where trade was more or less restricted to the southern port of Guangzhou (Canton), refused to open its ports to British ships. For China, the Middle Kingdom, a country which considered itself superior to any other and self-sufficient, permission to trade was a special privilege bestowed on other countries by the Emperor. Within China, according to the Confucian social hierarchy, merchants were accorded a very low status, the lowest of four categories, beneath the warrior-administrators at the top, the peasants, or primary producers, next, and the artisans, or secondary producers, third. For the aristocrats who created this order, the economic value of merchants was dubious.[2] In Britain, the birth-place of Adam Smith, author of *The Wealth of Nations*, and the land of the 'merchant venturers' or 'merchant princes', trade was viewed as an essential source of a nation's prosperity and a universal right. Merchants were due a status equal to that of any other before the law.

Sino-British trade, in the 18th century, was very one-sided. The British people developed an insatiable thirst for tea, which, along with silk, was imported from China in large quantities. The Chinese, however, considered themselves self-sufficient and had little desire to import any of the manufactures which Britain was beginning to export so successfully to other parts of the world. The China trade was a considerable cost, therefore, to the British balance of payments, while the large amounts of silver coming into China as payment for the tea and silk were much welcomed by the Chinese Government. Towards the end of the 18th and, increasingly, into the 19th century, there was

3

one product for which the British did begin to find a market. This was opium, a substance which was produced in increasing quantities in British-controlled India. The opium trade was to lead to major misunderstandings between Britain and China and eventually to war.

The difficulties experienced by the two proud nations in communicating with each other were highlighted in two abortive missions by British emissaries to China, in 1793 and 1816, in attempts to establish diplomatic and trade relations. The failure of the first, which culminated in a refusal by its leader, Lord Macartney, a cultivated man who had successfully negotiated earlier with Catherine the Great of Russia, to perform the kow-tow, or ritual prostration, to the Chinese emperor, Qianlong, has been taken as a symbol of the difficulty the two nations had in coming to a harmonious relationship.[3] For Macartney, the representative of the British King, prostration in front of another nation's leader was inappropriate; the King and the Emperor should communicate on the basis of equality. For the Chinese, on the other hand, all foreigners were considered to be *yi*, meaning uncultured, but usually translated as 'barbarian'. Representatives of foreign countries were treated as tributaries, or supplicants. For this reason, Emperor Qianlong could not accept the British request to, as he put it in a letter carried back by Macartney to the British King, George III, 'send one of your nationals to stay at the Celestial Court to take care of your country's trade with China'. Such an idea was 'not in harmony with the state system of our dynasty and will definitely not be permitted.'[4] As to the British request for a small island from which they could conduct their trade with China under their own rule of law this too was totally out of the question, although it was an idea that was to be taken up again at a later date by the British.

The main motive for the second British mission to the Middle Kingdom, in 1816, this time led by Lord Amherst, was again trade and a desire for the Chinese to open up more ports to British ships. 'The causes... which have rendered a mission from this country expedient are the insolent, capricious, vexatious procedures... by which they [Chinese Government officials] have obstructed trade.', according to the East Indian Company, which sponsored Amherst's expedition.[5] This mission was again unsuccessful.

'The insolent, capricious, vexatious procedures' imposed on British trade referred to above were as follows. Those British and other European merchants who were allowed to trade with China were established at Guangzhou, but were subject to many restrictions. They were only allowed to remain in Guangzhou during the trading season, from October to May, and were not permitted to go outside a small area set aside for Europeans, where their 'factories' or warehouses were situated, on the river to the south-west of the city; women were not allowed; neither were firearms; Europeans were prohibited from learning Chinese; in principle, Chinese servants were not allowed. On the Chinese side, trade was controlled by a monopoly of merchants, called the *Co-Hong*, who owned the factories used by the Europeans. The *Co-Hong* were viewed as a source of revenue for the Chinese Government and thus needed to levy various taxes and charges on the Europeans, who were allowed to trade with no others. Communication with the local Mandarins, or government officials, had to be conducted through petitions sent through the *Co-Hong*. These various restrictions, however, were not enforced strictly – for example, the regulation regarding the employment of Chinese servants was quite openly flouted – but were rather available as and when the Chinese wanted to put pressure on the Europeans. This inconsistency was galling for the British, who came from a society which prided itself on the importance of the impartial application of the rule of law.

Until 1833, trade with China, on the British side, was conducted by a monopoly held by the Honourable East India Company. However, the Company increasingly found its business being taken away by unlicensed traders, many of whom passed themselves off as honorary consuls of other countries, thereby putting themselves beyond its control. Many of these illicit merchants dealt increasingly in opium, a product which the Company was not at liberty to deal with in China, but which it produced in large quantities in India. In order to dispose of this opium, the Company had no other option but to allow it to be sold by the private merchants. By 1833, largely due to pressure from merchants who had been based at Guangzhou and manufacturers in Britain who wanted to open up the China market, the monopoly was officially broken by the British Government. Justifying a monopoly of any kind was difficult at that time, when free trade (as it still is today) was the predominant theory of political economy. As the Tory *Quarterly Review* reported: 'From the moment, indeed, that the "FREETRADE mania" became the order of the day, the China monopoly received its death-blow.'[6]

The East India Company monopoly having been broken, more and more merchants began to participate in the China trade, through the factories in Guangzhou. Pre-eminent among the merchant houses, or *hongs*, which benefited from the dissolution of the monopoly were those of Thomas Dent and Jardine-Matheson, the latter company remaining to this day an important player in the Hong Kong economy. Opium was a growing part of the trade of most of these *hongs*. Produced in British India, the drug was shipped through Guangzhou, although, from the 1820s, most of the trade, which was in theory illegal, was conducted at Lintin island in the Zhujiang (Pearl River) Estuary, off Guangzhou.

China had issued various edicts during the 18th century prohibiting the smoking of opium and, in 1799, a law was introduced forbidding its importation. For various reasons, however, the trade continued to flourish. First, the disreputable European merchants were willing to take considerable risks, given the large profits which were to be made. Second, China did not have the ability to enforce the ban. There was no efficient customs service, local officials were corrupt, and the fast smuggling boats were armed. On the British side, the opium produced considerable revenue for the government in Calcutta and the drug was not illegal in Britain. One of the leading importers of opium at Guangzhou, William Jardine, of Jardine-Matheson, attributed any blame for the trade in the drug to the Chinese: 'We are not smugglers, gentlemen! It is the Chinese Government, the Chinese officers who smuggle, and who connive at ... smuggling; not we!' Because the trade was carried on outside British jurisdiction, the British argued that they were unable to take legal action to stop it, a point which the Chinese, who were unfamiliar with the British notion of a judicial system independent of the government, found difficult to comprehend. The Chinese periodically made token attempts to curb the trade, but the amounts of opium entering China continued to increase throughout the 1820s. The balance of trade had already been moving to Britain's advantage, with the increase in illicit traders outside the East India Company monopoly. Once the monopoly was broken, the balance swung firmly in Britain's favour. Where, in the past, there had been a net inflow of silver to China, to pay for tea and silk, now silver flowed out, to pay for opium.

Once the East India Company's monopoly had been revoked the question arose as to who was to regulate and represent the European merchants in Guangzhou. The merchants wanted someone who could develop business relations with the Chinese. 'We must have a commercial code with these celestial barbarians ... We have the right to demand an equitable commercial treaty' wrote William Jardine. The British Government, with Lord Palmerston as Foreign Secretary, created a new position, Superintendent of Trade, appointing Lord Napier to be its first incumbent.[7] The brief of the new Superintendent was conciliatory; he was not to coerce the Chinese into further opening up their markets as the Guangzhou merchants wanted. His instructions were worded in terms which made it clear that he was to observe a high level of sensitivity to Chinese conventions and feelings. In his letter of instructions from Palmerston, Napier was told that he should refrain from 'all such conduct, language and demeanour as might needlessly excite jealousy and distrust' and to emphasis to the merchants at Guangzhou 'the duty of conforming to the laws and usage of the Chinese Empire.'[8] In spite of this very conciliatory approach, Palmerston's instructions contained one fatal sentence which was to contribute to the disaster that Napier's mission became: 'Your Lordship will announce your arrival at Guangzhou by letter to the Viceroy', this sentence stated.[9] Such a course of action might have seemed normal courtesy, but it infringed Chinese protocol. As a visitor to China, Napier had to be treated as either a tributary, as Macartney and Amherst had been, in which case he would proceed to Beijing, or as a merchant, in which case his destination could only be Guangzhou, after acquiring the necessary permission. In the latter case he would be required to communicate through the Hoppo, the head of the South Sea Customs, in the form of a petition, and not directly with the Viceroy.

While the breach of protocol embodied in the letter directly addressed to the Viceroy could be put down to the fact that Napier was following a specific instruction from Palmerston, some of his other actions betrayed a disregard for the overall emphasis Palmerston had put on guarding against damaging Chinese sensitivities. On arrival in Macau, Napier wasted no time in proceeding directly to Guangzhou, when protocol demanded that he should have first informed the Hoppo at Guangzhou of his arrival, and the latter would in turn have petitioned the Viceroy to allow him right of entry. The Viceroy's indignation and perplexity at Napier's affront to national dignity is evident in a letter from him to the Emperor: 'Whether the foreign chief Napier has any official title we are not in a position to find out. Even if he is an official of his country, he cannot claim equality with an important guardian of the territory of the Celestial Dynasty. This is a matter of national prestige . . . although the English barbarians are beyond the bounds of civilisation, yet having come to the inner country to trade, they should immediately give implicit obedience to the established laws. If even England has laws, how much more the Celestial Empire.' Nevertheless, the Viceroy was willing to give Napier the benefit of the doubt, stating that ' . . . in tender consideration of his being a newcomer strict investigation will not be made'.[10] Such consideration was wasted on Napier, however. When sent representatives by the Viceroy, he reprimanded them for being late, for thereby committing 'an insult to His Britannic Majesty', and threatened that Britain would be prepared to go to war, if necessary, if it did not have its way. To back up his threat, in a very dangerous operation, which came to be referred to as the Battle of the Bogue, Napier had two British frigates brought up the Zhujiang (Pearl River), at the cost of a number of casualties from Chinese fortress-based guns.

The response of the Viceroy to this act of aggression was quite simply to suspend all trade, an action which was obviously unpopular with the European merchants, especially those who were not British, and to blockade Napier at Guangzhou, by laying barriers across the river. Within a short time, Napier had no choice but to ask for permission to return to Macau, under Chinese guard, where he shortly died of a fever. He had ignored his instructions for dealing with the Chinese and had violated established forms of communication and behaviour. The Chinese, on the other hand, while doing nothing to relieve the frustration of British merchants, had respected the appropriate protocol in every respect.

In spite of the difficult relations between the British merchants and the Chinese authorities, the illegal trade in opium continued to flourish. In response to this deteriorating situation, the Chinese Emperor decided to take action and, in 1839, he appointed Lin Zexu as his special commissioner, to stamp out the opium trade in Guangzhou. On his arrival, Lin took the British by surprise, ordering them to hand over all the opium in their possession and to sign an undertaking to the effect that no more of the drug would be imported in future, subject to the death penalty. In addition, he ordered that the 16 most notorious drug smugglers be handed over as hostages and he put the factory area under siege. By this time, the British Superintendent of Trade was Captain Charles Elliot. Summoned from Macau, he too was besieged in the factory area with the merchants, but after some weeks organised the surrender of the opium. For Lin, this might have been the end of the matter, but the British merchants refused to sign the bond committing them to abandoning the opium trade in the future. Elliot called for the suspension of all business and led a withdrawal of the British community to Macau. Lin put pressure on the Portuguese Government and forced the British community to take to merchant ships and take shelter off Hong Kong.

Palmerston decided at this point that there should be an end to the Sino-British disputes. He demanded either a commercial treaty from the Chinese, on equal terms, or the cession of an island, where the British could operate under their own laws and be free from Chinese interference. In this he seems to have been following the advice of Jardine, who recommended that:

- the principal ports of China should be blockaded
- an apology should be demanded for insults to the British merchants
- payment should be demanded for the surrendered opium
- an equitable trade treaty should be negotiated
- Chinese should be forced to open up other ports to trade.[11]

In order to achieve these ends, Jardine advised that various islands off the Chinese coast should be temporarily occupied. In addition, he counselled that it might be necessary to take permanent possession of some island with a safe anchorage, for the future conduct of British trade.

Some months earlier, predicting trouble of the sort that had arisen, Elliot had summoned military help from London. Palmerston now informed him that a naval force was on its way and that it would arrive in March 1840. Its purpose was to blockade the two rivers leading to Guangzhou and Beijing. The arrival of this fleet and accompanying expeditionary force was to signal the beginning of the first Anglo-Chinese, or Opium War. The campaign demonstrated the Chinese to be woefully unable to counter the superior weaponry of their adversaries. When the British landed at Xiamen, for example, they suffered no casualties, but over a hundred Chinese were killed by British musket fire. Hostilities continued, interrupted by negotiations, from June 1840 until January 1841, when the so-called Convention of Chuenpi was signed by Elliot and Lin's replacement, Qishan. The terms of this agreement were humiliating for the Chinese. China was to pay a large indemnity; British merchants were to be re-established at Guangzhou; relations between Britain and China were to be established under conditions of equality; and the island of Hong Kong was to be ceded. In return, Britain was to give up the island of Zhoushan, which had been occupied. Not surprisingly, the Chinese Emperor refused to ratify this agreement when he was informed of it. More surprisingly, the Convention was also repudiated by the British Foreign Minister, Palmerston, who was upset at Elliot's relinquishment of Zhoushan in favour of Hong Kong, which he referred to as 'a barren island with hardly a house on it ... the desert island of Hong Kong'.[12]

Palmerston was also upset that Elliot had not used the force at his disposal 'for the very purpose for which it was sent'. As a result of what he referred to as his disobeyal of his instructions, Palmerston dismissed Elliot from his post, but not before a landing party, under the latter's instructions, had formally occupied Hong Kong and established a settlement. Both sides repudiating the treaty, hostilities soon recommenced in August 1841. Elliot was replaced by Sir Henry Pottinger, who conducted operations with vigour, attacking up the Changjiang (Yangtse River). Suzhou, Shanghai and Qiantang were all bombarded and captured. With Nanjing being threatened, hostilities were brought to an end with the Treaty of Nanjing, signed in August 1842.

By this time, there had been a change of government in Britain and Palmerston had been replaced as Foreign Secretary by Lord Aberdeen. Aberdeen's position on Hong Kong was not quite as negative as that of Palmerston. He accepted that it might be taken as a temporary possession to be used as a bargaining chip with China, if a satisfactory treaty on trade could not be negotiated. However, Pottinger, like Elliot, had been convinced of Hong Kong's longer-term value and was of the opinion that it should be taken as a British possession. He went beyond the terms of his instructions, therefore, and claimed Hong Kong for Britain, as part of the agreement he concluded with the Chinese. On receiving his copy of the treaty, which included the annexation of Hong Kong, Aberdeen was willing to accept the acquisition of Hong Kong as a *fait accompli.*

While from afar, in London, the attractions of Hong Kong might not have seemed great, for those present in Southern China they were numerous: first and foremost it offered a territory from which British merchants could operate under British law and unhindered by Chinese interference; it could also be easily protected, given British naval supremacy; it covered a small area and had a negligible indigenous population, which would make it easy to administer;[13] it had ample supplies of fresh water; and last, but by no means least, it offered one of the few natural deep-water safe harbours along the whole of the Chinese coast.

The terms of the Treaty of Nanjing were even more onerous than those of the earlier Convention of Chuenpi. In addition to ceding Hong Kong, in perpetuity, the Chinese undertook to open five ports to international trade: Xiamen, Fuzhou, Ningbo and Shanghai, as well as Guangzhou. Each of these cities would have a British consul, who would be responsible for trade and for the welfare of British citizens, and who would be subject to consular, not Chinese, law. All future dealings between China and Britain would be on equal terms, between two sovereign states. China would pay Britain $21 million in reparations, much more than the cost of the war. British warships would be allowed to patrol the Chinese coast and rivers and a naval base would be established at Shanghai. Soon after, similar privileges were granted to France and the United States.

The Opium War and the ensuing Treaty of Nanjing were a humiliation for China in the extreme. The war showed up China's technical and military backwardness and its vulnerability to military incursion. The treaty forced it to relinquish an important part of its sovereignty.

* * *

The signing of the Treaty of Nanjing did not mark an end to Britain's rapacious behaviour towards China, however. Under the terms of the treaty, British ships patrolled China's coast and rivers and were ruthless in their attacks on pirates. It was a Chinese attack on a vessel flying the British flag, in 1856, however, which precipitated the Second Opium War of 1856–8. Although it is doubtful whether the vessel, *The Arrow*, was in fact British, the British Consul in Guangzhou used the incident as a pretext to give a warning to the Chinese authorities against interfering with trade and to settle the question of his right to deal directly with Chinese officials in Guangzhou, by having the city bombarded by British naval ships. At the same time, the French used the killing of a missionary as a pretext to send ships to join the British, and the city of Guangzhou was taken with minimal resistance. During this period, Lord Elgin was summoned from Britain to take charge of a land-based expedition. After a combined British and French force moved north and captured a fort guarding the river leading to Beijing, in June 1858, these hostilities came to an end, with the signing of the Treaty of Tianjin, separate versions of which were signed by Britain, France, the United States and Russia.

The resulting peace was short-lived, however, and Elgin had to be recalled to settle matters once again, as a result of Chinese unwillingness to apply the terms of the treaty. In 1859–60, an Anglo-French expedition led by Elgin marched on Beijing and, in late 1860, the terms of the Treaty of Tianjin were ratified in the Convention of Beijing. According to the terms of this treaty, further commercial benefits were offered to the Europeans: diplomatic embassies were now allowed in Beijing and foreign diplomats were excused from performing the kow-tow; foreigners could travel anywhere in China; Christian missionaries were allowed; a total of ten treaty ports were

opened up to foreign trade; opium was legalised; the recruitment of
Chinese labour for work overseas was allowed; finally, Britain took
possession of another piece of land, the Kowloon Peninsula, some
three square miles of the Chinese mainland, facing the island of Hong
Kong. The second military expedition had camped there before moving north and had found the area healthy. Given earlier misgivings
about the lawlessness of the inhabitants of the area and that it was
within cannon range of Hong Kong and could thus prove dangerous
if it fell into foreign hands, the British decided they would keep it as a
military cantonment.

It was the military campaign leading up to this final treaty which
probably left the greatest mark on the Chinese collective conscious-
ness, culminating as it did in the occupation of the nation's capital,
Beijing. Not only that, but considerable looting accompanied the
campaign and the Imperial Summer Palace, a symbol of Chinese
imperial power, was burned down, on the instructions of Elgin.

In the space of twenty years China had submitted to three wars,
which had been conducted by Britain in the name of free trade.
National shame was compounded by the realisation that China, with
its ancient civilisation and huge population, was powerless in the face
of the modern technology of the British, wielded in the hands of very
few men. Although Britain had no territorial ambition, because of
what it considered to be Chinese intransigence, in refusing to engage
in trade and to negotiate on an equal footing, Britain had decided to
seize the island of Hong Kong and the adjoining territory.

Although Britain was the country with most to gain from access to
China's markets, because the terms of the treaties extended to all-
comers, other Western powers also benefited. Indeed, these other
powers had ambitions of their own. Russia had its eyes on Korea, a
tributary province of China, while France had ambitions in Indo-
China, another Chinese tributary. China's weakness also sent a signal
to Japan, which would later exploit China's predicament.

For the forty years from 1860 to the turn of the century, Britain had
a stranglehold on China's trade. By 1895, two thirds of China's foreign
commerce was in British hands. Topping the list of imports was opium,
followed by Lancashire cottonware. From 1853, the Chinese customs
were under British control. The head of the Chinese customs service,
Sir Robert Hart, had a staff of 89 Europeans, half of whom were
British. The service, of course, was backed up by the Royal Navy.

If, by 1895, British commercial influence was at a high point, its
political pre-eminence was already beginning to decline. No doubt alerted

to the opportunities by earlier British incursions, in that year Japan routed China in the Sino-Japanese war (1894–5). Japan claimed sovereignty over Taiwan and demanded a large financial indemnity for the cost of the war. The jealous French, Russians and Germans, who had cynically banded together to protect China against the Japanese demands, were also rewarded with various commercial prizes. In 1897, Germany used the pretext of murdered missionaries to occupy Jiaozhou, which became a naval base, while, in 1898, Russia took over Lushun (Port Arthur). In the same year, to counter the increasing naval power of the other European nations in the region, Britain leased Weihai as a naval base.

At the same time, Britain obtained from China an extension of its territory in Hong Kong, an area which was to become known as the New Territories. Britain argued that it needed the Kowloon hinterland and surrounding islands as security for the urban areas of Hong Kong Island and Kowloon. Technical advances had increased the range of artillery considerably and, to assure the safety of these areas, the defensive cordon would need to be more widely spread. In fact, the area taken over represented more than ten times the amount of territory already ceded. However, China did not want to cede the additional territories in perpetuity and Britain accepted a 99-year lease, on the grounds that leases were also being given to the other imperial powers at the time.[14] The British did not insist on complete cession, as they had done for Hong Kong Island and Kowloon, as this might have encouraged the other powers to demand similar terms, and Britain wanted to curtail the influence of its rivals as much as it could.

\* \* \*

All this imperialistic activity provoked xenophobic feelings in China. A powerful group, the I-ho chuan (Boxers), whose members were violently anti-foreign, rapidly grew. The Boxers mounted vicious attacks on foreign missionaries, Chinese Christians, and anyone who used foreign manufactured goods. They won support from the ultra-conservative members of the ruling establishment, as a means of deflecting mounting criticism of the imperial regime. As a result of the attacks on the missionaries, ships of the European powers gathered in Chinese waters, within striking distance of Beijing. Fearing foreign intervention, early in 1900, the Dowager Empress Tzu-hsi joined imperial troops with the Boxers in a desperate siege of the walled area of the capital occupied by the foreign legations. The foreign powers sent an 18 000-strong expeditionary force to successfully relieve the legations and suppress the up-rising. As reparation for the damage done to the embassies, the cost of the expedition, and the murder of some 200 Europeans, the Western powers demanded a huge sum in compensation, payable over 39 years. To make sure of payment, in the ultimate humiliation, Beijing was occupied by foreign troops.

The Boxer rebellion provided a further pretext for more foreign incursions, and Russia shortly sent 200 000 troops, in the annexation of Manchuria. This Russian advantage was not to last for long, however. Due to the increasing presence of its imperial rivals in the region, by this time Britain could no longer afford enough ships to maintain naval supremacy over the combined forces of Russia, France, and Germany. In 1902, the British, accordingly, concluded a treaty with Japan, under the terms of which each nation would help the other if attacked by more than one other. This alliance with Japan allowed Britain to withdraw some of its naval forces from Asia. One result of the agreement was that it opened the way, in 1904, for Japan to defeat the Russian navy and land forces, thus allowing it to annex significant parts of China, in what was to be just the start of the fulfilment of its own growing imperial ambitions in the Middle Kingdom and which eventually culminated in total domination during World War II. Japanese incursions were helped by the 1911 Chinese revolution, which overthrew the imperial dynasty and was the start of internal divisions and upheavals.

In 1931, the Japanese took control of Manchuria, the northern part of China, and established a puppet Emperor, Pu-yi, head of the Chi'ing imperial dynasty. In 1932 they attacked Shanghai. The following year they took Jehol and Chahar, leading to control of Inner Mongolia. In 1935 they brokered a North China Autonomous Region, which meant the northern part of China would come under Japanese control. Full scale war between China and Japan broke out in 1937, merging into World War II. During this period, the Japanese army was responsible for many atrocities, including the Nanjing massacre, when hundreds of thousands of men, women and children were savagely killed by Japanese soldiers.

After Japan's defeat in World War II, civil war still raged in China between the Guomindang (Nationalist Party of China) and the Communists. In spite of considerable assistance from the United States, in 1948, the Guomindang was defeated and the People's Republic was established. It was only then that China became unified and free from foreign interference, although Hong Kong, which had been returned to Britain (in spite of Guomindang claims that the colony should be returned to the Motherland), the Portuguese enclave of Macau, and Taiwan, where the Guomindang had established a stronghold, remained apart.

\* \* \*

The preceding account shows Chinese humiliation at the hands of foreigners, a humiliation which has been carried down in the minds of the Chinese people to the present day. Although most cruelty and suffering was meted out by the Japanese, Britain was the instigator and dominant player for most of the period and Britain, even after the unification of the country under the Communists, in 1949, still retained sovereignty over a part of Chinese territory, Hong Kong, right up until 30 June 1997. Li Ruihuan, a senior Chinese official, evoked the theme of national shame in relation to the return of Hong Kong, as follows:

> Hong Kong's return is a major event in Chinese history. China was bullied by imperialists, and gradually became a semi-colony and a semi-feudal society from the time Hong Kong was ceded by the Treaty of Nanjing after the Opium War in 1840.
>
> After this, all the other imperialists invaded China ... killed our people, seized our wealth, occupied our lands and established their spheres of influence. It has been a heart-breaking matter for many generations of Chinese. After Hong Kong's return we can wipe out our ancestors' disgrace, console their spirits and tell our successors that Chinese should stay strong, or else we will be bullied, invaded and grabbed by others.
>
> We should look at Hong Kong's return in the context of Chinese history. Taking Hong Kong back to the mainland is ... a very important turning point of history.[15]

# 2 From Early Development to the Beginnings of Retrocession

As indicated in Chapter 1, the British took control over what is now known as Hong Kong in three stages. First, Hong Kong Island was ceded, in perpetuity, in 1842. Next, the Kowloon peninsula was ceded, in 1860. Finally, the New Territories came under British control, according to the terms of a 99-year lease, in 1898.

Following the establishment of the colony in 1842, conditions in the early years of Hong Kong were difficult. A sizeable proportion of the population was wracked with fever and much damage was done by the typhoons which regularly lash the China coast during the summer months. There were many unruly elements among the population and crime was rampant. But in these difficult conditions Hong Kong did progress, with the island becoming a centre of trade with China, as the colonists had foreseen. Because of the prevalence of the China trade, the silver dollar was adopted as the currency, rather than the British pound.

Helped by the Treaty of Tianjin of 1858 and the Convention of Beijing of 1860, which provided for the right to travel in China and the opening up of more treaty ports, by 1880 Hong Kong handled 21 per cent in value of China's total export trade and 31 per cent of its imports. The security of British-governed Hong Kong and the accompanying rule of law made the colony a convenient base for the larger firms. Supporting the trading houses were associated accounting, banking, insurance and shipping services. As a measure of Hong Kong's growing success as a trading centre, the number of ships passing through the harbour grew from 538, in 1844, to 2889, in 1860, and to 4558, in 1864.[1] Opium was still an important part of Hong Kong's trade, accounting for as much as 45 per cent of the total value of China's imports in some years.[2] The enclave also became a centre of emigration for Chinese seeking to work overseas and a vast network of links with the various Chinese communities spread about the world was established, a network which has been strengthened in more recent years, with the rise of emigration which has followed the Sino-British Joint Declaration.

16

On annexation, on 14 May 1841, the indigenous population was estimated at 4350; by 1862, the total population had risen to 123 511, of whom 120 477 were Chinese; by 1895 it had reached 248 498, of whom 237 670 were Chinese.[3] The large Chinese influx was surprising to the colonists, because it had not been expected that they would want to live under a foreign flag. Hong Kong was seen by Chinese, however, as a place of refuge from disturbances at home on the Mainland, and there was a demand for labour. The population increased during times of trouble, but then declined again, when things settled down. Right up until 1970, the majority of Hong Kong's population had always been born outside the territory.[4]

As in other British colonies, from 1843 Hong Kong was administered by a Governor, nominated by Whitehall, and an Executive (Exco) and a Legislative Council (Legco), each nominated by the Governor, with the majority of their members drawn from official positions. The Exco is the decision-making body, while the Legco passes laws and authorises public expenditure. Indicative of the importance ascribed to business by the Hong Kong Government, one of the first non-government appointees to Legco was William Jardine, head of the Jardine-Matheson trading house. The appointment of a representative of the so-called 'Princely Hong' was to continue right through to recent times.

The Governor had great individual power. The only form of control on him was the possibility of the people appealing to the Secretary of State in London. Hong Kong's first official Governor, Pottinger,[5] exploited his autonomy to the limit by appointing the same three paid government officials (the minimum allowable) to both Exco and Lego. In 1850, Hong Kong's fourth Governor, Bowring, however, tried to introduce an element of democratic reform, with a proposal to introduce three new directly-elected members of Legco. These councillors would be elected by all those, irrespective of race, who held land worth £110 per year. The Colonial Secretary of the time, Labouchere, would not accept Bowring's proposal, however, arguing, in effect, that the Chinese population of Hong Kong was not to be trusted with such a responsibility and that the minority British population, especially given its transient nature, should not be allowed to rule over the large Chinese majority. He suggested, instead, the appointment of reputable Chinese to official positions. It was not until 1880, however, that the first Chinese was appointed to Legco, with representation of this race on Exco having to wait until 1926.[6] As Welsh points out,[7] it was to be a century and a quarter before an element of democracy was introduced into the Hong Kong legislature, and then a less radical one than that proposed by Bowring.

* * *

The attitude of the British to the Chinese was to allow them to follow their own customs and laws. Elliot decreed that 'the natives of the island of Hong Kong and all natives of China thereto resorting, shall be governed according to the laws and customs of China, every description of torture excepted'.[8] Initially, there was to be a separate Chinese legal system, with magistrates brought in from China, but this idea had to be abandoned, mainly through the sheer weight of crime. In its place, in 1865, a system of equality of all races before the British law was established. Nevertheless, in practice, the Chinese followed their own customs, British norms applying only if they were involved in any sort of criminal activity. Footbinding, infanticide, concubinage, child marriage, and opium smoking were all prevalent and were not interfered with by the British administration.

In general, the two races were content to go their separate ways, with the main point of contact being business and the workplace. Among the most successful Chinese were the compradors, or middlemen, who acted on behalf of the European firms, or *hongs*, and the Chinese business community. Such men were essential for a successful business, as it was almost impossible for a foreigner to negotiate the alien language, customs and human networking systems (*guanxi*) of the Chinese. Pidgin English had developed in Guangzhou to facilitate basic human intercourse, but at the higher levels bi-lingual and bi-cultural experts were required. Chinese were only co-opted into the British colonial establishment as and when they were required. Increasingly, however, Chinese were operating companies on their own account. Endacott reports that in 1881 there were 18 ratepayers with property rated at over $1000 per quarter and that 17 of these were Chinese, the remaining one being the largest British *hong*, Jardine-Matheson.

In 1865, the instructions to the Governor were amended so that he should refuse to assent to ordinances 'whereby persons of African or Asiatic birth may be subjected to any disabilities or restrictions to which persons of European birth or descent are not also subjected'. In practice, however, racial discrimination in Hong Kong was rife. In 1888, the European District Reservation Ordinance, which effectively restricted the upper central parts of the town (known as Victoria Peak, or The Peak) to Europeans, was published.[9] This was followed, in

1902, by an ordinance setting aside an area of Kowloon for European occupation. Attitudes towards Chinese on the part of Europeans were often offensive. 'You cannot be two minutes in Hong Kong without seeing Europeans striking coolies with their canes or umbrellas,' Welsh cites a Miss Bird, for example, as recording.[10] Polite society effectively excluded Chinese. Tea- and dinner-parties, garden parties, sporting activities, amateur theatricals and musical performances were almost exclusively European. The Jockey Club, the Hong Kong Club, the Victoria Recreation Club and the Amateur Dramatic Corps had not a single Chinese member between them, Welsh notes.[11] One area where the two races did mix was less respectable. Because there were so many single men in Hong Kong, both Chinese and Western, prostitution was rampant. Many Western men frequented Chinese brothels and/or took Chinese concubines.

\* \* \*

Many historical accounts of Hong Kong describe both the British and the Chinese races as equally arrogant and happy to get along without each other where possible. However, on a number of occasions Chinese resentment against British domination rose to the surface. In 1857, during the Second Opium War, arsenic was placed in the bread distributed by a Chinese-owned bakery, in an attempt to poison foreigners in the colony. The amount of arsenic used was easily detected and no great harm was done.

Following the cession of the New Territories, in 1898, anti-British feeling reached its highest expression, with local residents organising themselves into military groups to actively resist the British take-over. Given that the cession was an agreement imposed on China by Britain to which the indigenous residents of the area, who would become British subjects instead of Chinese, had not been a party, this action was hardly surprising. Following several days of sporadic resistance, on 17 April 1899, a grouping of several thousand armed Chinese was put down by British forces. This put a stop to active resistance, but local inhabitants remained uncooperative and resentful against the presence of the British.

In 1922, there was a strike by Chinese seamen, who were paid much less than their European counterparts for doing the same work and were generally exploited by their employers. On 13 January, the seamen withdrew their labour and departed for Guangzhou. They were soon followed by other workers – domestic servants, engineers and coolies – who had similar grievances. Having forbidden these workers, who represented, in fact, the majority of the work-force, from leaving the colony, the Government sent police and troops to prevent them from crossing the border. Indian colonial troops opened fire on a large crowd, killing five Chinese.

The seamen's strike was followed, in 1925–6, by a general strike and boycott of British goods. This action resulted from what Endacott refers to as 'a political movement arising from popular feeling against the privileged status of foreigners.'[12] Starting in Shanghai as an anti-Japanese demonstration, the movement quickly became largely anti-British, because Britain was the predominant foreign power in China and because the public disorder was put down by British-led troops, at the cost of 11 lives. The unrest spread along the China coast to Guangzhou, where, following the killing of a further fifty-two demonstrators, a boycott of foreign goods and a total withdrawal of Chinese labour from Hong Kong was organised. Over a million workers left Hong Kong for Guangzhou. The strike eventually fizzled out, but the boycott of goods continued until October 1926 and a special loan had to be arranged to support the foreign merchants who had been affected by the boycott.

\* \* \*

From the turn of the century, Hong Kong experienced steady growth as a centre of trade and commerce. In 1898, for example, 11 058 ships of 13 252 733 tons used the port; in 1913, the figures rose to 21 867 ships of 22 939 134 tons; in 1918, there was a slight decline, due to the demands of war, with the figures dropping to 19 997 ships of 13 982 966 tons. However, even with this small decline in 1918 these figures indicate that Hong Kong had established itself as one of the world's leading ports.[13] Hong Kong was primarily an entrepot. Important commodities shipped in and out included coal, rice, sugar, flour, and kerosene. Human traffic was also an important boost for the port, with huge numbers of Chinese both leaving for and returning from America, the Pacific, Southeast Asia and Australia. In 1913, for example, there were 142 759 departures from Hong Kong, while in 1914 there were 168 827 arrivals.[14]

The period between 1911, the year of the Chinese revolution and overthrow of the imperial dynasty, and 1941, when Japan entered World War II and Hong Kong was invaded, was marked in the colony by various influxes of population from the Mainland as a result of the instability with which the country was afflicted. While the Manchu regime had been overthrown in favour of a republic there was no agreement on what form the new government should take. Within five years, central government had totally collapsed. In its place, China was divided among various warlords who fought with each other for power. By 1928, a Guomindang-backed nationalist government was set up, gradually extending its power during the years leading up to 1937. By that time, however, Japan, alarmed at the prospect of a unified China, had taken over Manchuria and established the puppet state of Manchukuo, leading to full-scale war between Japan and China. This was to merge into World War II, when Japan initiated hostilities against the Western allies on the side of the Axis powers, in 1941. A further destabilising factor was the rise of the Chinese Communist Party (CCP) whose army was sporadically either allied with the Guomindang against the Japanese or fought against them for political control.

As a result of all this, by 1920 the population of Hong Kong had reached 600 000; and by 1938 it had increased to over a million. The Japanese aggression in 1937 and the fall of Guangzhou, in 1939, saw the greatest influxes: 10 000 in 1937; 500 000 in 1938; and 150 000 in 1939. By 1941, Hong Kong's population had risen to 1.6 million, with some 500 000 forced to sleep on the streets.

Japan bombed Hong Kong at about the same time as it attacked Pearl Harbour, on 7 December 1941 (Hong Kong time), and a swift land invasion quickly disposed of the badly prepared and organised opposition from the colonial defence forces, making a mockery of Churchill's message to his troops that, 'by a prolonged resistance you and your men can win the lasting honour which we are sure will be your due'.[15] The brutal Japanese occupation lasted 3 years and 8 months, during which time the population was reduced from 1.6 million to 600 000.

\* \* \*

At the end of the War, President Roosevelt and the United States State Department wanted to hand Hong Kong back to the Chinese. The United States was against colonialism and Roosevelt supported the Guomindang leader, Chiang Kai-shek, who had called for Hong Kong's return. Churchill, on the British side, had other ideas, however. Helped by the death of Roosevelt and his replacement by President Truman, who was not so favourably disposed towards Chiang, the new Labour Party British Foreign Secretary, Bevin, persuaded Truman that it should be the British navy which recovered Hong Kong following the Japanese surrender and not Chinese Nationalist troops.

The Guomindang might have tried to seize the colony, as they had forces in the area, but they were preoccupied with their civil war against the Communists, the pursuance of which depended on American support. In 1949, the Communists defeated the Guomindang, who withdrew to Taiwan, and proclaimed the People's Republic. While Jiang and the Guomindang had demanded Hong Kong be retroceded, the Communists, who were grateful for British neutrality in the war against the Nationalists, were less hostile, their representative in the colony, Quiao Guanhua, expressly stating that a Communist China would not seek to take Hong Kong by force.

According to one commentator, recent evidence from the Soviet archives suggests that Mao Zedong, the Chinese leader, had already decided well before his army reached the frontier with Hong Kong that he wanted to leave the colony in British hands as a base for foreign trade.[16] In addition, Hong Kong may have been kept as a possible future venue for developing relations with the West.[17] The British were encouraged by this attitude and later concluded that Hong Kong under British rule offered benefits to the Communists which would mean they would not seek to take the territory back. China needed Hong Kong for trade with the outside world and for much-needed foreign exchange. During the Korean War, the People's Republic was able to depend on Hong Kong merchants for supplies, to break a UN-imposed international embargo.

* * *

After the war, the British approach to Hong Kong changed. British colonial policy, set by a newly-elected Labour Party, was now concentrated on preparing the various colonies of the Empire for independence. On resuming his governorship, which had been interrupted by the war and his internment by the Japanese, Sir Mark Young stated that he wanted Hong Kong people to have 'a fuller and more responsible share in the management of their own affairs . . . the fullest account being taken of the views and wishes of the inhabitants'.[18] Young planned a revision of the Municipal Council along democratic lines and the expansion of representation in the Legco. He attempted to consult with various sectors of Hong Kong society about his plan, which had been drawn up by the Colonial Office, but as Cameron notes 'there seemed to be an innate reluctance on the part of Hong Kong people of all stations in life to join in political debate'.[19] Of course, this is hardly surprising, as the vast majority, whether new immigrants from China or long-term Hong Kong residents, had never been given this opportunity before. After what consultation and discussion in the community he could manage, Young presented his plan to London. There were to be elections for two-thirds of the Municipal Council seats, split equally between Chinese and non-Chinese constituencies, with the remaining third appointed by representative bodies. On the Legco, there would be equal numbers of government appointees and non-official members. It was not until 1949, however, that detailed bills were prepared to put the Young Plan into law. By this time Young had been replaced as Governor by Alexander Grantham, who was less enthusiastic about reforms. Grantham presented a much-watered-down version of the Young Plan to the British Government. Even after this plan had already been approved by the British Cabinet, however, Grantham allowed himself to be persuaded by a delegation of Executive and Legislative Councillors to drop the idea of constitutional reform altogether. The Colonial Secretary, acting on Grantham's advice, informed the Cabinet that he had changed his mind and that the reforms would now not go ahead 'until conditions are more settled'.[20]

By this time it had become clear that a serious problem had developed that made the plan impracticable, or so the government claimed. As a result of the Communist victory, there had been a further tremendous influx of refugees from China. Following the liberation of Hong Kong, by 1946, the population had already got back to 1.6 million. But between 1946 and the end of 1950, it rose to 2.36 million. Between October 1949, when the Communists captured Guangzhou, and May 1950, alone, it is estimated that 700 000 refugees entered the territory. Clearly, any reforms based on proportional representation according to race, as contained in the Young Plan, would be unworkable, given the tremendous increase in the Chinese population. Accordingly, in October 1952, London announced that the time was not opportune for constitutional reform.

From that time until the 1970s, there were no significant moves in the direction of greater democracy. The Hong Kong and British governments' line was that whereas in other British dependent territories democracy had been promoted in preparation for independence, because of its unique situation such constitutional development was not appropriate in Hong Kong. The British Hong Kong Government's attitude during this period was, first, that the main priority should be the absorption of the tremendous numbers of immigrants who were flooding into the territory. It was argued that these people had come to Hong Kong seeking social stability and prosperity, not representative government. Other arguments in favour of inaction on the constitutional front were that party politics might encourage political rivalry between Chinese Communist and Guomindang sympathisers, and that moves in the direction of greater autonomy might upset Mainland China and jeopardise the territory's status as a colonial enclave. On this latter point, Sir David Trench, who was Governor from 1964–71, stated as follows:

> If Hong Kong could be towed 100 miles out to sea it would be quite a different, and not necessarily a better place. But, since it can't be, every single policy – social, political or economic – is coloured by China's nearness, China's attitudes, and the consequent difficulty of being certain of an assured future... This situation demands great realism in all our thinking; and many fine judgements have to be made as to what is best to be done. In any given situation, Hong Kong cannot afford the luxury of [making] mistakes, and particularly of well-meant mistakes, in any of its policies.[21]

One democratic development which did take place, but did not require constitutional reform, was the increasing involvement of Chinese in matters of government. The numbers of Chinese members of Legco, Exco, the Urban Council and charitable and advisory bodies consistently increased, in a process which Ambrose Yeo-chi King called the administrative absorption of politics.[22]

* * *

After a period of stagnation brought about by the United Nations embargo on trade with China during the Korean War, the Hong Kong economy began to take off. The huge rise in population meant that the economy could not operate solely on trade, as it had tended to do in the past. Helped by the capital and expertise which had flowed in from Shanghai, following the Communist take-over, industrial manufacturing began to establish itself. This was the beginning of the economic miracle which has continued in Hong Kong right up to the present time.[23] The important industries were initially cotton, woollens, and made-up garments, with man-made fibres, plastic flowers, toys and basic electronics soon following. Shanghai entrepreneurs were also active in shipping and the film industry.

A number of reasons are usually put forward for Hong Kong's great economic success. These include the expertise brought to Hong Kong by the Shanghai and other Chinese entrepeneurs, the strong work ethic of the Chinese, a low tax rate and low government spending, a government policy of so-called 'positive-non-intervention' in the economy, and a solid legal framework within which business can operate. Spurring the strong work ethic, others have noted, was the absence of social welfare benefits, lack of free education (in the early years), and the sojourner mentality of Hong Kong people, which encouraged them to make as much money as they could in a short space of time. To this list, one might also add Chinese Mainland acquiescence in Britain's continued presence and food, water and manpower at low cost.

To keep pace with the population explosion, in the early 1950s the Hong Kong government embarked on an ambitious public housing scheme, which was initiated due to a fire in 1953 which destroyed squatter dwellings and as a result of which 53 000 people had nowhere to live. By 1975, 1.7 million people were living in public housing, a figure which has subsequently increased to over 3 million. During this period great strides were also made in public education, so that by 1971 compulsory schooling was provided up to the age of 15.

One hiccup along the road to the economic prosperity of the 1960s occurred in 1967, when the effects of the Cultural Revolution in China spread to Hong Kong, with rioting, temporary paralysis of the economy, and a death toll of over 50. However, this unrest was relatively short-lived and the colony soon got back on the path of economic progress (although it did bring to public attention some of the serious social iniquities prevalent in the colony).

\* \* \*

The year 1971 was a watershed for Hong Kong. In that year, a new Governor, Sir Murray (later Lord) MacLehose, took over. MacLehose, generally described as a man of great integrity, vision and energy, presided over a period of rapid economic and social development. Much as Patten was to do later, MacLehose demonstrated the common touch:

> MacLehose immediately began to dismantle much of the pomp associated with the post. He dispensed with the use of the Governor's limousine for the short journey from Government House to Legco Chambers, preferring to walk there for meetings. A common touch quickly became apparent as the new Governor took regular

walks, in short-sleeved, open-necked shirts, through densely populated residential areas. All indications were that here, at last was a
governor of the people. This in itself came as quite a shock to the
colonial system.[24]

Unlike Patten, MacLehose, with a background in the diplomatic
service, also knew China and Hong Kong well and spoke Chinese.

Scott remarks that: 'The first years of MacLehose's governorship
were remarkable years for Hong Kong. They dispelled the image of a
government previously thought to be uncaring and unresponsive.'[25]
During the period of just over a decade during which MacLehose
was Governor Hong Kong experienced average annual economic
growth of over 9 per cent.[26] Such tremendous economic development
created higher government revenues and allowed for greater social
spending, without the need to raise taxes.[27] MacLehose set a pre-
cedent in his first policy speech, which again was to be reflected
later by Patten, of setting specific targets for what his government
wanted to achieve. As Scott argues, with more representative institutions and direct elections out of the question, government sought to
establish its legitimacy by setting targets for meeting the aspirations of
the public in terms of social provision and letting the public evaluate
the government on the basis of the extent to which these targets
were met.[28]

MacLehose's speech announced increased provision for housing,
education, and social welfare, with health care added the following
year. Although MacLehose did not achieve all he set out to, it is
generally agreed that he improved the lot of the Hong Kong people
considerably in each of these areas.[29] In housing, the tremendously
ambitious 'new towns' plan was set in train. These towns, which are
actually cities of well over half a million inhabitants, form a network
of satellite conurbations consisting of huge high-rise blocks of over 30
storeys. In education, MacLehose planned that, by 1979, all children
would receive three years of secondary education; this target was in
fact met a year earlier than anticipated. In social welfare, public
assistance was introduced for those who did not have adequate
income to support themselves, facilities for the disabled and the
elderly were provided, and social and recreational facilities were
improved. During MacLehose's period of office, welfare spending as
a percentage of total government spending nearly doubled. In health
care, there was similar expansion of provision, with new hospitals,
more doctors and nurses, and better equipment.[30]

Another achievement under MacLehose was the great progress made in developing a sophisticated infrastructure of roads, urban railways, port facilities, and what is now one of the world's busiest airports. The construction of the Mass Transit Railway (MTR), a much needed facility given Hong Kong's congested conditions, has in particular been widely admired. The railway was built ahead of schedule and under budget (an occurrence which has subsequently proved to be almost the norm for construction projects in Hong Kong) and is widely praised for its efficiency.

MacLehose's reputation for integrity was enhanced by his management of the problems of rampant corruption in the Hong Kong police force and public service. In response to a particularly serious corruption scandal, in 1973, MacLehose established the Independent Commission Against Corruption (ICAC), a body with strong powers and independent of the police and civil service. Corruption was so endemic, however, during the early period of the ICAC, that their investigations led to a revolt and the storming of their offices by a group of police who were under suspicion. In order to avoid a total breakdown in law and order, MacLehose was forced to offer an amnesty in all but the most serious cases. Nevertheless, through perseverance, the body's reputation was salvaged and later increases in prosecutions restored public confidence to a considerable degree.[31]

Although MacLehose took a number of measures to make the civil service more efficient (he employed a private consultancy firm to report on what needed to be done) and measures were taken to improve communication between the government and the public at large, through a Community Involvement Plan and a policy of assiduous public consultation on all new policy initiatives, during his long term of office, from November 1971 to April 1982, there was no serious attempt at any sort of constitutional reform.[32] The Government's view under MacLehose seemed to be that they knew best how to provide for the physical and economic welfare of the people and so long as these needs were catered for, there was no requirement for any sort of more formal democratic representation.

\* \* \*

In the same year that MacLehose became Governor of Hong Kong, 1971, a new era of Sino-American co-operation began, with the visit of the United States table-tennis team to a China which until then had been virtually shut off from the Western world. This became possible because of President Nixon's new policy of withdrawal from Vietnam and a gradual thawing of relations between the world's greatest power and the People's Republic. The table-tennis team's visit was followed up by a private visit by the US Secretary of State, Henry Kissinger, and, in 1972, an official visit by President Nixon. This was the start of China's new 'open door' policy, but also represented a more relaxed position on the part of the United States with regard to that country. The People's Republic of China was admitted to the United Nations in place of the Republic of China (Taiwan), which the United States, until then, had supported as the official representative of China. The United States now accepted that there was one China and that Taiwan was a part of that China (the so-called 'one China' policy). This new American policy was to have an immense effect on Hong Kong and its status as a British colony. If the United States and the international community now recognised that Taiwan was a part of China, how could the British Government maintain the status of Hong Kong as anything different?

Since 1947, Hong Kong had been treated by the United Nations and its Special Committee on Decolonization as a country which was moving towards self-determination. The British Government had, accordingly, every year, provided the Special Committee with information on Hong Kong's constitutional development. In 1972, with the accession of the People's Republic to the United Nations, their ambassador asked that Hong Kong be taken off the list of colonial territories, on the grounds that 'settlement of the question of Hong Kong and Macau is entirely within China's sovereign right and they do not at all fall under the category of colonial territories.'[33]   Britain made no public objection to this request and it was accordingly accepted. The Chinese Ambassador had also stated that the Chinese Government would settle the issue of Hong Kong 'in an appropriate way when conditions are ripe'.[34] This, of course, left Hong Kong in a state of limbo. China had established the right to reclaim Hong Kong, but the people of Hong Kong had no indication of if and when this claim would be exercised.

The question arises as to why Britain did not object to China's claim of sovereignty over Hong Kong. Wilson reports that, as early as 1955, Britain and China had come to an understanding over the territory, when the then Hong Kong Governor, Grantham, had paid an unofficial visit to Beijing and met with Chinese Premier Zhou Enlai. The message Grantham returned to Hong Kong with was that China considered the Hong Kong question to be a problem left over by history and that the colony would be recovered at a time suitable to China. In the meantime, China accepted the British presence, as long as Britain did not allow the territory to become self-governing or a base for the Guomindang.[35] The willingness of China to allow the British to remain was confirmed in 1967, when the Portuguese government offered to hand back Macau, which suffered similar public disorder to that of Hong Kong during the Cultural Revolution. The Chinese refused the offer, presumably because to accept it would have created instability in Hong Kong over fears of a similar take-over of the British colony.

From China's point of view, it was difficult during this period to justify allowing the British to remain in Hong Kong, when anti-colonial struggles – which as a revolutionary regime it supported – were going on around the globe. The Russian leader, Krushchev, for example, embarrassed China when he referred to what he called 'the stench of colonialism' on China's doorstep.[36] It would have been easy to get rid of the British. Hong Kong was dependent on the Mainland for food and water supplies and these could easily have been cut off. There were important reasons, however, for allowing the status quo to prevail. Most importantly, perhaps, China relied on Hong Kong for much of its foreign exchange, through exports and remittances from overseas Chinese. After 1972, China was developing its rapprochement with the United States and the international community and Britain was America's closest ally and a permanent member of the United Nations Security Council. Any action to recover Hong Kong would have been likely to jeopardise China's relations with the United States – which was coming round to China's point of view over Taiwan, the first priority as far as reunification was concerned – as well as its position in the United Nations.

A further reason for Britain not reading any particular significance into the Chinese action at the United Nations is the perception that the statement was the reiteration of a long-held official position. China was merely setting the record straight, now that it was a member of the United Nations. Finally, in removing Hong Kong from the list of territories due to become independent, China's action, in fact, allowed Britain to maintain the status quo. No measures would be needed to introduce representative government in preparation for self-government as Hong Kong would no longer be prepared for independence.

Although China had not specified publicly any time for the possible recovery of Hong Kong, there were private indications to British representatives that 1997, the year of the expiry of the New Territories lease, was a likely date. Although China did not accept the treaties which ceded Hong Kong Island and Kowloon to Britain, it was aware that the British did. Hong Kong and Kowloon would not be viable, however, without the New Territories, so by waiting until 1997 and the expiry of the lease, China could at the same time most conveniently lay claim to the whole territory. Cradock notes that, in 1971, Zhou Enlai remarked to Malcolm Macdonald, the former British Commissioner for South-East Asia, that China would only reclaim Hong Kong once the lease on the New Territories had expired.[37] Edward Heath stated in an interview, in 1995, that in the spring of 1974, immediately after he was defeated as Prime Minister in a general election, he met privately with Mao Zedong and agreed future priorities to ensure a trouble-free handover, in 1997, with Hong Kong as an integral part of China.[38]

\* \* \*

From the Hong Kong perspective, in the late 1970s, as the date of the termination of the lease over the New Territories drew nearer, both local and foreign businessmen began to express concern about the future. Already in 1976 the director of the Hong Kong Chamber of Commerce, Jimmy McGregor, had stated that large-scale businesses would need some indication from China about Hong Kong's future, before committing themselves to investments.[39] Businessmen were anxious about the uncertainty of the individual land leases, all of which were due to expire three days before the lease on the New Territories itself, in June 1997. But they were also concerned about the effect the end of the New Territories lease would have on the future of Hong Kong in general.

By 1978, Deng Xiaoping had consolidated his position as the Chinese leader, following the death of Mao in 1976 and an interim period under the leadership of Hua Guofeng. One of the first things that Deng did was to create a Special Economic Zone (SEZ) at Shenzen, on the border with Hong Kong. The idea was to learn from the British-controlled capitalist enclave and develop an equally successful commercial and industrial centre. This was the beginning of China's successful experiment with market economics, later dubbed 'Socialism with Chinese Characteristics'. If China was now willing openly to seek to learn from Hong Kong, the thinking went in the territory, then perhaps China would look favourably on co-operation over the question of the lease.

As awareness grew of the potential damage to investment and business, the British and Hong Kong Governments began to discuss ways of resolving the problem. In March 1979, the Hong Kong Governor, MacLehose, visited Beijing and raised the issue of the leases, in an interview with the Chinese leader, Deng. He put forward a plan whereby the Hong Kong Legco would unilaterally rescind the 1997 deadline, but without Britain making any permanent claim to the territory. China would retain sovereignty, but Hong Kong businessmen would continue to be able to use the land. Deng, who had not been prepared for the question, merely restated China's official position on Hong Kong, saying that China would either take back the territory, or that the status quo would remain. In either event, he reassured MacLehose, businessmen need not worry, because China would take care of the Hong Kong question in good time and business interests would be safeguarded.

In April 1981, the question of Hong Kong's future was again raised with Deng, this time by British Foreign Secretary Lord Carrington. Deng's response, on this occasion, was that Hong Kong would be dealt with in the same way as China planned for the reunification with Taiwan and he encouraged Britain to study in detail this plan when it was made public. In September of that year, China unveiled the formula for reunification with Taiwan, under the principle of 'one country two systems'. As a Special Administrative Region (SAR) of the reunified country, Taiwan would retain a high degree of autonomy and its current way of life would be preserved. The central Government would not interfere in local affairs. Taiwan would even be able to retain its own armed forces.

In mid-1982 China revealed its plan for Hong Kong, according to the slogan that became known as the 'sixteen character solution':

- Recover sovereignty.
- No change in social systems.
- Hong Kong people ruling Hong Kong.
- Preserve stability.

In order to prepare Hong Kong people for what they had in store for them, from June 1982 groups of influential Hong Kong Chinese were invited to Beijing to be informed by high officials about China's plans for the territory and the 'one country two systems' concept. Also in 1982, Deng Xiaoping described the plan in some detail to former British Prime Minister Edward Heath, who was visiting Beijing as a 'friend of China'. Deng told Heath that China planned to take over Hong Kong according to the 'one country two systems' formula and that the British would have to withdraw.[40]

# 3 The Negotiations and the Joint Declaration

In September 1982, Margaret Thatcher, fresh from her victory in the Falklands war, visited Beijing.[1] By this time, it was clear to British diplomats that China intended to reclaim Hong Kong in 1997. Taiwan was no longer to be seen as the model which Hong Kong would follow. Instead, Hong Kong would provide the model for reunification with Taiwan. Thatcher states in her memoirs that Britain's negotiating position was founded on 'Britain's sovereign claim to at least a part of the territory', but that she 'could not ultimately rely on this as a means of ensuring the future prosperity and security of the Colony'. Britain's aim was 'to exchange sovereignty over the island of Hong Kong in return for continued British administration of the entire Colony well into the future.'[2]

In Beijing, Thatcher first met with Zhao Ziyang, the Chinese Prime Minister. She argued that it was important to maintain confidence in Hong Kong and that in order to do this, Britain should continue to administer the territory. If an arrangement could first be come to with China over continued British administration, then the question of sovereignty could be considered. Zhao replied that China was not willing to compromise on sovereignty. From China's point of view, the people of Hong Kong were Chinese and not British. China would recover sovereignty over the whole of the territory, not just the New Territories, in 1997, although Hong Kong would be allowed to maintain its capitalist system and way of life. When Thatcher expressed concern that such a course of action would provoke financial instability, Zhao responded that China put sovereignty before prosperity.[3]

On leaving the meeting with Zhao, Thatcher slipped on the steps leading down from the Great Hall of the People, a mishap which was recorded by photographers and widely circulated in the press. This misfortune, along with the fact that Thatcher was suffering from a severe cold during her visit, was widely interpreted by the deeply superstitious Hong Kong Chinese as an ill omen for the future. Some members of the Hong Kong press also joked that the British Prime Minister had finally submitted to kow-tow to Chairman Mao, whose image looked down over the square.

The day after the meeting with Zhao, Thatcher met Chinese Leader Deng Xiaoping, who was also adamant on China's claim to sovereignty, although this need not be announced immediately, but in a year or two's time, when China was ready, he said. Deng rejected Thatcher's argument that the sovereignty issue could be settled later, if agreement was first reached over continuing British administration. At one point, he threatened that the Chinese could walk in and take Hong Kong that day, if they wanted to.[4] According to press reports, when Thatcher referred to the treaties, Deng retorted with so many expletives, that his interpreter could not translate for her. From Thatcher's point of view, 'the Chinese, believing their own slogans about the evils of colonialism, just did not realise that we in Britain considered we had a moral duty to do our best to protect the free way of life of the people of Hong Kong'.[5] She nevertheless felt that 'For all their difficulties, however, the talks were not the damaging failure that they might have been.'[6] The official communiqué, indeed, betrayed no measure of ill-feeling:

> Today the leaders of both countries held far-reaching talks in a friendly atmosphere on the future of Hong Kong. Both leaders made clear their respective positions on this subject. They agreed to enter talks through diplomatic channels following the visit with the common aim of maintaining the stability and prosperity of Hong Kong.

While this positive statement gave the impression that the meetings had been successful and betrayed no major disagreement between the two sides, the Chinese used a tactic, which was subsequently to be found to be a feature of their negotiating style, of releasing a separate statement to the press expressing their own position. As Thatcher was giving a press conference and trying to calm nerves, a Xinhua (New China News Agency, NCNA[7]) statement was relayed from Hong Kong in which the Chinese Government stated its position that China would regain sovereignty over the whole of Hong Kong, not just the New Territories, as the whole of the territory came under Chinese sovereignty.

On 26 September, after visits to Shanghai and Guangzhou, Thatcher arrived in Hong Kong. At a press conference the next day she maintained that the treaties ceding the island of Hong Kong and Kowloon were valid under international law and, in a comment that was certain to antagonise the Chinese Government, that: 'If a country will not stand by one treaty, it will not stand by another.' She also made the point that Britain had a moral responsibility to the people of Hong Kong. The Chinese Government soon reacted to these remarks, in a long Xinhua commentary of 30 September, which set out its position on the treaties, that is that they were 'unequal' and therefore not valid, having been imposed on China by Britain, following acts of aggression. As for Thatcher's claim over a moral responsibility to Hong Kong people: 'The Government of the People's Republic of China alone is in a position to state that, as the government of a sovereign country, it has a responsibility and duty to the Chinese residents in Xianggang [Hong Kong],' the commentary said.

This megaphone diplomacy, which was to remain a feature of Sino-British relations over Hong Kong right up until the handover in 1997, created great nervousness in the colony. On 27 September 1982, for example, the stock market dropped 10 per cent, and during this period the Hong Kong dollar also fell sharply. David Bonavia, *The Times* correspondent in Hong Kong at the time, wrote of Thatcher's visit: 'Mrs Thatcher left the next day, somewhat like one of those typhoons which run in from the Western Pacific, leaving a trail of destruction behind them. Seldom in British colonial history was so much damage done to the interests of so many people in such a short space of time by a single person.'[8]

The Prime Minister's interpretation was, needless to say, rather different. From her point of view, her visit to China and Hong Kong had three beneficial effects. She wrote, in her memoirs:

First, confidence in Hong Kong about the future had been restored. Second, I now had a very clear idea of what the Chinese would and would not accept. Third, we had a form of words which both we and the Chinese could use about the future of Hong Kong which would provide a basis for continuing discussion between us.[9]

While the first of these points is debatable, to say the least, the other two are probably correct. Until Thatcher's visit, various attempts to initiate a dialogue over Hong Kong had failed. China's attitude had been that they would act over Hong Kong when the time was right. If Britain felt there was a problem over the lease, then that was Britain's problem, not China's. At least now China recognised that some sort of formal agreement needed to be negotiated. At the same time, both China and Britain now publicly agreed that negotiations should be based upon the objective of maintaining Hong Kong's prosperity and stability.

* * *

Further progress following Thatcher's visit was slow in coming. 'Talks about talks' began in October 1982, but did not get beyond discussion of an agenda and procedure for negotiations. The British negotiating team was headed by Sir Percy Cradock, Ambassador to Beijing, a figure who was to remain close to Sino-British-Hong Kong affairs in various capacities right up until 1992.[10] Cradock was assisted by Robin McLaren, Hong Kong political adviser, another figure who was to feature in later episodes of Sino-British relations over Hong Kong.

Thatcher writes in her memoirs that, by January 1983, the British were concerned that no significant progress had been made in the negotiations. In the absence of any initiative from China, she considered the idea of proceeding as if Britain were preparing Hong Kong for independence or self-government, and developing a democratic structure. She was persuaded against this course of action by the ministers, officials and the Hong Kong Governor, Sir Edward Youde (who had replaced MacLehose in May 1982), with whom she discussed it. Instead, she wrote to Zhao Ziyang, softening the British position on sovereignty, stating that she would be prepared to recommend to the British Parliament that sovereignty over the whole of Hong Kong should be allowed to revert to China, if administrative arrangements which would guarantee prosperity and stability and which were acceptable to Britain, the people of Hong Kong and China could be worked out. Indicative of later differences between the British Government and the Foreign Office, Foreign Office officials wanted to go further and concede that British administration would not continue. Thatcher, however, 'wanted to use every bargaining card we had to maximum effect'.[11]

Over the summer. there were three further rounds of talks, but no progress. In fact, by the autumn, signs of panic in Hong Kong had begun to appear. On 23 September, talks ended without the usual words 'useful and constructive' in the communiqué and without a date being set for the next round. This led to a flight of money out of the territory and a collapse of the Hong Kong dollar, 10.3 per cent of its value being lost in just three hours. The next day, 24 September, there was a further fall, by which time the Hong Kong unit had been reduced to a value of $9.5 to the US dollar, compared to $6.5 at the end of 1982. The situation was exacerbated by a statement from Prime Minister Thatcher that there was great financial and political uncertainty about Hong Kong's future. Earlier, on 13 September, former Prime Minister Edward Heath had walked out of a meeting and dinner given for him by the Hong Kong Exco and Legco, on the grounds that members had criticised him for taking China's line on

Hong Kong's future.[12] In August, the Hong Kong Governor, Sir Edward Youde, was reprimanded by the Chinese Government for stating that he represented the people of Hong Kong at the negotiations. As far as the Chinese side was concerned, he could only be considered as a member of the British delegation, responsibility for the people of Hong Kong resting with China.[13]

As for the attitude of the people of Hong Kong in all this, opinion polls were consistent in indicating that they wanted to keep the status quo. Hong Kong people were enjoying the new prosperity of the economic boom of the 1970s. They could see the wide disparity between their standard of living and that of the Mainland. The younger members of the society had been born in Hong Kong and were beginning to identify with it as their home, whereas, in the past, Hong Kong had been viewed as a temporary refuge and/or place to make money.[14]

During this period, China had been increasing the pressure on confidence in the territory. On 13 August, a Chinese official said that China would not share administration with Britain over Hong Kong.[15] On 15 August, Hu Yaobang, Communist Party Secretary-General, announced to a group of Japanese journalists that China would reclaim Hong Kong in July 1997. This statement was reaffirmed on 20 August: 'There is no argument on whether or not to take back Hong Kong. What we are talking about now is what we are going to do during the transitional period and also the policies after the recovery of sovereignty.'[16]

On 14 October, in a softening of the British position, Thatcher sent a message to Zhao Ziyang expressing willingness to explore Chinese ideas and holding out the possibility of a settlement on those lines. This was followed up by a message from the British ambassador in Beijing spelling out that Britain now envisaged 'no link of authority or accountability between Britain and Hong Kong after 1997'.[17] Thatcher had decided that the overriding British priority should be that the negotiations not be allowed to break down.

At this time, Thatcher also sought advice from Lee Kuan Yew, Prime Minister of Singapore, who advised that Britain should send a very senior minister or emissary to convey Britain's proposals at the very highest level. Lee emphasised that the British should present themselves as 'neither defiant nor submissive, but calm and friendly'.[18] He stressed that Britain should clearly accept that 'if China did not wish Hong Kong to survive, nothing would allow it to do so'.[19] In her meeting with Deng, when the Chinese leader had made this very point,

Thatcher had responded that there would be an international price to pay if China took over Hong Kong without regard for its prosperity and way of life. In response to Lee's advice, she now modified her position: 'I now had to accept that China's concern for its international good name would allow us only so much latitude.' This is a surprising admission on the part of the Iron Lady and victor of the war over the Falklands. It makes the refusal to heed such cross-cultural advice and kow-tow to China by Hong Kong's last Governor, Chris Patten, and Thatcher's successor as Prime Minister, John Major, in subsequent negotiations, stand out even more strikingly.[20] In China, of course, Thatcher had a much more powerful country to contend with than Argentina, her opponent in the Falklands. The victory in the Falklands would be shown to have boosted her popularity enough to enable her to win the up-coming British general election in 1983; she did not need a major confrontation over China, as well.

From now on, Britain's position was to try to win as much autonomy and preservation of Hong Kong's system as possible, accepting that neither continuing sovereignty nor administration were possible. Britain's new stance was welcomed by China and the fifth round of formal talks were followed by the words 'useful and constructive' in the press communiqué.

\* \* \*

By the seventh round of talks, which took place from 7 to 8 December 1983, China for the first time formally tabled its blueprint for the handover. In keeping with China's tactic of releasing to the press their negotiating position while the supposedly confidential negotiations were actually going on, this plan had already been published on 5 December in the Hong Kong newspaper, *Ta Kung Pao*. The plan, presented as twelve points, stated that China would leave Hong Kong's social and economic systems unchanged for 50 years. It drew attention to the new article in the Chinese constitution which allowed for the setting up of a Hong Kong Special Administrative Region (SAR) in Hong Kong, to be governed by the local people. And it stated that a Basic Law would be drafted, which would be Hong Kong's mini-constitution. The twelve points were to prove to be the basis for the final outcome of the negotiations, the Joint Declaration.

From this point in the negotiations, the emphasis changed. Until now, the talks had been characterised by China's insistence that it would take over both sovereignty and administration of Hong Kong, set against Britain's persistence in its wish to maintain administration.

Now that China had put forward its own plan, Britain took the initiative, trying to get more specific and detailed information put into the blueprint, which China preferred to keep, for the time being, in terms of broad principles. (From Beijing's point of view, the details would be a question for China, when it later drafted the Basic Law.)

Keeping up the pressure on Britain through the mass media, on 23 January 1984 an interview in *Newsweek* reported Li Chuwen, Deputy Director of Xinhua in Hong Kong, as having said that the Chinese hoped to work out an agreement with Britain by September 1984.[21] If this was not possible, China would make a unilateral announcement of its plans to recover sovereignty. After the British had explained in the negotiations the difficulty of meeting such a deadline, due to the fact that the British constitutional system required that the agreement had to be first put before Parliament before it could be ratified, the Chinese brought forward their deadline to July, thus putting further pressure on Britain. All China wanted from the British was agreement in principle that China would take over Hong Kong sovereignty and administration. They would work out the details of how this would work out in practice. The British, on the other hand, wanted to put as much detail into the agreement as possible, in line with their claim of moral responsibility for the welfare of the people of Hong Kong and their wish to preserve the interests of British and other international investments.

In the ninth round of talks, the Chinese introduced a new idea into the negotiations. They now proposed that there should be a supplementary protocol to the main handover agreement, which would provide for a joint Sino-British commission to oversee all major aspects of British administration, including financial policy, civil service appointments, land sales and constitutional developments, leading up to the handover in 1997. This was something of a bombshell to the British, who decided that this issue would have to be handled at a higher level. As a result, in mid-July, British Foreign Secretary Geoffrey Howe visited Beijing and conducted high-level talks with the Chinese administration.

Howe's visit was a success and considerable progress was made.[22] In meetings with various officials, including Zhao Ziyang and Deng Xiaoping, Howe agreed that September would be the deadline for initialling the agreement, with ratification to follow later. The Chinese agreed to allow more detail, in the annex of the main agreement, as long as their main principles remained as the central core of the document. Agreement was reached to set up a separate Sino-British group which would be responsible for the actual drafting of the document, while the main negotiating teams would continue to focus on issues of principle. China continued to insist on the protocol concerning the joint commission, however. Deng was concerned that Britain would try to siphon money out of Hong Kong during the transitional period, by selling off large amounts of government land, committing money to expensive new government spending programmes, or reducing the government's monetary reserves.[23] In an apparent reference to a recent announcement by Jardine-Matheson (of opium-trading fame), one of Hong Kong's largest companies, that they would move the official domicile of their holding company to Bermuda,[24] Deng stated that: 'Some parties are working to leave Hong Kong in a mess.'[25] Deng also emphasised that he wanted the People's Liberation Army (PLA) to garrison troops in Hong Kong, a point the British had been resisting.

On his way back to London, Howe called in at Hong Kong. On 20 April 1984, at a press conference in the Legco, he announced that Britain no longer considered it possible to attain the goal of continuing British administration in Hong Kong and that Britain was negotiating for an agreement with China which would provide for a high degree of autonomy. Although widespread speculation had already suggested that such a position had been taken, now that it was stated officially, as Cradock, Britain's chief negotiator (after Geoffrey Howe), notes in his memoirs, 'It was an emotional moment.'[26]

In the months following Howe's visit, in spite of the progress made, the talks again became bogged down over the joint commission idea. In June, a visit had been arranged to Beijing for three executive councillors, led by S.Y. Chung, to express Hong Kong's concerns about the handover issue. Their misgivings were not well received by Deng, who said that if they had concerns about Hong Kong, so did the Chinese Government and for this reason they were proposing the setting up of a joint working group in Hong Kong to monitor the transitional period. Howe, again, had to visit Beijing to unblock the impasse.

On the first day of the visit, Ambassador Cradock had a private lunch with Chinese Assistant Foreign Minister Zhou Nan. By this time, the British diplomat had finished his term of duty in Beijing and had been made personal adviser to Margaret Thatcher on foreign affairs, with special authority to oversee the Hong Kong negotiations from London. Zhou explained that there were important meetings of Chinese leaders approaching and that they would affect Hong Kong. For this reason, it was important to resolve all outstanding issues in the next few days. To allay Britain's concerns over the joint commission, China would accept its ideas on this issue, but if overall agreement could not be reached, the Chinese would withdraw all their previous offers and withdraw from the talks. The British sent a telegram to London asking the Prime Minister if they could proceed along these lines. The reply was that they could do so, in principle, but that they did not have carte blanche. This gave the British negotiating team the leverage they wanted and in the ensuing meetings rapid progress was made on outstanding issues. Importantly for the British, the Chinese accepted that the joint commission, or Joint Liaison Group (JLG), as it would now be called, would have terms of reference which would extend beyond the handover, until the year 2000, that it would meet on a rotational basis in London, Beijing and Hong Kong, but that it would start to meet in Hong Kong only in 1988. In this way, Britain would have the right to monitor Chinese compliance with the agreement as well as China monitoring Britain. At the same time, the authority of the body would be reduced; it would be 'an organ of liaison, not of power'. Other agreements were that the policies contained in the agreement would be set out in the Basic Law and that passages referring to imperial history, which the British did not like, would be struck out. Most importantly, statements were added to the draft document making it clear that both sides considered it to be a legally binding international agreement.

In a concluding meeting with Deng, who had returned specially from a seaside holiday, the Chinese leader expressed his satisfaction that the agreement was finally tied up, barring a few loose ends. He proclaimed the agreement, or Joint Declaration, as it was to be called, to be 'an example to the world, for settling questions between states, left over from the past.' He also invited both Margaret Thatcher and the Queen to visit China.

* * *

On his return to London, Howe again stopped over in Hong Kong. The British had kept the Hong Kong Government in the dark over the Beijing visit, not wanting any premature disclosure of the outcome. There was general satisfaction when the Hong Kong Government and public were informed by Howe of the result. The following is the impressive list of points that he was able to report had been negotiated:

• Hong Kong's unique economic system and way of life would be preserved

- the agreement would be legally binding
- there would be liaison between China and Britain after conclusion of the agreement
- the arrangements would prevail for 50 years and would have sufficient clarity and precision to command the confidence of the people of Hong Kong
- the common-law legal system would be preserved
- Hong Kong's own trade policies, free port status, and manufacturing and trading economy would be maintained
- rights of ownership of property would be preserved
- Hong Kong would continue to be a separate customs entity
- Hong Kong would continue to be represented in international organisations such as GATT
- Hong Kong people would retain the right to travel in and outside Hong Kong
- fiscal policy, freedom to move capital, and a convertible currency would be maintained
- the education system would remain the same
- all rights and freedoms now enjoyed would be preserved.

Following Howe's visit, the two negotiating and special drafting teams continued to work over the Declaration until the final version was ready by the third week of September. One of the last ministerial exchanges occurred on 15 and 16 September, when Howe sent a note to his Chinese counterpart insisting that the governor and the legislature should be democratically elected.[27] The Chinese agreed to the inclusion of a statement that the legislature 'shall be constituted by elections' and that the executive would be accountable to the legislature. However, they refused to define the term 'elections' in any way – a point which was to lead to a lot of controversy later – and insisted that the procedure for the appointment of the future Governor, or Chief Executive, would be 'by election or through consultations held locally'.[28]

It seems odd that such a fundamental issue as how the government would be chosen in the future SAR should have been left until such a very late stage in the negotiations. British thinking, presumably, was that raising this issue earlier in the negotiations would have been likely to antagonise the Chinese and result in a possible breakdown in the talks. After all, the British had refrained from introducing any democratic development in Hong Kong, at least partly because of a fear of provoking conflict with the Mainland Government. Democracy would have suggested self-determination, which China did not agree with, in accordance with its view of Hong Kong as an integral part of China. Now that they were in a situation of not having introduced democracy and that they continued to run Hong Kong on colonial lines, how could the British justify suddenly recommending that democracy should be introduced?

So the reference to 'elections' was left deliberately vague and the Joint Declaration was initialled in Beijing, on 26 September. As part of the consultation process, the Hong Kong people were given the opportunity to express their view on the outcome. A referendum had been ruled out. The specially set up Assessment Office gave people little option but to respond positively; they had to say whether they preferred the agreement being offered or no agreement; they were not given the option of saying that they wanted a better agreement, although the report produced by the assessors did state that many, while accepting the agreement, did so with reservations. In general, however, press reaction and the reaction of the international community was very positive. The United Nations Secretary General, no less, described it as 'one of the most outstanding examples of effective quiet diplomacy in contemporary international relations.'[29] The ratification period over, on 19 December 1984, the Joint Declaration was duly signed in Beijing by Margaret Thatcher and Zhao Ziyang, with the diminutive, beaming Deng Xiaoping looking on and sharing in the toast.

\* \* \*

By any criteria, the Joint Declaration was a remarkable achievement and Deng was justified in his comment that the agreement 'showed the world that problems left over by history can be resolved through peaceful negotiations'. All of the points outlined by Howe in his press conference were incorporated into the document. On rights and freedoms, Annex 1, Chapter XIII had this to say:

> The Hong Kong Special Administrative Region Government shall protect the rights and freedoms of inhabitants and other persons in the Hong Kong Special Administrative Region according to law. The Hong Kong Special Administrative Region Government shall maintain the rights and freedoms as provided for by the laws previously in force in Hong Kong, including freedom of the person, of speech, of the press, of assembly, of association, to form and join trade unions, of correspondence, of travel, of movement, of strike, of demonstration, of choice of occupation, of academic research, of

belief, inviolability of the home, the freedom to marry and the right to raise a family freely.

Every person shall have the right to confidential legal advice, access to the courts, representation in the courts by lawyers of his choice, and to obtain judicial remedies. Every person shall have the right to challenge the actions of the executive in the courts.

\* \* \*

During a visit to the territory, in 1982, when 'talks about talks' were going on, Lord Belstead, British Minister of State with responsibility for Hong Kong, used the analogy of a three-legged stool, to describe the support that any agreement over Hong Kong's future would have to have. An agreement would have to be acceptable to China, to Britain and to the people of Hong Kong, he declared.[30] Governor Youde, in his inaugural speech, had also referred to Hong Kong's future and suggested that the views of Hong Kong people should be taken into account in any decisions that might be made.

Hong Kong's role in the negotiations, in practice, was limited, however. The two sovereign nations both had reasons for excluding the colony. From China's point of view, Hong Kong was a part of its sovereign territory and therefore could not participate on an equal footing with Britain and China, the two sovereign states. Having Hong Kong representatives on the opposite side of the negotiating table would have been tantamount to being confronted by their own citizens, as far as the Chinese were concerned. As already mentioned, Governor Youde was considered to be a member of the British team at the negotiations, not a representative of the people of Hong Kong. The British Government, who claimed to represent the interests of Hong Kong, were not keen to involve the territory, for two reasons. First, because they knew that insistence on Hong Kong participation would antagonise China. Second, because they knew that Hong Kong would take a stronger negotiating position, which they thought might lead to a breakdown in the negotiations. Throughout the talks, Youde presented the Hong Kong view and tried to persuade the British to take a tougher stance. The Hong Kong Exco and Legco thought that China would put economic interests first and could therefore be persuaded by economic arguments. The Foreign Office, however, felt that sovereignty would always be foremost for China, if the two criteria of economic benefit and sovereignty came into conflict.[31]

Hong Kong's frustration at being kept to the sidelines was high-lighted on various occasions. The attitude of Deng Xiaoping to the misgivings expressed by the Executive Councillors whom he met with in June 1983 has already been mentioned, and the confrontation between Edward Heath and the Hong Kong Executive and Legislative Councillors, in September 1983, is another example of a clash between Hong Kong and British attitudes. In May 1984, a delegation of unofficial Exco and Legco members lobbied the British Parliament in London, expressing their concerns about the likely agreement and asking, in particular, how the British Government would ascertain the agreement's acceptability to the people of Hong Kong and what the British Government would do if the agreement was not to the Hong Kong people's liking. They also asked what guarantees the British Government could offer to those Hong Kong residents who held British Dependent Territories passports (about half of the population) and whether these people would be allowed to settle in Britain if they did not wish to live under Communist authority. The delegation received short shrift in London, however, with Edward Heath saying that they 'did not represent the views of the people of Hong Kong'.[32] On the right-of-abode issue, Sir Geoffrey Howe stated in Parliament: 'I do not believe that either this Parliament, or a successor, would favour changes which stimulated emigration from Hong Kong to the United Kingdom, or elsewhere.'[33]

The most overt manifestation of the frustration felt by the Hong Kong general public during the negotiation period occurred in January 1984, when a strike by taxi-drivers was provoked by clumsily introduced legislation allowing for an increase in registration and license fees. In the course of a few days, the strike action, which had begun with drivers using their cabs to block traffic, escalated into a full-scale riot, involving some 10 000 people. Such unrest had not been experienced in Hong Kong since 1967 and the rioting provoked by the Cultural Revolution. Although the action was short-lived, it was serious enough for Governor Youde to tell Margaret Thatcher that Hong Kong was becoming 'restless' and that reassurance was badly needed about the negotiations.[34]

On the political front, the pressure was kept up by the Exco and Legco. In March 1984, a motion introduced by the senior member, Roger Lobo, was unanimously passed in the Legco, calling for any proposals on Hong Kong's future to be debated in the Legco, before any agreement was reached. The announcement of the motion provoked a strong reaction from China, with Zhou Nan accusing the

British of organising the debate as a pressure tactic in the negotiations. He insisted that: 'There are only two parties in these talks: Britain and China.'[35] On 13 July 1984, Richard Luce, British Foreign Office Minister, was told by Legco that it was about time that the Hong Kong people were told what was going on. Further pressure came from Hong Kong, with the announcement by Jardine-Matheson that they were moving their domicile to Bermuda.

Although participation by Hong Kong was minimised by both Britain and China, both sides tried to influence Hong Kong public opinion.[36] The statements by Lord Belstead and by Governor Youde, in his inaugural speech, are examples of this. In the White paper accompanying the draft Joint Declaration document published by the British Hong Kong Government, four quite lengthy paragraphs are included under the heading, 'Consultation with the People of Hong Kong'. The Government Information Service (GIS) provided information to the mass media, putting forward the British/Hong Kong view, on a daily basis. On the Chinese side, the number of Hong Kong representatives on various Chinese bodies, including the National People's Congress (NPC), was increased. As previously mentioned, groups of influential Hong Kong Chinese were invited to Beijing to be informed about China's plans. Between November 1982 and September 1984, more than 33 such delegations visited the Chinese capital, many of them meeting with important leaders.[37] To counter the GIS, the Chinese used Xinhua and Chinese-backed Hong Kong newspapers to put forward their view and win support for it.

* * *

Some commentators have criticised the British negotiators for being too soft and not holding out for a better deal. As already noted, the Hong Kong Executive and Legislative Councillors wanted a stronger line. Martin Lee, the pro-democracy leader, who was soon to come into prominence, has criticised Cradock, the chief British negotiator, and the British approach, saying that they do not have a 'bottom line' when they negotiate with China.[38] As Cradock points out, on the other hand, there were innumerable occasions when Britain might have withdrawn, but this would have resulted in China taking unilateral action in recovering the territory. Cradock accordingly describes the situation as 'a highly unequal negotiation' and says that 'The Chinese held virtually all the cards.'[39]

The negotiations represented an attempt to find agreement between two countries with totally different ideologies. Given the gulf separating the two parties and the mutual ignorance of each other's constraints and presuppositions, it is perhaps surprising that the negotiations were so successful. Although, by the early 1980s, China was beginning to open up to the outside world, Chinese politicians still viewed the international arena as a place for dialectical struggle between the forces of Western capitalism and their own version of Marxist/Leninism. From China's point of view, Britain's main motive, as a capitalist nation, was financial gain.[40] This had been what motivated the establishment of Hong Kong and the British opium traders and others who had forced open China's markets. Allied with the goal of financial gain, according to the Chinese view, Britain's other motive for trying to negotiate a continuing presence in Hong Kong was to establish Western/Capitalist hegemony, or influence, and perhaps extend it into China and undermine the Chinese political system. Given this perspective, the Chinese found it difficult to comprehend the British claim to have a moral responsibility towards the people of Hong Kong and to want to get the best possible terms and guarantees of freedom under Chinese sovereignty possible.

Britain's position was built partly on a feeling of guilt that they were not able to offer the people of Hong Kong the self-determination that they had offered to their other colonies. In addition, British negotiators knew that they could not offer the option of emigrating to Britain to those who did not want to live under Communist rule; the immigration act of 1962 had removed the rights of Hong Kong residents to settle in Britain. These again were doubts that China found difficult to understand. Attempts to negotiate guarantees for Hong Kong's future autonomy were seen by the Chinese as a way of prolonging British rule.

While it may not be the case with the British diplomats, who were for the most part experienced sinologists, there was perhaps on the British side an inability to understand the intense feeling of national shame and humiliation that China experienced from continuing British presence on what it considered to be Chinese territory.[41] Notwithstanding its veneer of Marxist ideology, Chinese society is rooted in traditional Confucianist teachings of ancestor worship, filial piety, and shame on those who do not live up to their duties.[42] If Hong Kong was Chinese territory, why should China have to enter into negotiations to assert its sovereignty? This might explain the intense anger felt at Margaret Thatcher for insisting that the treaties were legally binding and the more co-operative attitude once she had accepted that sovereignty and administration would return to China.[43] Similarly, British attempts to include Hong Kong representatives in the negotiations were an affront to Chinese sovereignty. How could China agree to their own compatriots lining up on the opposite side of the negotiating table with the British?

* * *

While some of China's negotiating behaviour can be interpreted as a reaction to what China felt to be the unacceptable British point of view, other parts can be interpreted as simply tactics to gain the best advantage possible. A number of commentators have attempted to characterise the Chinese negotiating style, both in business and in politics.[44] The tactics preferred by the Chinese can be presented as maxims, as follows.

**Be patient and use time pressure on the other side:**
Britain wanted to settle the 1997 question quickly, because of the problem of the leases. China was able to put the British off by simply saying that it would recover Hong Kong 'when the time was ripe'. This encouraged Britain to adopt a more flexible approach. Chinese delays also led to Britain first giving way on the sovereignty issue and then on administration. It is clear from Thatcher's memoirs that she was impatient to settle matters. The Hong Kong lobby wanted to hold out longer for better terms, on the grounds that China was primarily motivated by financial arguments. The inevitable economic crisis which would follow from lack of agreement on the lease, according to this line of argument, would have put pressure on China to be more flexible. Cradock and others have argued, however, that China would always put sovereignty before economic gain.[45]

**Choose the venue:**
In making Beijing the venue for the negotiations, Britain was put in the place of the supplicant. Because of the time constraint, presumably, Britain accepted this arrangement. However, this put Britain at a disadvantage in a number of ways. First, there were considerable logistical problems in communicating with London and Hong Kong. Second, from the psychological point of view, conducting the negotiations in Beijing gave support to the argument that Hong Kong was a Chinese issue. The British position on sovereignty was already, therefore, weakened. Third, the Chinese reduced any possible pressure from the Hong Kong lobby. As hosts, it was easier for the Chinese to insist that Governor Youde could only participate as a member of the British team, not as a representative of Hong Kong.[46]

**Put the other side in the position of the supplicant:**
Choice of venue was one way of putting the other side in the position
of the supplicant. Another way China did this was in failing to
respond to the initial enquiries by the British on the question of the
New Territories' lease. Some have argued that if Britain had not taken
the initiative, then China might have had no alternative but to offer an
extension of the lease or some other way of prolonging the status quo.
On the other hand, the question of the importance China attaches to
the sovereignty issue is again crucial. Such a strategy would have
created the risk of China acting unilaterally and using some sort of
economic blockade or even force.[47]

**Let the other side reveal their hand:**
Here China waited until the British had conceded on sovereignty and
continuing administration, before revealing its twelve-point plan, in
the seventh round. Of course, China had revealed its general position
that it would retake Hong Kong 'when the time was ripe' and in
stating that 'Hong Kong people could put their hearts at rest', during
MacLehose's visit. But China did not reveal how this would be carried
out, until Britain had yielded on sovereignty and administration.

**Establish principles and avoid legalistic details:**
The Chinese were unwilling to proceed with the negotiations until
Britain had first backed down over sovereignty and then over administration. These were China's two basic principles. Once these had
been agreed, the Chinese wanted to finalise the agreement as quickly
as possible, based on its twelve points. The British achievement was to
persuade the Chinese to add as much detail to the Joint Declaration as
they did, although details concerning the constitutional arrangements,
for example, were to be left to the Basic Law, a document which
would be drawn up by China alone.[48]

**Demand a high price first, even if unrealistic:**
This is a basic negotiating tactic, used by both sides. For the British,
Thatcher first demanded that sovereignty remain with Britain, although
her position was that she was willing to relinquish sovereignty in return
for continuing British administration.[49] On the Chinese side, China
threatened to act unilaterally, if Britain did not agree to its demands.
Without access to the Chinese archives, it is not possible to know to what
extent this was a realistic threat or not. In persevering at all costs to get an
agreement, it seems that the British took this threat seriously, however.

**Establish your bottom line and stick to it:**
Thatcher's first negotiating position was to hold out for retention of both sovereignty and administration. When she was forced to give in on sovereignty, her next position was to hold out for administration. But this was also yielded. It seems that Britain, although starting with a bottom line, failed to keep to it and refused to walk away from the negotiations. At this stage, the Chinese were ready with their bottom line, the twelve-point plan, which remained the basis of the final agreement. In subsequent negotiations over Governor Chris Patten's 1992 political reform plan, Patten claimed that this time Britain did have a bottom line.[50] In this case, however, the negotiations were aborted and China did take unilateral action.

**Foreclose the negotiating position of the other side by rejecting it publicly prior to a negotiating session:**
The Xinhua statement prior to Thatcher's press conference following her meeting with Deng is an example of this tactic. In saying that China had sovereignty over the whole of Hong Kong, not just the New Territories, the Chinese pre-empted Thatcher's position on the validity of the treaties.

**Maximise media pressure by issuing public statements:**
China consistently used the pro-China Hong Kong press to reveal its negotiating position while the supposedly confidential negotiations were actually going on. In this way it put pressure on the negotiators. The twelve-point plan was published in a Hong Kong newspaper, as mentioned above, before it was revealed in the negotiations. When negotiations were going well, from the Chinese point of view, the megaphone was turned off. When things were not going as they would have liked, it was switched on again. In this way, public opinion was affected in Hong Kong, and this put pressure on the British negotiators. Of course, the British also revealed their position, through 'leaks' to the press, when it suited them, but, as a proponent of a 'free' press, their scope for propaganda was restricted.

**Use extreme language:**
Deng's foul language during the Thatcher meeting is an example of this tactic. His threat that the PLA could take Hong Kong that day was another example. Press reports heaped personal abuse on the British Prime Minister, denouncing her, for example as a 'stinking woman'.[51] Such threats and abuse are designed to unsettle the

other party, as one never knows how much truth, if any, there is in them.[52]

**Shame the other side:**
During the negotiations China presented itself as the injured party. The China-backed media put out a steady stream of statements and articles detailing alleged British injustices in Hong Kong and its other colonies throughout history. The Chinese wanted the final declaration to describe the imperial background to Hong Kong. This was only taken out in the last round of negotiations.

**Use a 'friend of China' to pressure the other side:**
China makes great efforts to cultivate foreign dignitaries with whom it has established a co-operative relationship, with a view to enlisting their help at some future date. These people are referred to as 'old friends of China'. President Nixon (the first Western statesman to have dealings with China, following its espousal of the 'open door' policy of the seventies), American Secretary of State, Henry Kissinger (the architect of Nixon's China policy), President Bush (an ex-ambassador to Beijing) all became 'old friends of China' and China sought to maintain the relation with them and use their influence long after they had left office. On the British side, Edward Heath, as the first British Prime Minister to visit China and hold talks with Chairman Mao, is a good example of a 'friend of China'. Heath makes regular visits to the PRC, where he is well received, as if he were an official visitor. Considering himself an expert on Chinese affairs, he is often outspoken in Britain on China-related issues, often taking a pro-China line. As noted in the previous chapter, it was Heath who conveyed the initial message to the British Government that China planned to take back Hong Kong. Heath's encounters with Hong Kong representatives in London and Hong Kong are also good examples of the 'old friend of China' tactic being used to China's advantage during negotiations. Heath was also used as an intermediary in conveying a message that China would act unilaterally if an agreement was not reached by September 1984.[53]

**Do not view an agreement as a completed transaction:**
In business negotiations, it has been noted that Chinese negotiators may want to re-negotiate after their interlocutors believe everything to have been signed and sealed. In the field of international relations, at the signing ceremony for the Joint Declaration, Zhao Ziyang made

the point that China has a very good track record of complying with its obligations.[54] Nevertheless, there still remains the question of different interpretations of the agreement. This may be why the Chinese prefer broad principles to legalistic details. The decision not to spell out the constitutional arrangements is a case in point here. Even the statement: 'The legislature shall be constituted by elections.' has been open to different interpretations, as will be seen in later chapters of this book.

The above negotiating maxims will be returned to in considering later dealings with China during the Patten governorship.

* * *

The question remains. Was the Joint Declaration the best deal that Britain could get for Hong Kong, in the given circumstances?

In March 1992, the International Commission of Jurists produced a report of a mission sent to Hong Kong to investigate the human rights situation in the territory.[55] While applauding the Joint Declaration as 'in many ways a highly creditable achievement and...a much better deal for Hong Kong than it would have been reasonable to expect before the start of negotiations', the Commission argues that Britain should have obtained the authority of the Hong Kong people both before entering into the negotiations leading up to the Joint Declaration and before signing the final agreement.[56] It rejects the view that China would not have allowed such a procedure. Arguing from a slightly different perspective, Scott also criticises the British side for not conducting an official measure of popular opinion before the negotiations were started. Unofficial opinion polls before and during the negotiations clearly favoured the status quo. An official measure, showing the same attitude, might have allowed the British to have argued a stronger case on behalf of the people of Hong Kong.[57]

Scott has various other reservations about the way the agreement was negotiated by the British. First, Britain might have played the economic card more forcefully, as the Hong Kong lobby wanted them to. Perhaps Hong Kong could have withstood some sort of economic stand-off better than the British negotiators claimed it could.[58] Second, Scott notes a failure on the part of the British negotiators to stipulate how the document would be interpreted if there were disputes over its meaning. In including the provision that China alone would draw up the Basic Law, based on the Joint Declaration, Britain effectively granted the sole right of interpretation to China. Third, Scott argues that, in consistently giving ground to the Chinese, Britain set a pattern of backing down to the Chinese side which it would prove difficult to break during the transitional period.[59] Following the signing of the document, it was indeed the case that, as the following chapters will show, the pattern of British accommodation to China's wishes continued. When finally Britain tried to break the pattern and take a stronger line, with Patten's 1992 electoral reform proposals, China was not prepared and a crisis developed in the Sino-British relationship.

One final caveat which might also be mentioned regarding the final settlement is that there must also be a suspicion regarding the conviction with which Britain argued Hong Kong's case. There are some in the British camp who view long-term relations with China as more important than Hong Kong. Since its acquiescence to China's demand that Hong Kong be taken off the United Nations list of colonies which were due for self-determination, it was clear that Britain had decided to relinquish Hong Kong as and when China decided it wanted to reclaim it. By entering into the Joint Declaration, Britain washed its hands of Hong Kong, this line of thinking goes, and left the way open for improved British relations with China, the most populous nation in the world and an important market for British goods.[60]

In addition to this self-interest, there was another possible reason for Britain being willing to give up Hong Kong. During the anti-China period of United States foreign policy and the wars in Korea and Vietnam, it suited the United States to have a friendly ally in East Asia in British-controlled Hong Kong, which it could use as a staging post and information-gathering centre. Once President Nixon and, later, President Reagan decided that China should become the United States' ally in its cold war against the Soviet Union, then Britain would have realised it would receive little support from the United States in maintaining its colony in the face of Chinese claims.

With Hong Kong being effectively kept out of the negotiations, it is not possible to know to what extent these lines of thinking may or may not have prevailed. But the suspicion must always remain.

In weighing up the available evidence, however, the Joint Declaration still remains a remarkable document, negotiated by two countries with proud histories and totally divergent ideologies. In the words of *The Times,* the agreement was probably, 'as good as Britain and Hong Kong can expect to get'.[61]

# 4 Representative Government and the Basic Law

It is ironical that the introduction of democratic reform in Hong Kong only really started to be put into effect once the British Government had decided to allow the colony to revert to Chinese sovereignty. It was the statement incorporated at the last minute into the Joint Declaration, to the effect that 'the legislature of the Hong Kong SAR shall be constituted by elections' and that 'The executive authorities shall abide by the law and shall be accountable to the legislature' which prepared the way for such a course of action. From the shelving of the Young Plan, which had been introduced in 1945, the British and the Hong Kong-British Governments had consistently back-pedalled on the issue of constitutional reform.

Already, as the final stages of the negotiations leading to the Joint Declaration were going on, in July 1984 the Hong Kong Government set about the task of planning for democratic development, producing a consultation Green Paper which set out its intention 'to develop progressively a system of government the authority for which is firmly rooted in Hong Kong, which is able to represent authoritatively the views of the people of Hong Kong and which is more directly account-able to the people of Hong Kong'.[1] This Green Paper was quickly followed four months later by a policy White Paper, which proposed that for the first time, in 1985, 24 members of the 57-member Legco should be elected.[2] However, arguing that Hong Kong was not ready for direct elections based on universal suffrage and that the adversarial politics which was likely to ensue from such a procedure might lead to social instability at a crucial time, elected members were to be selected by other means. Half would be chosen by electoral colleges made up of members of various local councils. The other half would be elected by functional constituencies, that is, individuals grouped according to professional and corporate interests, such as commercial, industrial, legal, medical, and educational. In both types of election the electorate would be very small and often close-knit. When the first election took place in 1985, for example, the number of eligible voters in the electoral college constituencies ranged from a minimum of only 27 to a maximum of only 63. In the functional constituencies, 5 of the 12 candidates were elected unopposed.[3] For lobbying, most candidates sent personal letters to their constituents or approached them individually. In many cases, the support of key individuals had an important influence on the result. The whole process ensured that those returned tended to be conservative in outlook, pro-Government and pro-business. In addition to these restrictions on representativeness, it also needs to be noted that in all discussion of electoral reform for the legislature in Hong Kong, the Exco, which is the policy-making body, would continue to be made up of appointees and ex-officio members.[4] The Legco is only able to vet legislation introduced by the government. Private members' bills can be introduced, but only if there are no budgetary implications, and the bill does not relate to political structure or the operation of the government. Real power lies with the Governor (or Chief Executive, after the establishment of Hong Kong as an SAR), and his personally chosen Exco, not with the Legco.

In spite of its rejection of the idea of direct elections in 1985, the White Paper stated that 'the bulk of public response from all sources suggested a cautious approach with a gradual start by introducing a very small number of directly elected members in 1988 and building up to a significant number of directly elected members by 1997'.[5] While not categorically committing the Hong Kong Government, the White Paper therefore created the strong expectation of a start to direct elections in 1988, followed by a significant increase by 1997. A final decision on direct elections would be made, the White Paper stated, in a further review of constitutional arrangements, to be made in 1987.

The expectations concerning direct elections were confirmed when the British Parliament debated the Joint Declaration shortly after the Green and White Papers were published. During this debate, members of parliament emphasised the importance of the provisions in the Joint Declaration for constitutional reform. It is possible that members were not fully aware of the limited scope for democratic development that the Joint Declaration actually provided for. Speaking for the government, on 5 December 1984, Minister of State at the Foreign Office Richard Luce stated that 'We all fully accept that we should build up a firmly based democratic administration in Hong Kong in the years between now and 1997'.[6] This was a very ambitious goal, however, given the limited scope for democratic development contained in the Joint Declaration. The emphasis of the Sino-British document on executive-led government, the fact that the chief execut-ive would be selected 'by election **or through consultations held locally**' (emphasis added), and the fact that the term 'elections' was not defined meant that a fully elected government was out of the question.

The promised 1987 review did not live up to this expectation created by the Green and White papers and the British parliamentary debate. The White Paper that was issued in February 1988 stated that direct elections would now be deferred until 1991, when ten members would be chosen by direct election. These would be as a replacement of those previously elected by the electoral colleges, not in addition to them. In 1988, the only change foreseen was an increase from 12 to 14 in the functional constituency seats. The White Paper justified this slowing down in progress to the need for a smooth transition to Chinese rule and continuity thereafter. It further stated that any further democratic development must wait for the promulgation of the Basic Law. This was the beginning of the new policy of 'convergence', meaning that all future change in Hong Kong's constitutional arrangements should conform to China's plans, as stated in the Basic Law.

\* \* \*

Britain's change in policy came about as follows. Initially, China did not publicly complain about Britain's constitutional proposals for Hong Kong, although Britain must have been aware that they would not be well received by the Chinese side. The reference to elections in the Joint Declaration, as noted in the previous chapter, was only accepted at the last minute. Percy Cradock, the chief British negotia-tor, has subsequently written in his memoirs that there was no ques-tion of referring to 'direct' elections.[7] Similarly, when Thatcher tried to raise the question of constitutional development at a meeting with Zhao Ziyang on the day she was to sign the Joint Declaration, in December 1984 (therefore after the Green and White Papers had already been published), Zhao told her that 'the Chinese Government was not prepared to make any comment on constitutional develop-ment in the transitional period'.[8] Perhaps, during the honeymoon period of the signing of the Joint Declaration and its aftermath, China did not want to ruffle feathers. It was only on 27 May 1985 that the two countries officially ratified the agreement, after all, at a ceremony in Beijing. In June of that year, on a visit to Britain to discuss trade, Zhao Ziyang was still able to say, in a reference to the implementation of the Joint Declaration, that Britain and China 'share[d] identical views on this question'.[9]

After officially showing no concern about the British constitutional proposals, by November 1985 China's growing suspicions of Britain's intentions were made public. In an indirect reference to the British-Hong Kong Government, the Head of Xinhua, Xu Jiatun, stated in his first press conference in the two years he had been in Hong Kong that it was essential that both Britain and China abide by the Joint Declaration, but that: 'It is not difficult to detect that somebody has already deviated from the Joint Declaration.'[10] He continued that it would be most unfortunate if changes were made to Hong Kong's political system before the publication of the Basic Law, China's mini-constitution for Hong Kong.

By this time, China had set about creating its own constitutional arrangements for post-1997, with the creation of the Hong Kong Basic Law Drafting Committee (BLDC). The BLDC had its first meeting at the beginning of July 1985, in Beijing. Its job was to flesh out the provisions of the Joint Declaration into the Basic Law. Although the laws of Hong Kong were draconian in many cases and gave the colonial authorities considerable scope to deny personal freedoms, if they wanted to, in practice these powers, since the 1967 disturbances, had been fairly sparingly used and Hong Kong people enjoyed personal freedom equivalent to that of many Western countries. In order to guarantee that this freedom was preserved, democratic provisions would be written into the Basic Law. Most areas had already been negotiated between Britain and China in drawing up the Joint Declaration and in many cases the Basic Law simply repeated what was already stated in that earlier agreement. On the question of elections, however, as this was a new development for Hong Kong, there was a problem, because the Chinese had insisted that the Basic Law was their responsibility alone and not the joint responsibility of both China and Britain. Britain, however, had already committed itself to introducing electoral reform during the transitional period.

Clearly, there was a problem in having both the British-Hong Kong Government and the Chinese Government working on separate electoral arrangements for the post-1997 period. One party's arrangements would have to be scrapped, and as China had responsibility for Hong Kong post-1997 it would be more reasonable that it should be its arrangements which should prevail. One can only assume that the British, in starting early in developing constitutional reform, were hoping to present the Chinese with a *fait accompli* in the form of a set of democratic arrangements which they would feel obliged to incorporate into the Basic Law. The British had not anticipated that the

Chinese would start work on the Basic Law so soon.[11] But the Chinese, after their initial hesitation, had other plans. They insisted that any electoral arrangements made by the British would have to conform with the Basic Law. Although they started work on the Basic Law in July 1985, it was not due to be promulgated until 1990. The Chinese thus presented the British with the choice of either holding up their plans until the Basic Law was promulgated (and thereby effectively postponing or cancelling any democratic reform) or continuing with their plans (and thereby creating conflict with China and the possibility that whatever arrangements they set in place would be scrapped in 1997).

Its bluff in moving quickly to introduce an element of democracy in Hong Kong having been called by China, Britain was now in a dilemma. Its attempts to move towards democracy were being blocked by China, but the British Government had promised Hong Kong a steadily increasing degree of democratic development leading up to the handover. The British Government had also promised that Britain would not allow any Chinese interference in Hong Kong's affairs during the transitional period. If these promises had not been made, it is unlikely that the Joint Declaration would have been accepted by the British Parliament or the people of Hong Kong.

\* \* \*

The way the British tackled the problem was not an honourable one. As had been promised, in May 1987 the Hong Kong Government issued a Green Paper to assess public opinion on the question of electoral reform. Probably the most important question to be addressed, as indicated in the earlier 1984 Green and White Papers, was that of direct elections. However, while the Green Paper focused upon just about every other issue, that of direct elections was, as one commentator has stated, 'carefully buried'.[12] A Survey Office was set up to collect opinions on the Green Paper. This office commissioned two public opinion polls. In accordance with the apparent aim of keeping attention away from the issue of direct elections, there was no direct question along the lines of : 'Do you think that there should be direct elections in 1988?' There was also evidence of manipulation of the data collected by the Survey Office. The responses of those in favour of direct elections in 1988 were apparently played down. A petition containing 230 000 signatures in favour of direct elections, for example, was accepted as a single opinion, on the grounds that only signed letters would be counted as submissions. The majority of signed letters received were, in fact, pre-printed form letters distributed by Chinese-backed companies to their employees, who were required to sign them and send them in. These letters, of course, were not in favour of direct elections.[13]

According to independent opinion polls, the majority of public opinion was clearly in favour of direct elections in 1988. When the outcome of the consultation was published in October 1987, however, the government reported that this was not the case and that the majority of Hong Kong people did not favour direct elections in 1988. It was this controversial finding which the Hong Kong Government used to justify the decision in the 1988 White Paper to hold off on direct elections and thereby tacitly accept China's insistence on convergence. According to Roberti, indeed, the British had already secretly agreed with the Chinese Government, at a meeting of the JLG in November 1995, soon after the Xu Jiatun press conference, that the British Government would put off 'all major constitutional changes'.[14] Ensuring minimum adverse public reaction, the White Paper was published a day before the eve of the lunar new year, the most important public holiday in Hong Kong and a time when up to 15 per cent of the population travel to China for family reunions and those who remain are focused on family visits and festivities. As well as putting off the introduction of direct elections until 1991, the White Paper further watered down its proposals, by having the directly elected seats replace those which were already indirectly elected, not those which were appointed, as had been anticipated. In this way, the Government not only ensured that it fitted in with China's wishes, but also that the British Hong Kong Government, which for so long had operated without interference from elected representatives, would itself keep its built-in majority until 1994.

Britain used the cosmetic term 'convergence' to describe its policy of dovetailing its electoral reform plans with the Basic Law. There is some doubt about who invented the metaphor. According to Roberti, it was the British representatives on the JLG, David Wilson (the future Governor) and Anthony Galsworthy.[15] Cottrell, however, attributes the term to Ji Pengfei, head of the Hong Kong and Macau Affairs Office and Chairman of the BLDC, who used it with a group of visiting Hong Kong architects to Beijing, in October 1985.[16] The expression seems to have been used for the first time in public by an official on the British side by the Minister of State with special responsibility for Hong Kong, Timothy Renton. Renton explained the idea following talks in Beijing, in January, 1986: 'By convergence I mean two or more [parties] moving in the same direction in order to arrive at approximately the same place at approximately the same time.'[17] It is perhaps significant that in Renton's description both sides are moving, while in the account given by Cottrell of Ji's description it is only Britain that should converge with the Basic Law, but not vice-versa.

\* \* \*

The BLDC consisted of 59 appointed members. 36 of these were from the PRC and 23 from Hong Kong. In addition to the BLDC, there was a Basic Law Consultative Committee (BLCC), all of whose 180 members were from Hong Kong. Although Britain and China had together drawn up the Joint Declaration, the drafting of the Basic Law, which was to be based on the Joint Declaration, was seen as a matter for China alone. This was very important, not least because the Joint Declaration left it to the Basic Law to specify the arrangements which would be set in place for forming the legislature, which the Joint Declaration only stated 'shall be constituted by elections'. In addition, the Basic Law would interpret just what was meant by the statement: 'The Executive shall be accountable to the Legislature.' As already indicated, Britain and China had very different views on this issue of constitutional arrangements. How the Basic Law interpreted the Joint Declaration would determine to a considerable degree what was meant by the 'high degree of autonomy' which Hong Kong was promised.

Both the BLDC and the BLCC had a large representation from the Hong Kong business community, including some of its most wealthy and influential tycoons. China viewed appointments to its transitional committees as an extension of its 'united front policy'.[18] By co-opting business people it was hoped that there would not be a flight of capital out of Hong Kong, as there had been from Shanghai at the time of the Communist take-over. Both the Chinese Government and the Hong Kong business community wanted to make sure that the Basic Law should provide for only limited democracy. The business community had traditionally had an important say in government policy in Hong Kong, through their representation on the Exco and Legco, and the Chinese envisaged maintaining this status quo. China wanted Hong Kong to play an important role in its economic development; it therefore wanted to continue the pro-business stance of the British administration. From the Hong Kong business people's point of view, they had become increasingly dependent on Chinese banks and Chinese-backed companies, which were becoming more influential in the territory, and they wanted to ensure that they were viewed positively by the Chinese authorities after the handover. The business people, in the

main, were opposed to democratic development because they feared
that it might lead to increased social expenditure and higher taxes, on
the one hand, and social instability on the other. T.S. Lo, an Executive Councillor who resigned from the British Hong Kong Government
and threw in his lot with the Chinese, made a statement on the day of
his resignation that expressed the business people's attitude well:
'Hong Kong people should spend less energy and time in politics',
he said, 'and concentrate more on business, which is more helpful to
China. If Hong Kong can suit the needs of China, then it will have a
better future. If not, its future will not be as bright.'[19]

The business interests organised themselves into the Business and
Professional Group of the Basic Law Consultative Committee
(BPG).[20] In August 1986, they issued a manifesto for the future political structure. The plan called for a powerful Chief Executive, no
political parties, and an independent judiciary. The Chief Executive
would be chosen by an electoral college of 600 people. There would be
80 Legislative Councillors. Half would be elected in functional constituencies, a quarter by the electoral college, and a quarter by democratic
election. The group advocated no direct elections in 1988. It was widely
believed that the plan had the backing of the Chinese Government.[21]

China's anti-democracy stance was emphasised in a BLDC meeting
in April 1987, when they were addressed by Deng Xiaoping. Deng
warned the drafters that Hong Kong's system of government should
not be 'completely westernised' and that it should not be modelled on
a British or American style parliamentary system. People should not
judge whether Hong Kong's system was democratic on the basis of
whether it had those features, he argued, specifically stating his opposition to general elections: 'Hong Kong's administrators should be
people of Hong Kong who love the Motherland and Hong Kong. But
will a general election necessarily bring out people like that?'. He
referred to a recent statement by Governor Wilson that things should
be done gradually, a view he agreed was realistic.[22]

In response to the BPG initiative the liberal lobby set up their own
organisation, The Joint Committee on the Promotion of Democratic
Government, in October 1986.[23] They proposed that the Legco should
be composed of over half directly elected members, a quarter from the
functional constituencies, and a quarter from local councils. The Chief
Executive would be elected by universal suffrage.

The conflicting approaches to the constitutional issues of the business and liberal groups represented the beginning of active politics in
Hong Kong. The BPG, as well as a pamphlet, produced a video

presenting their case. The liberals, however, organised public demonstrations and a candlelight vigil, activities which have since come to be part of Hong Kong's way of life. At one rally, on 2 November 1987, more than 1000 people, representing 127 organisations, attacked the BPG proposal.[24] Denis Chang, Chairman of the Bar Association and a leader of the democratic coalition, warned that by barring popular participation the BPG model risked encouraging radicals and unrest. Radicals and unrest were, of course, exactly what the business lobby claimed would be the outcome of more democratic arrangements. Huang Dhen-ya, President of the Hong Kong Affairs Society, warned that, 'What these people are trying to do is to preserve the type of society which allows under-the-table deals, insider trading, corrupt practice and monopoly by a few.' The ensuing period of consultation was a period of heated political debate in Hong Kong. The China-backed newspapers produced a barrage of editorials and commentaries arguing against direct elections, while the liberals were active in street and signature campaigning in favour of them.

\* \* \*

On 6 December 1986, Governor Youde died unexpectedly, in his sleep, while on a visit to Beijing. The Unofficial members of the Exco requested that a politician of considerable standing be appointed to replace Youde, instead of a diplomat, as had been the practice until then. They wanted someone who could provide leadership over the transitional period. They had in mind someone like Lord Soames, who had overseen Rhodesia's independence. According to Roberti, however, Percy Cradock advised the Prime Minister to appoint another diplomat who knew how to deal with China, and David Wilson, one of 'Cradock's people' (the name given to those foreign office officials who specialised in Hong Kong and China affairs)[25] was chosen.[26] Wilson had long experience of China and Hong Kong. On appointment to the Foreign Office he had spent two years in the colony, studying Chinese. After this, he had spent two years as First Secretary in the embassy in Beijing. In the late sixties he had resigned from the Foreign Office to prepare a PhD thesis at the School of Oriental and African Studies in London and then to edit the *China Quarterly*, a prestigious academic journal. On rejoining the Foreign Office, he had been political adviser to Governor MacLehose, from 1977–81. He was involved in the Joint Declaration negotiations with Cradock. On Wilson's approach to the governorship, Roberti states that 'he saw things much the way Cradock and the other "Old China Hands" did'.[27]

Approaching six months into his appointment, on 23 September 1987, Wilson made a visit to Beijing to try to make progress on the elections issue.[28] Although the report of the Survey Office had not yet been completed, Wilson indicated in a meeting with Zhou Nan that the results so far showed that the Hong Kong public was in favour of direct elections, but not until 1988. (He was probably able to make such an early determination from the biased way in which the survey had been structured and conducted.) Zhou stated that the Chinese Government could accept a small number of directly elected seats in 1991, subject to the framework developed for the forthcoming Basic Law allowing for it. While retaining a semblance of the independence of the BLDC in determining the post-1997 electoral arrangements, the way was thus opened for Chinese drafters, prompted by Zhou, to argue for a political system which included a small measure of direct elections. This would allow the British Hong Kong Government to incorporate direct elections into the arrangements for 1991 (though not 1988). In a subsequent visit, on 3 December, to brief him on the survey report and forthcoming White Paper, Wilson announced that Zhou had told him that China would accept some element of direct elections before 1997, if this was provided for in the Basic Law. The *quid pro quo* was thus that the Chinese would allow for limited direct elections in the Basic Law, starting in 1991, in return for Britain's agreement to hold off on direct elections in 1988.

Shortly after Wilson's announcement, no consensus being possible on the draft of the Basic Law, the Committee decided to include various models as alternatives. In accordance with the Zhou-Wilson *quid pro quo*, although the Hong Kong members of the BLDC did not know about it, each of these models for the post-1997 Government allowed for some element of direct elections. The decision to present the alternative models was taken on 4 December 1987. The draft of the Basic Law was issued on 28 April 1988 for a public consultation period extending to the end of September.

When the first draft of the Basic Law was published, it received a lukewarm reception in Hong Kong, except from the business lobby and the China-backed newspapers, who supported it. A poll conducted on behalf of the *South China Morning Post* found that less than half of respondents were confident that the Basic Law would effectively implement the policy of 'one country two systems'.[29]

The problem was not so much that the document was not a fair reflection of the Joint Declaration. Most of the provisions on individual freedoms included in the Joint Declaration were also spelt out in the draft of the Basic Law. What troubled many people was the underlying feeling that China might not honour what was set out. The Chinese Constitution, like the Basic Law, also spelt out individual freedoms – of speech, of assembly, of the press, of association, of demonstration, for example – but these freedoms were clearly interpreted in a different way to how they would be in a western-style democracy. In China, the individual is subordinate to the collective, which is embodied in the Communist Party.[30] The Party is the agent of the people. The law and its interpretation follow the policy as laid down by the Party. Under the Chinese system, accordingly, the Party may have recourse to such procedures as administrative detention and secret trials, in what for Westerners is a contradiction of the individual rights expressed in the Constitution. People in Hong Kong were worried, therefore, that the concerns of the CCP might overrule what was set out in the Basic Law.

A more specific concern along the above lines, which also made people feel uneasy, was that the power to interpret and amend the Basic Law did not rest with Hong Kong's courts, as Martin Lee and others argued it should do, but with the National People's Congress (NPC) of China. The NPC, an organ of the CCP, would thus be able to change or interpret the text of the Basic Law at will, without having to consult Hong Kong people.

During the consultation period, some 74 000 submissions were received by the BLCC, whose job it was to collect public opinion on behalf of the BLDC. At the beginning of the consultation period, leading officials of the BLCC insisted that they would look for quality rather than quantity and that they would not conduct opinion polls, given the general apathy among Hong Kong people in general concerning political arrangements. This approach was a convenient way for the BLCC to de-emphasise the views of those who wanted a more radical approach, in favour of the conservative, business-dominated elite. In a pattern that was to be repeated often in matters which concerned China's plans for Hong Kong, there was widespread community dissatisfaction with this approach, however, and the Committee back-tracked and said they would consider both quality and quantity.

In October and November 1988, following the consultation period, there was continued public debate over various proposals for a revised version of the Basic Law. The main conflict continued to be between the pro-China business lobby, or BPG, and the pro-democracy liberals, or Joint Committee. Although there were various meetings between representatives of the two groups, they were still unable to come to a compromise plan. In the end, at a meeting of the BLDC, in mid-November, the so-called 'mainstream model' was formally adopted. According to this model, 15 out of 55 Legislative Councillors would be elected by democratic elections in 1997, a figure which would increase to half by 2003, the legislature's third term. Later, there was the possibility of a referendum to determine whether the entire legislature should be chosen by universal suffrage, in 2012. In 1997, a preparatory committee would be appointed by the Chinese Government, consisting of 60 Hong Kong and Mainland people. Its job would be to establish an election committee of 400 Hong Kong residents who would choose the first Chief Executive. The election committee would increase in size to 800 for the second term. There was again the possibility of a referendum to decide whether the Chief Executive would be chosen by universal suffrage, in 2012. According to the BLDC's second draft of the Basic Law, Hong Kong would therefore be offered the possibility (not the certainty) of a directly elected legislature and Chief Executive some 15 years after the enactment of the Joint Declaration and 30 years after it had been signed by Britain and China. This model was voted on by the BLDC and accepted by all members, except the two pro-democracy representatives, Szeto Wah and Martin Lee.

As discussions were going on in the BLDC, the British and Chinese Governments were again conducting secret negotiations regarding the post-1997 constitutional arrangements. At meetings in Hong Kong with Li Hou and Lu Ping, in September, and with Zhou Nan, in Beijing, in early November, the two sides agreed on arrangements whereby legislators and senior civil servants in post prior to the handover would be allowed to remain in office under Chinese sovereignty. It was argued by the British side that this would ensure continuity and protect stability during what might otherwise be a nervous transitional period. Legislative Councillors and senior civil servants would be able to keep their positions under Chinese sovereignty, taking a simple oath of allegiance to the Chinese Government at the time of the handover. Legco elections would be arranged, in 1995, for a four-year period of office, removing the need for fresh elections in 1997. The two sides agreed that the exact method of elections in 1995 would be subject to further negotiation and that it would, accordingly, not be specified in the Basic Law. The arrangement came to be referred to as the 'through-train model', after the direct rail link between Hong Kong and Guangzhou.[31]

On 22 February 1989, the second draft of the Basic Law was approved by the Chinese NPC. It incorporated the agreement made between Wilson and Zhou that there would be no specification of how the first government would be structured. This would be settled by an NPC resolution. Meanwhile, in an expression of their frustration with the outcome of the drafting process, on 4 December 1988, a group of some 600 protesters, led by Martin Lee and Szeto Wah, had torn up and burned copies of the Basic Law outside Xinhua's Hong Kong headquarters. Lee cried: 'We have become the pioneers of the democratic movement in China. We hope that the torches of democracy will light up every corner of China. Today's action is not aimed to fight for democracy in Hong Kong, but on the Mainland. We hope Hong Kong, after 1997, can become a special *democratic* region of China.'[32] This statement was a blatant challenge to China's policy of 'one country two systems' and insistence that Hong Kong should not interfere in Mainland politics. It was therefore exactly what China did not want to hear.

# 5 Tiananmen and After

On 4 June 1989, events in Tiananmen Square in Beijing created a tremendous impact on Hong Kong and shattered any confidence that had remained after the signing of the Joint Declaration. The chain of events leading to the tragedy began on 15 April 1989, with the death of former CCP General Secretary Hu Yaobang, who had been dismissed in 1986 for not being harsh enough on student demonstrations in 1986.[1] Hu's death led to a wave of pro-democracy demonstrations throughout China. The dissension was given added impetus three weeks later, on 4 May, with the commemoration of the seventieth anniversary of the May Fourth Movement.[2] On 13 May, students in Beijing started a mass hunger strike and occupied Tiananmen Square, the spiritual heart of the nation, demanding democratic reforms and anti-corruption measures. The students were joined by workers, swelling the demonstrations to over a million people. By 20 May, martial law had been proclaimed and, on 4 June, tanks and soldiers entered the Square, indiscriminately firing on the protesters.

These events were watched on television by millions of people in Hong Kong. On 20 May, there was already a mass rally of some 80 000 people in the territory in support of the students, despite a typhoon. On 21 and 28 May there was a march of a million people. After the military intervention, on 4 June, over a million protesters again marched, this time in silence.

A whole range of other actions was taken by people and organisations in Hong Kong in sympathy with what was happening in China. On 20 May, Szeto Wah and Martin Lee, along with other pro-democracy advocates, created the Alliance in Support of the Patriotic Democratic Movement in China (the Alliance). The Alliance received massive support and sent considerable donations of money and supplies to the protesters in Beijing. The Alliance took the position that so long as there was no democracy in China there could be no democracy in Hong Kong. Szeto and Lee also suspended their membership of the BLDC, until such time as Deng Xiaoping, Li Peng and Yang Shangkun were replaced as China's leaders.[3] On 21 May, two other members of the BLDC resigned. One of them, Louis Cha, had been largely responsible for drawing up the compromise 'mainstream model' of the Basic Law. On 24 May, the unofficial members of the Legco and Exco (OMELCO), in contrast to their normally conservative approach, reached a consensus agreement that half the legislature should be directly elected by 1995 and that it should be fully directly-elected by 2003.

By 11 July, China had begun to respond to developments in Hong Kong. Jiang Zemin, the new CCP General Secretary, warned Hong Kong people not to interfere in Mainland affairs when he uttered the proverb: 'The well water does not interfere with the river water.'[4] The 'one country two systems' policy required that China would not interfere in Hong Kong affairs, but that neither should Hong Kong interfere in China. On 21 July, the leaders of the Alliance, Szeto Wah and Martin Lee, were criticised in an article in the *People's Daily* for 'subversive activities'.[5]

\* \* \*

In the face of the events of Tiananmen and the resultant developments in Hong Kong, the British Government was called upon to respond. The new-found pro-democracy solidarity in Hong Kong created pressure for Britain to do something about safeguarding civil liberties post-1997 and speeding up the pace of electoral reform, in order to safeguard Hong Kong's autonomy. At the same time, the brutality of the Mainland regime, which in 1997 was due to take over the colony, led to renewed calls for Britain to soften its position on the right of abode of Hong Kong people in the United Kingdom. In July 1989, the British Government announced that it had decided to enact a Hong Kong Bill of Rights,[6] to speed up the pace of the local democratisation process, and to offer British nationality, with full right of abode in the UK to selected Hong Kong residents.[7] These measures had been recommended in a multi-party Parliamentary Foreign Affairs Select Committee report on Hong Kong that was released in July. In particular, the report had argued that half of the Legco should be directly elected in 1991 and that it should be fully directly elected by 1995.

None of these actions was straightforward. China objected to all three, for various reasons. When the Bill of Rights was enacted, overriding all other laws, in June 1991, Chinese officials made it clear that China reserved the right to repeal it if it was judged to be incompatible with the Basic Law. On the issue of elections China had already made its opposition to universal suffrage clear in the BLDC. On the question of right of abode China claimed the granting of British passports to Hong Kong Chinese citizens to be an infringement on its sovereignty and an infringement of the Joint Declaration. An exchange of diplomatic memoranda had allowed for Hong Kong holders of British Dependent Territory passports to continue to use them, while noting that these passports did not confer the right of abode in Britain. Full British passports, China maintained, which did confer the right of abode, went beyond what was stipulated in the memoranda. Britain's position was that the memoranda only set out the situation in 1997. Prior to 1997, Britain was still free to make changes in its policy. China made it clear that holders of full passports issued by Britain would not be treated as foreign nationals or allowed British consular protection after 1997; neither would they be allowed to hold senior positions in the civil service. A provision in the Basic Law was also introduced which limited the number of Legislative Councillors who held foreign passports to 20 per cent.

There was also a serious problem for Britain concerning passports on the home front. Giving passports to all of Hong Kong's 5.6 million residents, or even the 3.3 million who had the right to British Dependent Territories passports, was out of the question. With unemployment in Britain running at over 3 million and both the Conservative and Labour Parties committed against mass immigration, the granting of any passports to Hong Kong residents would be difficult to sell to the British public. In the face of heavy lobbying from Hong Kong, a decision was taken to issue full British passports to a maximum of just 225 000 Hong Kong people or 50 000 qualified households. Given that the purpose of the measure was to boost confidence, passports would be allocated to those judged to hold positions important to the smooth running of Hong Kong. Having a British passport to fall back on, it was argued, would encourage people in important positions to stay on in Hong Kong. By the time the passport package was announced, Geoffrey Howe had been replaced as Foreign Secretary by Douglas Hurd. Announcing the package in the House of Commons, in late December, Hurd declared: 'It's not just our duty to look after Hong Kong – it's a matter of honour. It is also in our national interest.' Hong Kong was 'the last main chapter of the country's empire' and it 'should not end in a shabby way'.[8] For the first time, a representative of the British Government was talking publicly about not just Britain's moral obligation to the people of Hong Kong, but also the need to consider how Britain's actions in what was its last significant colony would be judged by history.

For some years, by 1989, the Hong Kong Government had been considering the building of a new airport and various feasibility studies had been commissioned. In his October policy address, Governor Wilson announced that a decision had now been made to go ahead, not only with the airport but also associated port and other infrastructure developments, to be completed by early 1997. The plans were massive and would involve tremendous investment. The project would be one of the largest civil engineering projects anywhere ever, at an estimated cost of HK$127 billion. The announcement was widely seen as a confidence-boosting measure, as an indication of confidence in the future of the territory.

At the same time as these confidence-boosting measures, Britain tried to draw on international opinion in support of Hong Kong's autonomy. Prime Minister Margaret Thatcher spoke on the Hong Kong question at important international gatherings such as the European Meeting of Heads-of-Government in Madrid, the Group of Seven economic summit in Paris, and the Commonwealth Heads-of-Government meeting in Kuala Lumpur.[9] China claimed that this internationalisation of the Hong Kong issue was a breach of the Joint Declaration and the Basic Law and commentaries to that effect appeared in the Chinese and pro-China Hong Kong press.[10]

\* \* \*

During the events of Tiananmen and the immediate aftermath, work on the Basic Law had come to a halt. The consultation period on the second draft was therefore extended until the end of October. In November, when work was about to be resumed, Lee and Szeto were barred from rejoining, because of their actions over Tiananmen and their role in the Alliance, which had been labelled a subversive group.

At about the same time as the BLDC was again becoming active, in early December, secret negotiations were re-started between Britain and China on electoral reform. This development followed a secret visit to Beijing by Percy Cradock. Initially the Chinese rejected any speeding up of democratic reform, but they agreed to continue contacts.

In December, rather than softening their approach, the Chinese representatives on the BLDC took a harder line and introduced a number of new clauses, each of which would require new legislation by the first SAR Government. The first new clause prohibited acts of subversion against the central government. This was widely seen as being directed at activists such as Lee and Szeto who had sent funds and other support to the Tiananmen protesters. The second new clause outlawed foreign political groups in Hong Kong and contacts by Hong Kong political groups with outside groups. This was thought to be aimed at dissidents who were using Hong Kong as a base against the Mainland. The third new clause stated that no law could be given status above the other laws of Hong Kong. This was directed at the Bill of Rights, which Britain had introduced, and which would have power to override other laws. Because the Mainland representatives were in the majority, they were able to push all these measures through, in spite of opposition from Hong Kong representatives. In the past, Hong Kong drafters had been listened to by their Mainland counterparts, but now confidence had been lost and co-operation declined.

In spite of diplomatic pressure from Britain, arguments from Hong Kong members of the Committee and public opinion in Hong Kong, the Mainland Drafters did not allow any concessions on electoral arrangements, either. The final plenary meeting of the BLDC adopted a package for the first SAR Government which allowed for 18 seats to be directly elected, 12 seats to be elected by an electoral committee, and 30 seats to be elected by functional constituencies. In accordance with the 'through-train' agreement, this legislature would be elected in 1995. In 1999, the directly elected seats would increase to 24, with a commensurate reduction in the number of seats allotted to the electoral college. In 2003, the electoral college would be eliminated and there would be a fifty-fifty split between directly elected and functional constituency seats. In 2007, there would be the possibility of a fully directly elected legislature, but this would require a two-thirds majority of all members and the agreement of the Chief Executive.

On the final day of the meeting, there was a last minute amendment to what had been decided. Diplomatic negotiations between Britain and China had arrived at an agreement and it was now allowed that there would be two more directly elected seats in the 1997 legislature, bringing the number up from 18 to 20.

Immediately following the announcement of the agreement by the BLDC, the Hong Kong Government announced that there would be 18 directly elected seats in the 1991 elections and 'not less than 20' in 1995. Britain had managed to extract from the Chinese two more directly elected seats for the 1995 elections – a far cry from the 50 per cent directly elected legislature in 1991 and the fully directly elected Legislature in 1995 called for by the Foreign Affairs Select Committee. The use of the expression 'not less than' seemed to offer the possibility of a further increase, but this may have been face-saving on the part of the British, to justify their return to the policy of convergence.[11]

* * *

When China had signed the Joint Declaration and had agreed to 50 years without change to Hong Kong's way of life and capitalist system, there are grounds to believe that it had assumed that this would be based on the status quo in 1984. It had not anticipated that Britain would attempt to change the system, and, in particular, introduce democratic elections in the lead up to the handover in 1997. After all, the reference to elections in the Joint Declaration had only been introduced at the last minute, as an afterthought almost. The term 'elections' was not defined. China had just as much right, it could be argued, as Britain to interpret the word 'elections' in the way this was meant in China, as a process of consultation, rather than universal suffrage, as elections were understood in the West. Evidence for the view that China anticipated that the status quo in 1984 would be maintained until the handover is to be found in the memoirs of Xu Jiatun, head of Xinhua leading up to Tiananmen, who defected to the United States following those events. Describing the proposed electoral reforms as '13 years of great change and 50 years of no change', Xu argued in his report on the 1984 Green and White Papers for a shift from a policy of passively reporting to his superiors on the British proposals to one of actively opposing them.[12]

Having changed their attitude towards British constitutional proposals, China had set up the Basic Law Drafting and Consultative Committees, as a means of retarding and controlling Britain's plans. Nevertheless, China had been willing to accept a measure of democratic reform, albeit within a firmly executive-led system of government. This is apparent from the acceptance of the Drafting Committee of suggestions from the Hong Kong representatives, some of whom – Martin Lee and Szeto Wah, for example – were in favour of universal suffrage. Faced with China's new policy, the British Government had had to choose between accommodating its reform plans with those of China, as would be specified in the Basic Law, or going it alone and risking a break-down in bi-lateral relations, along with the likelihood that in 1997 China would unilaterally replace the system introduced by Britain with what it specified in the Basic Law anyway. Britain had chosen the former of these alternatives and instituted the policy of 'convergence'. This was in spite of the fact that political reform had been one of the arguments used by Britain in persuading the Hong Kong people and British Parliament to accept the Joint Declaration.

Following Tiananmen and calls in Hong Kong and the British Parliament for a faster pace of democratic reform and other assurances for the future, Britain had again seemed to take a more radical line and made noises about increasing the pace of electoral reform, introducing a Bill of Rights, and offering more passports. However, once order had been restored in China and the Chinese Government again started to assert itself, Britain again backed down from its more assertive position, in spite of a consensus having been developed in previously divided Hong Kong political circles for a faster pace of democracy in the form of the OMELCO consensus. By this time, however, China had been alerted to the possibility of subversive activity in Hong Kong post-1997, following the pro-democracy movement in Hong Kong's support for their counterparts in China. Its position consequently hardened and new clauses were introduced to the Basic Law putting restrictions on civil liberties. Notice was also served that the Bill of Rights envisaged by Britain would be overridden by the Basic Law. Where previously the Drafting Committee, with its Mainland majority, had tried, to a degree, to accommodate to the positions taken by the pro-democracy liberals, now Lee and Szeto were excluded from the Committee and the conservative line taken by the Group of 97 business representatives was favoured. As a sop to Britain's return to the path of convergence, however, China allowed for a token two additional directly elected members of the Legco in 1995.

\* \* \*

Having re-established its control over the electoral reform process, by 1990, China was ready to assert its influence over other Hong Kong matters. Shaken by what it saw as Hong Kong interference in Mainland affairs during the crisis period over Tiananmen and British connivance in allowing the pro-democracy movement to operate in Hong Kong, China was now more suspicious than ever of British motives. As Governor (now Lord) Wilson put it, in 1995, in a collection of reflective memoirs by Hong Kong personalities: 'The Chinese had programmed their minds to think that almost anything we did was somehow directed against them or was just a straightforward reaction against Tiananmen.'[13] On 28 April 1990, Guo Fengmin, leader of the Chinese JLG team, stated that China now expected to be consulted on all major Hong Kong decisions.[14] In the ensuing period, Britain, which had sold the Joint Declaration to the people of Hong Kong on the basis of Hong Kong retaining a high degree of autonomy and no interference in Hong Kong affairs by China before the handover, tried to assert Hong Kong's autonomy. But there were a number of opportunities for China to intervene.

The first area where China tried to make its presence felt in Hong Kong affairs was the airport and associated infrastructure project. In September, Ji Pengfei, Director of the Hong Kong and Macau Affairs Office asked Britain to send a group of experts to Beijing to consult on the project.[15] Hong Kong Government officials, however, insisted that the project was purely a local affair that did not need China's approval. By September, however, the British had changed their mind and Lord Caithness, the Foreign Office Minister with responsibility for Hong Kong, on a visit to the territory, accepted that China should be consulted.[16] In announcing the project, Wilson had, apparently, naively assumed that it could go ahead without the need to consult China. However, banks were not willing to put up finance for a project which was not supported by the incoming sovereign. China, understandably, was not willing to endorse a project which it did not have information about. It had genuine concerns about the cost, financing, timing, and location of the project. Above all, in line with Deng Xiaoping's concerns expressed during the negotiations over the Joint Declaration, China was worried that Britain might be trying to bleed the territory of its financial resources before the handover.

During the negotiations leading to the Joint Declaration, China had made Britain agree to a separate annex in the agreement concerning land issues. The annex specified that, during the transitional period, a joint Sino-British commission would be set up to monitor Government leases and land sales. In addition, the annex stated that a fund would be set up to share all proceeds from government land sales equally between the British Hong Kong Government and the Government of the future SAR. Revenue from land sales in Hong Kong constitutes a considerable part of government revenue. The annex was specifically designed to allay Chinese suspicions that Britain would try to sell off large quantities of land in the lead-up to 1997 and abscond with the revenue. Now that Britain was planning the airport and related projects, China saw this as a further ploy to gain economic advantage for Britain. Most of the work on the infrastructure project would be done by foreign firms and consortia, many of them British or with British involvement.

Before consultations could take place on the infrastructure projects, creating further affront and suspicion on China's part, the Hong Kong Government announced that the first stage of the project, one of the bridges linking the airport (to be built on a small outlying island, Chek Lap Kok) with Kowloon, would go ahead, with government finance. It seemed as if the Hong Kong Government, although agreeing to consultations, was asserting the right to go ahead with the project anyway. Not surprisingly, when the consultation meeting did go ahead, China did not agree to endorse the project.

During the following months, there was a continual series of meetings, including trips to Beijing by Governor Wilson and Foreign Secretary Hurd, to try and win Chinese agreement. The British Hong Kong Government was willing to consult with the Chinese over the project, but was not willing to give China the power of veto. This would be giving up Hong Kong's autonomy. Finally, in June 1991, Sir Percy Cradock was (again) sent on a secret mission to Beijing to negotiate. The outcome of his discussions with the Chinese Government was a Memorandum of Understanding, announced by Wilson on 4 July, which allowed for the airport to go ahead. Key clauses of the agreement were as follows:

- The Hong Kong Government agreed to retain at least HK$25 billion in the reserves by 1997.
- Any debts over a certain amount, due to be repaid under Chinese sovereignty, after 1997, had to have China's approval before being taken on.
- A Chinese representative would sit on the Airport Authority.
- An airport consultative committee would be set up, with Chinese representation.
- The British Prime Minister, John Major, would visit Beijing to sign the Memorandum. (This was a very significant concession on the part of the British, as Major would be the first Western leader to visit China since the Tiananmen incident. His visit would, therefore, in a way, mark Beijing's return to the international community.)
- The British and Chinese Foreign Ministers would meet twice a year and the Governor would meet regularly with the Director of the Hong Kong and Macao Affairs Office.

The agreement was presented by the British as a good one, as it offered the prospect of the airport project going ahead and of better Sino-British Hong Kong relations. On the other hand, it signalled much greater Chinese participation in Hong Kong affairs while the territory was still under British sovereignty. In addition, it was viewed by many commentators as a continuance of the rather humiliating stance – referred to in political circles and the media as 'kow-towing' – adopted by the British side, especially in the stipulation that the British Prime Minister should visit Beijing. And, of course, the agreement had been achieved in secret, without the participation of the Hong Kong Government.

* * *

The second area where China tried to intervene in Hong Kong affairs was on the Court of Final Appeal (CFA). Under British sovereignty, the Privy Council in London was the court of last recourse for Hong Kong. According to the Joint Declaration, the Privy Council would be replaced by a CFA to be set up in Hong Kong. According to the Joint Declaration, again, and later the Basic Law, the Hong Kong court would be allowed to invite judges from other common law jurisdictions to sit on it. For a long time Britain and China had remained deadlocked in negotiations over setting up the court. Rather than unilaterally going ahead, the British Hong Kong Government, in line with its policy of convergence, continued to negotiate with China. Finally, in a JLG meeting in late September 1991, the two sides reached agreement and it was announced that the court would be set up in 1993, so that by the time of the handover it would be well up and running. As part of the agreement, however, in spite of what is said in the Joint Declaration and Basic Law about overseas judges, the two sides agreed that there would be a maximum of only one overseas judge who could sit on the Court.

A second point of contention concerned the inclusion of the term 'act of state' into the bill setting up the court. Cases involving acts of state would not be within the court's jurisdiction, instead coming directly under the authority of the Mainland courts. Under common law, the term 'act of state' is narrowly defined as relating to either defence or foreign affairs. In China, however, acts of state can refer to anything that the state or Communist party is involved in. In the Basic Law, article 19 refers to 'acts of state such as defence and foreign affairs', thus allowing the future sovereign to argue that there are other acts of state besides those relating to defence and foreign affairs. Acceptance of this much broader Chinese definition would allow China, rather than the CFA of the SAR, to rule on any politically sensitive case, therefore. For example, a political demonstrator in Hong Kong could be dealt with by the Mainland, not the SAR. Similarly, a business deal involving a Mainland company and a local Hong Kong or – importantly for the international business community – an international company could be deemed outside the jurisdiction of Hong Kong's courts.

The JLG accord was condemned in Hong Kong, in particular by the legal profession. On 4 December 1991, in spite of intensive lobbying from the government, the Legco voted against the agreement and called for a larger number of overseas judges.[17] For the first time the Legco had voted against an agreement reached between Britain and

China. Following the Legco's rejection of the JLG accord, China argued that it had no right to reject an international agreement, as it was only an advisory body under the British colonial system. In statements which were claimed to be an infringement of the autonomy granted to Hong Kong under the Joint Declaration, the Chinese side argued that if the agreement was not passed by the Legco, then legislation would be introduced by the NPC to set up the court in 1997.

At least two important factors can be identified as impinging on the negotiations leading up to the agreement on the CFA. First, as with other Sino-British negotiations over Hong Kong, Britain was under pressure of time. The alternative to what was offered was no agreement at all, which meant in effect that China could wait until 1997 and then do whatever it wanted. Time was on the side of China, not Britain. In the issues at stake in the CFA negotiations we see again the importance of language and the contrasting interpretations put on the wording of documents and agreements, the key issue here being the term 'act of state'. Britain, with its legalistic approach to international agreement, strove for clear definition of this term. China, on the other hand, with no tradition of a legal culture, preferred a more general principle which allowed greater leeway for interpretation.

* * *

One reason why the Legco now felt confident enough to reject an agreement which had the support of the Chinese, British and Hong Kong Governments was that its make-up had fundamentally changed. On 15 September 1991, in accordance with the electoral reform that had been put in place, the first-ever direct elections had been held in Hong Kong.

Although there were 18 seats, there were only 9 geographical constituencies, with two seats assigned to each. This would allow weaker candidates to be elected in each constituency, as well as stronger ones. Opinion polls and earlier local elections had indicated that the United Democrats of Hong Kong (UDHK), the leading pro-democracy party, under the leadership of Martin Lee, and the smaller liberal groups and independents had a high level of support. Allowing two seats in each constituency, it was thought, would enable pro-China or conservative candidates to win seats, as well as liberals, thus creating a less radical legislature. This might in turn encourage China to be more tolerant of direct elections, the thinking went, and allow more directly elected seats in 1995. (At the same time, a less radical legislature would also suit the Hong Kong Government in the final years of colonial rule, although this was not stated.)

The plan backfired, however, due to a clever strategy adopted by the Democrats. They decided to field two candidates in each constituency and told their supporters that they needed to vote for both. The strategy was a dramatic success, with the democrats winning 12 of the 18 seats and three of their close allies another three. No pro-Beijing candidates were successful in winning a seat. The turnout, 39.1 per cent, was rather low, considering that this was the first time that Hong Kong people had had the opportunity to vote in direct elections, and that nearly two million (1 916 925) people had taken the trouble to get their names on the electoral register.[18] Critics of greater democracy for Hong Kong, including Chinese officials, argued that the low turnout rate demonstrated that Hong Kong people were not very interested in democracy. Pro-democracy supporters, on the other hand, argued that the low turnout might be explained by the fact that such a small number of directly elected seats as were on offer would not really affect the way Hong Kong was governed. With fully democratic elections, the turnout would likely be higher, they argued. What the election certainly did show, however, was that on the first occasion Hong Kong people were given the opportunity to express their political preference they had decided overwhelmingly to support the democrats and their policy of greater autonomy and democracy in Hong Kong.

\* \* \*

Commentators have sought to explain the strong support for the pro-democracy parties in the 1991 direct elections in terms of the development of a growing, educated, Hong Kong-born middle class. As noted earlier, since the establishment of the colony, the majority of Hong Kong's population had been born outside the territory. Most had received only basic, if any, formal education. Many saw themselves as temporary sojourners (whether or not this turned out to be the case). By the beginning of the nineties, however, the situation had changed. According to the 1991 Population Census, more than 3 million out of the 5.5 million total population had now been born in Hong Kong.[19] They had benefited from the formal education that was made available, some of them (still a small minority) to university level. This generation also had access to the international mass media. As beneficiaries of the economic boom, their standard of living had increased. Already, by the seventies, in fact, a middle class group which started to question the political status quo had begun to develop. A small-scale study conducted by the Hong Kong Government in the late seventies identified a group of well-educated, middle-income executives, with an average age of 33, who were unanimous in the view that there was a credibility gap between the public and the government.[20] In the 1970s a group of middle-class student activists came together and, in 1975, created a grouping called the Hong Kong Observers. They acted as a pressure group, trying to make the government accountable and asking for dialogue. They made political proposals and offered alternative policies.[21] Many of the members of this group subsequently became democracy campaigners, Legislative Councillors and political commentators. One of the group's members, Anna Wu, has recently described her situation as follows:

> I am from the second generation of Hong Kong people who were born and brought up here. We consider Hong Kong our home. Our lives have been much easier than our parents'. They had to suffer the hardships of the 1940s and 1950s, but, as Hong Kong became more affluent so did they. It has been my generation which has been able to benefit from those who came and worked so hard...
>
> There were many factors pushing people onwards, to look for some kind of identity for themselves in Hong Kong. People like me had been pulled in different directions throughout our lives. There had been the colonial British influence, the impact of the Cultural Revolution, and the repercussions of that; and then, there were our parents, who kept on telling us what they did in China, why they had run away and, then, their plans to leave once again.
>
> In short, the demographics had changed, and people like myself no longer associated ourselves with China in the same way that our parents had. I've never thought of myself as someone who was a Chinese national. I thought of myself as a Hong Kong person, and there were many who thought like me.
>
> Together with the sense of belonging and identity came the wish to participate in the running of government. We were the second generation. We had grown up in Hong Kong. We were more affluent, better educated, more inquisitive, and it was quite natural to want to have a role in the running of Hong Kong, whether through community affairs, social affairs, or politics. It was one of the major issues that I, and others, became concerned with while I was at university in the early 1970s.
>
> Many have argued that Hong Kong people were not interested in elections or in politics. I would dispute that comment. Ever since I remember, from the 1970s on, quite a lot of people were talking

about politics. We began to wonder why 98 per cent of the population could not participate fully in community affairs or government administration.[22]

Until the 1970s, the colonial government had managed to run Hong Kong effectively by absorbing the Chinese elite into the system. As Hook has written: 'The administrative absorption of politics was achieved by the formal and informal absorption of Hong Kong Chinese civic and business leaders, who might otherwise have become foci of political activity, into the process of elite consensual government at various levels.'[23] Chinese were appointed as representatives of one form or another on the many consultative bodies which had been established by the government. These ranged from the Urban Council, at the bottom, right up to Legco and Exco, at the top. They also included semi-governmental bodies, such as universities and hospitals, and charitable organisations. The appointment of local Chinese representatives to these bodies gave a superficial legitimacy to the colonial government. At the same time, in assigning political power according to wealth, the business-oriented, free-market approach of the government was assured.[24]

The success of the colonial policy could be justified on a number of grounds, according to Hook. It had provided for economic success within a framework of the rule of law. It had met little resistance from the local population, whose culture was based on familism, patriarchy and the avoidance of politics whenever possible. And it had avoided the gap between social mobilisation and economic development which characterised the political instability of many developing countries.[25]

As Anna Wu has testified above, already by the 1970s, and increasingly into the 80s and 90s, a growing middle class was beginning to feel left out of the political process. With the impending departure of the colonial ruler and the worries engendered by the future sovereign, following Tiananmen, this group was beginning to be willing to assert itself. This was a growing force which Wilson and his government, with their emphasis on convergence, failed to accommodate.

\* \* \*

The group represented by Anna Wu would likely have been considerably stronger if it had not been for another option open to the growing middle class, post-Tiananmen: emigration. Indeed, throughout the 80s, emigration was already increasing.[26] In the early part of that decade, an estimated average number of 20 000 persons per year left the territory, but by 1987, this figure had risen to 30 000. By 1992, however, following Tiananmen, the figure jumped to 66 000, while in 1994 and 1995 there were 62 000 and 43 100 leaving, respectively.[27] Of those emigrating a large percentage were from the well-educated middle class. Of those who left in 1995, for example, the Government estimates that 15 700 were managers, administrators, professionals and associated professionals. To counter this brain-drain, the Government facilitated the return of former migrants and, by the time of the handover, returnees had become a significant group in Hong Kong's labour force. With a second passport in their pocket, these people have the assurance of being able to leave if things go wrong, a fact which the incoming sovereign, China, will necessarily need to take into account in planning for the future stability, prosperity and individual freedom of the SAR.

The preferred destination countries for emigrants are Australia, Canada, New Zealand, and the United States. Britain is low on the priority list. This is not surprising, given Britain's strict immigration laws and earlier treatment of the nationality of Hong Kong British passport holders. Until 1962, all Chinese born in Hong Kong were entitled to full British passports, with the right to settle and live permanently in Britain. In 1962, Britain passed a nationality act, stating that this right of abode in Britain would from then on only apply to those already living in Britain or those with at least one grand-parent born there. This effectively took away, therefore, the rights of Hong Kong British subjects to emigrate to Britain. According to Miners, the 1962 act was designed to stem immigration from the West Indies and East Africa, although 'British officials were well aware that the Lease on the New Territories would expire in 1997', and, 'wanted to take early precautions against a flood of Chinese immigrants holding British passports seeking to settle in Britain at that time'.[28] In 1981, another Nationality Act created a new category of British Dependent Territory Citizens. This did nothing to change the actual status of Hong Kong holders of UK passports, merely their official designation. However, it was seen as a sign that Britain was further downgrading Hong Kong citizens and further distancing itself from them. A decision to extend nationality to holders of British passports born in Gibraltar and the Falkland Islands in the same act of Parliament certainly did nothing to increase Hong Kong people's trust and confidence in the British Government.

* * *

Shortly after the Government defeat in the Legco on the JLG Court of Final Appeal agreement, the British Government announced that David Wilson would retire. The decision came as a surprise, as there had been no warning. Indeed, there was not even a formal announcement. Wilson's five year term of office was not due to expire until July 1992. In the New Year's Honours List, however, it was announced that he was being given a peerage and that he was retiring. The retirement was only revealed in passing, as incidental to his being given a seat in the House of Lords.

Most commentators believed at the time that Wilson was being replaced, at least partly, because of the humiliating trip he had involved Prime Minister John Major in, as a result of his mishandling of the airport issue.[29] Compounded with this issue, there was widespread dissatisfaction with Wilson's overall approach to dealing with China and his capitulation to its increasing demands, a policy referred to by Wilson's political opponents as kow-towing to China. As well as the airport and the CFA, it was also strongly felt that Wilson had given in to Chinese pressure not to appoint Martin Lee, Szeto Wah, or other members of the UDHK to the Exco, in spite of the UDHK holding a large majority of the directly elected seats in the Legco.[30] Furthermore, he had given in to Chinese demands and cancelled plans to corporatise the government-backed Radio Television Hong Kong (RTHK).[31]

Before Wilson returned to Britain, he was invited by the Head of the Hong Kong and Macao Affairs Office, Lu Ping, to accompany him on a short holiday in China. Lu presented a small gift to Wilson and referred to him as 'a friend of China', an honour which can only have increased suspicion among Wilson's detractors.[32] At the time of the announcement of Wilson's impending departure, there was a general election in the offing in Britain and it was decided to put off naming his replacement. When, after the election, in April 1992, Major, now elected in his own right, named a 'heavyweight' politician, Chris Patten, to replace diplomat Wilson, the way was open for a change of approach.[33]

# Part II

# 6 Enter Christopher Patten[1]

Chris Patten was born in 1944, the son of a jazz musician and publisher. He was successful at his Catholic school, St Benedict's, Ealing, and won a scholarship to Oxford, where, according to one commentator, he was more interested in the theatre than politics, being quite effective in comedy roles. On graduating from Oxford he won a travelling fellowship to the United States, where he gained his first experience in politics as a political researcher for John Lindsay, who was campaigning to be Mayor of New York.

On his return to Britain, in 1966, his interest having been kindled in politics, Patten took up a position in the Conservative Party research department, becoming Political Secretary to Lord Carrington, Chairman of the Party, in 1972, and rising to be appointed as the research office's youngest ever Director, in 1974, at the age of 30. Following a previously unsuccessful campaign in the 1974 general election, in 1979 Patten was elected as MP for Bath.

Under Margaret Thatcher as leader, Patten held a number of junior ministerial positions, in Education, the Northern Ireland Office, and Overseas Development. In 1989, he was promoted to the cabinet, as Secretary of State for the Environment, where he had the difficult role of introducing the hugely unpopular 'poll' tax. During his time in Parliament, Patten had a reputation as a 'wet' and as belonging to the old school of 'one-nation' Tories who followed the doctrine of Disraeli, which favoured narrowing the gap between the privileged and less privileged. In her memoirs, Margaret Thatcher, accordingly, refers to Patten as 'a man of the left'.[2] During the Conservative Government 'coup', in November 1990, which overthrew Prime Minister Thatcher, Patten was one of those Tory ministers who told her that it was time for her to step down.[3]

Following the demise of Thatcher, the new Prime Minister, John Major, made Patten Conservative Party Chairman in his new cabinet. Patten, with his widely admired rhetorical skills, was an excellent choice. He had worked on many of Margaret Thatcher's best party conference speeches and was described by her as having 'a way with words'.[4] It was not long before Major went to the country again, in April 1992. It was Patten, as Party Chairman, who master-minded the election campaign and achieved another five years in office for his party. The victory went against what many thought, based on the opinion polls, were impossible odds in favour of the opposition Labour Party. Although the Tories were successful, Patten failed to win re-election in his own marginal constituency of Bath. Shortly afterwards, Major asked him to take the position of Governor of Hong Kong. After some reflection, Patten accepted this offer from his colleague and close friend.

* * *

Patten has been described by one commentator, on a personal level, as 'a complex, interesting man of many interests; easily likeable; he speaks openly and honestly, and doesn't attempt to hide facts or feelings'.[5] On a political level, Patten was already tipped as a possible future Prime Minister even before he arrived in the House of Commons, in 1979.[6] He has been described by his namesake and Conservative ministerial colleague, John Patten, as: 'widely regarded as the most gifted politician of his generation. [If he had been re-elected to Parliament in 1992] he would plainly have been in a major position in the British Government, in one of the highest offices of state. I would have expected him to be Home Secretary. And if Douglas Hurd had retired, Chris would have been a natural successor to the Foreign Office.'[7] Alan Clark, in his *Diaries*, refers to Patten as 'brilliant'[8] and 'a good guy'.[9] In 1996, following a visit to Hong Kong, British Prime Minister John Major said that, if he was to step down, Patten would be a likely possible successor.[10] Outside the Conservative Party, however, Patten's reputation was not so brilliant. The voters of Bath rejected him and he was unpopular in many quarters because of the way he had tried to impose the 'poll' tax, when he was Minister of the Environment, getting himself a reputation as a political 'bruiser' in the process.

Given his high-flying profile, why did Patten accept the job of Hong Kong Governor, rather than waiting for a by-election, going to the House of Lords, or accepting a job in Europe or business? Patten explained his decision to take the Hong Kong job in an interview with the *South China Morning Post*. 'I knew enough about Hong Kong and relations between Britain and China', he said, ' to know how important the next five years would be. Not just up to 1997, but much beyond. I had the feeling, and I don't want to sound too sanctimonious that it was an honourable enterprise.'[11]

It is perhaps not coincidental that one of Patten's Conservative heroes was Ian Macleod, like Patten a 'one-nation' Tory, in the Disraeli mould.[12] In 1958, at the age of 46, just younger than Patten when he accepted the Hong Kong governorship, MacLeod was entrusted by the Macmillan Government with the responsibility of embarking on a radical colonial policy of bringing Britain's African territories to independence.

MacLeod's main role, not unlike that of Patten, was to negotiate with various stakeholders and make arrangements for the period following Britain's departure. MacLeod is described in Lawrence's *The Rise and Fall of the British Empire*, as 'a talented, sharp-witted and sometimes acerbic liberal Conservative who was temperamentally suited to carry out what were paternalistic colonial policies'.[13] Lawrence also describes Macleod as someone who was not afraid to stick his neck out. These are descriptions that well might fit Patten.

1997, the year of the return of Hong Kong to China, would be the 50th anniversary of the independence of India and Pakistan, a process which had been overseen by Lord Louis Mountbatten. With Hong Kong's retrocession, the colonial withdrawal begun by Mountbatten in the Indian sub-continent and continued by MacLeod in Africa would, save for a few minor vestiges of Empire, such as the Falkland Islands and Gibraltar, be completed, 50 years later, by Patten. No doubt the widely read history graduate would have been aware of the auspiciousness of the last five years of British Hong Kong and of the historic role to be played by its last governor. Certainly, when interviewed for this book, Patten agreed, as he put it, that '[he was] conscious that this period and the way we conduct ourselves will go into the history books'.[14]

\* \* \*

Patten arrived in Hong Kong on 9 July 1992, with his wife, Lavender, and two of his three daughters, Laura, 17, and Alice, 12. After a brief welcome and change of clothes at the airport, the family was taken to Kowloon Pier where they boarded the governor's launch, *The Lady Maurine*, for the ten-minute crossing to Hong Kong Island, for the official welcoming ceremony.

As the launch crossed Victoria Harbour, standing in the front of the craft, the Patten family had time to admire Hong Kong's spectacular waterfront skyline of ultra-modern skyscrapers, with its backdrop of Victoria Peak, the traditional home of wealthy earlier colonialists seeking to escape the heat and disease of teaming Victoria, or Central, as it is now called, below.

The official welcoming ceremony had much of the traditional colonial pomp which attends such proceedings. The governor's launch was followed across the harbour by the Royal Navy ship, *HMS Peacock*, two police launches, and two fireboats spraying water into the air. Overhead, there was a close-formation flypast of three aircraft and 12 helicopters, while on land there was the traditional 17-gun salute and, on arrival, the inspection of a guard of honour. What was most striking about the arrival, however, was Patten's decision to wear a sombre lounge suit, in preference to the traditional white tunic with brass buttons and gold epaulettes, ceremonial sword, and pith helmet crowned with ostrich plumes that previous governors had all worn. When asked about this, later, Patten explained the significance of his decision to wear a lounge suit to a local journalist as follows: 'I think in the last five years, a slightly different more accessible and less formal style is useful and relevant. I am going to be an open and accessible Governor of Hong Kong.'[15]

In addition to his dress, Patten reinforced his populist image and contrast with previous governors by waving to the hundreds of people who had come to welcome him, by shaking hands with some of them and by giving a double, arms-raised, thumbs-up salute. The populist image was reinforced further in Patten's maiden speech, when he moved inside the City Hall for the swearing-in ceremony. Here, in the first example of Patten's rather acerbic humour that Hong Kong was treated to (a brand of humour which was to so upset the Chinese Government in the ensuing months), he quipped that he particularly enjoyed hearing the speech of Baroness Dunn, the senior member of the Exco, twice: after she had given it first in English and then in Cantonese. In his own speech, he emphasised that he had 'no hidden agendas', and that, 'If you want to know what I believe, if you want to know what I think, and if you want to know what I intend to do, read what I say and listen to what I say.'

\* \* \*

Patten's conscious effort to cultivate the populist image was not lost on the local Hong Kong press. Under the headline 'Patten personality makes quick impact', The *South China Morning Post*, for example, reported as follows:

> The smack of firm government resounded around Hong Kong yesterday as Chris Patten delivered his first speech as Governor. All the sceptics who had doubted whether or not he could make a difference saw the living proof. His address at the City Hall was direct and decisive, while his handling of the arrival ceremonies showed how he intends to stamp his personality on the place.

The waves, the smiles, the gestures and the glad-handing of members of the crowd all testified to the populist skills of a master politician, deliberately distancing himself from the formalities of the past by wearing a business suit instead of the colonial uniform. The contrast in style with his predecessor was obvious to all, and Mr. Patten backed up that message with some powerful words.[16]

The *Hong Kong Standard*, under the headline 'Outlining a "clear and open agenda"', reported in similar vein:

Chris Patten gave a strong hint of the new style he intends bringing to Government House the moment he arrived in Hong Kong. It was smiles all round as Hong Kong's 28th and last Governor swept into Queen's Pier in the afternoon. Looking casual and relaxed, Mr Patten waved to the hundreds of people packed behind the barricades at Edinburgh Place and gave a thumbs-up salute, an apt echo of the old Tory catch-phrase 'five more years'.[17]

The Chinese language press was equally positive in its reporting of Patten's welcome. *Ming Pao*, for example, described how people rushed and pushed each other to shake hands with the new governor, whom they affectionately nicknamed '*fei*', or 'fatty', 'Pang'.[18]

\* \* \*

In the substantive part of his maiden speech, Patten listed five main points he intended to be the corner-stones of his policy. These points were, first, to make his governorship as open and accessible as possible, on the understanding that, ultimately, responsibility for leadership rested with him, as head of an executive-led government. This point seemed to be addressed to two specific audiences. On the one hand, it was designed to give hope for greater democracy to the UDHK and their supporters. On the other, it was a reassurance to China, which had expressed concern about any plans Patten might have had for moving from an executive-led system to a system controlled by the elected legislature, that that was not his intention, an important point that was to be overlooked by many, in the coming months and years of Patten's governorship. China had been concerned about a possible change of British policy which would be more amenable to the UDHK ever since Prime Minister Major and Patten had received Martin Lee and his deputy, Yeung Sum, in London, in May, shortly after the announcement of Patten's appointment.

Patten's second point focused on economic issues: the importance of a strong economy and the need to move forward. Here Patten was indicating to China the need for progress to be made on the airport, progress which had been held up by China's insistence than financing plans had to be approved by both the British and Chinese sides. In relation to the economy, Patten also stressed the need to battle inflation.

In his third point, Patten proclaimed the priority he gave to social issues: help for 'fellow citizens who fall by the wayside', support for education, care for the elderly and the disabled, housing, and the environment. These are issues which had been neglected by the previous British colonial governments. In spite of Hong Kong's high average per capita income – higher than that of Britain, the sovereign – income is spread very unevenly.[19]

Fourthly, emphasis should be given to law and order: the fight against crime and the importance of co-operation with China for cross-border crime.

Fifthly, and this he claimed to be his most 'vital and challenging' priority, Patten expressed the need to foster better relations with China. 'I have heard it said that the relationship between Britain and China, and therefore the position of Hong Kong, is still bedevilled by misunderstandings and the lack of trust', he declared. 'I will do all that I can to remove misunderstandings and to build up trust', he continued – on the proviso, however that 'Trust is a two-way street.'

* * *

As mentioned in the Introduction, Patten's governorship had a strong ideological and rhetorical dimension to it. In this chapter and those that follow, considerable emphasis will be put on Patten's ideology and the rhetoric he used to promote it. In Patten's maiden speech there were already a number of what were later to be recognised as hallmarks of his rhetoric. Throughout his governorship there was a range of rhetorical strategies which Patten consistently used to justify his policies and win over the people of Hong Kong.

**Stress the historical significance and momentous nature of the task of bringing about the transition:**
Patten stressed the momentousness of the task ahead in bringing about a smooth transition to Chinese sovereignty. He described the concept of 'one country two systems' as 'historic and far-sighted'. He described the task of bringing about the transition as 'historic', 'momentous', as Hong Kong's 'destiny', and as a 'symbol of

confidence and co-operation for the rest of humanity'. By stressing that he and the people of Hong Kong were jointly involved in this momentous task, he brought himself closer to the people.[20]

**Stress the value of the Sino-British Joint Declaration and the concept of 'one country two systems' as the basis for the transition:**
The British Hong Kong Government had based its policy and actions on the Joint Declaration. The Joint Declaration and the concept of 'one country two systems' had been promoted as guaranteeing continuity in Hong Kong's way of life beyond 1997. This strategy of presenting the Joint Declaration and the 'one country two systems' concept as guardians of Hong Kong's future was invoked by Patten when he pointed to the task ahead, a task shared between him and the people of Hong Kong:

> What we have to do in the closing years of this tumultuous century is to turn from earnest hope to firm reality, that historic and far-sighted concept 'one country two systems'. When we have achieved that, we will have fulfilled the promise enshrined in the Joint Declaration: a stable and prosperous Hong Kong, whose future – founded in that Declaration – is secure.

Significantly, there was no mention of the Basic Law, however. Patten's predecessor, Wilson, had set great store by adapting British policy to fit the requirements of that document, and had usually referred to the Joint Declaration and the Basic Law together, as the twin guardians of Hong Kong's future. There was not one single mention of the Basic Law in Patten's inaugural speech, however, an indication, perhaps, of a more independent policy on the part of Patten, a shift towards the UDHK, who had contested some of the provisions of the Basic Law as being contrary to the Joint Declaration, and a worry, therefore, for China.

**Praise Hong Kong people:**
A strategy very often employed by Patten is, whenever possible, to praise the people of Hong Kong. The purpose of this strategy, of course, is to get the people onto Patten's side and to support his governorship and policies. Patten used this strategy at numerous points in his maiden speech. He did this, first, by referring to Hong Kong as 'one of the world's greatest cities'. Hong Kong has achieved such a status through the efforts of the Hong Kong people: 'You the people of Hong Kong, have created here at the heart of Asia, a

wonder of the world, one of the most spectacular examples of the virtues of a free economy known to Man', he said. He later refered to the 'enterprise, energy, vitality and industry' of Hong Kong people, to their 'resilience, determination, and drive', and to how they care for the education of their children and for the welfare of the elderly and the disabled. Here, he was already positioning himself on the side of the people of Hong Kong and against China.

**Assert that Hong Kong's success is due to a felicitous combination of the character of its people and the social framework provided by the rule of law and associated democratic systems:**
Although Patten praised Hong Kong people, Hong Kong's success was not due only to its people, he claimed. It was due, also, to the sound political framework – a framework provided by the British (although this is by implication and is not stated) – within which the society had developed:

> Hong Kong has been made great not by the accidents of geography but by its most formidable assets, the enterprise, the energy, the vitality and the industry of its people, living, working and prospering *within a framework of sound administration and the rule of law* (emphasis added).

**Assert the democratic nature of Hong Kong's system:**
Although the British never developed a political system for Hong Kong based on universal suffrage, Hong Kong could nevertheless claim to be, in other ways, a free society. This was the basis for an important rhetorical strategy, consistently employed by Patten, which proclaims the essentially democratic nature of Hong Kong's way of life under British rule. 'What are the hallmarks of Hong Kong's system?', Patten asks, before himself providing the answer:

> The bedrock of your way of life is the rule of law that guarantees fair and equitable treatment for everyone. It governs all your dealings, personal and financial. You have an independent Judiciary in which every individual can have confidence. Because no one is above the law, the law serves everyone. People in Hong Kong enjoy the freedom to go about your business without constant interference from the government. You enjoy freedom of worship and speech. You have as well a government in which there is democratic participation by the people of Hong Kong at every level, a government supported by a fine public service.

**Stress that what is good for Hong Kong is good for China and Britain:**
As indicated in earlier chapters, since the signing of the Joint Declaration a considerable level of mistrust had existed in the tripartite relationship between Britain, China and Hong Kong.[21] There was mistrust by China of Britain's motives in wanting to leave behind more democracy, mistrust by Britain of China's commitment to carrying out the terms of the Joint Declaration, and mistrust on the part of the people of Hong Kong that Britain and China might be doing secret deals, to their mutual benefit, but to the detriment of Hong Kong. In order to counter this mistrust of Britain, Patten stressed the mutual benefit of any arrangements that they might make for Hong Kong. Thus, in referring to the impasse in the negotiations over the new airport, he made the claim that the project would act as a dynamo for economic growth, not just for Hong Kong, but also for the Southern Region of China. On a higher level, the whole transitional process would benefit all three parties: Hong Kong, China and Britain:

> That achievement [the fulfilment of the terms of the Joint Declaration] will be good for the people of today's Hong Kong; good for the people of the Hong Kong of tomorrow; good for China; good for Britain; good for the close relationship between our two ancient civilizations; and it will – as a new century unfolds – be good for the world.

**Stand up for Hong Kong (against China):**
At one point, which was widely reported in press accounts of the speech, Patten made the statement that he would 'stand up for Hong Kong as you would wish me to do, courteously and firmly'. This strategy of standing up for Hong Kong was to prove to be one of those most frequently used by Patten as his governorship developed and as he came into more and more conflict with China. Stated here, in the maiden speech, it could be taken as an indication of a change of stance of the British and Hong Kong governments in their dealings with China. The previous Governor, Wilson, had been criticised for kow-towing to China. A dissatisfaction with such appeasement, it was felt by many, was what had led the British Prime Minister, John Major, to replace Wilson with Patten.

**Stress the need to co-operate with China:**
Although willing to stand up to China, Patten was also guided by the strategy of stressing that co-operation was necessary for a successful

handover. Opinion polls consistently showed that good co-operation with China was a high priority of Hong Kong people. Patten described co-operation with China as the most challenging of the five tasks he had set himself. However, even here Patten attaches the proviso to this strategy, that co-operation has to be a two-way street: 'I will do all that I can to remove misunderstandings and to build up trust. Trust is a two-way street. Good co-operation with China is my sincere aim and my profound wish. It is vital for the next five years, vital for the future of Hong Kong.'

Co-operation with China, the months and years ahead would show, was not to be a feature of Patten's governorship; it was just the opposite, in fact. Nevertheless, on other occasions, Patten continued to claim that he wanted co-operation.

**Appeal to family values:**
Appeals to family values were tried as a vote-winner by John Major and his government in Britain, although the campaign back-fired, mainly because of the large number of Tory ministers and ordinary members of Parliament who were involved in scandals of various sorts which clearly demonstrated that they were not practising what they preached. The Patten family, however, was a very stable unit, Patten's Catholicism contributing to the overall picture of exemplary family behaviour.[22] As such an obvious outsider, it was important for Patten to demonstrate those attributes which he did have in common with the people of Hong Kong, if he was to win their support. Family values go down well with the ethnic Chinese in Hong Kong, who uphold a strong Confucianist tradition of filial piety and respect for the family.

It is not without significance that Patten was accompanied on his arrival and at his inauguration by his wife and two of his daughters.[23] During his swearing-in and the speech which followed, Patten's family were placed immediately behind him, in full view of the audience. This ensured that television coverage and press photographs showed Patten with his family. During his speech, Patten referred to the members of his family, individually, by name, and expressed their collective enthusiasm about Hong Kong and getting to know Hong Kong people. Patten's behaviour and many public pronouncements throughout his governorship involved the regular application of this strategy.

* * *

In terms of rhetorical style, Patten made use of three striking stylistic devices, in his maiden speech, which typify his rhetoric and which have been identified by earlier students of political oratory as creating a powerful impact on audiences and being highly memorable.[24]

The first of these devices is the use of lists. The main part of the speech was presented as a list of tasks which Patten had set himself to achieve. Each of these tasks was introduced by 'First', 'Secondly', 'Thirdly', 'Fourthly', and, for a little variation, 'My fifth task'. While this may seem rather predictable, it has the merit of clearly signalling each of the main points Patten wants to put over and thus making them easily comprehensible.[25] At the same time, the five-part list made this main section of the speech memorable and easy for media reporters to summarise. Reporters – as well as members of the general public – were able to use the fact that there were five points as a mnemonic when reporting and evaluating the speech. Lists are a favourite device which Patten used frequently in his speeches, interviews and other public pronouncements.

The second stylistic device used by Patten is referred to in the linguistics literature as parallelism, the rhythmic repetition of words and grammatical structures. It is a favourite device of political orators,[26] described in one handbook of persuasive techniques as the rhetorical device with the closest affinity to the direct expression of emotion.[27] The extract previously cited under the rhetorical strategy, 'Stress that what is good for Hong Kong is good for China and Britain', is a good example of Patten's use of parallelism, with its multiple repetition of 'good for', 'the people of', and 'will be'. This extract is also a good example of the third of Patten's rhetorical strategies, a heavy use of antithesis, with the parallel juxtaposition of 'Hong Kong', 'China', 'our two great civilizations', and 'the world', on the one hand, and the contrastive pair of 'of today' and 'of tomorrow', on the other.

Patten typically used parallelism and antithesis when he wanted to demonstrate his strong commitment to a particular point, or when he was trying to evoke the historical significance of his governorship. With this somewhat flowery rhetoric, it seems that already, in his maiden speech, Patten had the history books in mind.

\* \* \*

On the day following his arrival and inauguration, in his first full day as Governor, Patten continued what was turning into an almost triumphant reception by the press and public, with the emphasis again on accessibility and openness. The day began with an unprecedented early-morning press conference, in the grounds of Government

House. At the press conference, Patten announced that he would hold regular press briefings and that he would institute some sort of 'Question Time' in the Legco, where he would be answerable to legislators. In addition, he again spelled out some of the major aims of his governorship. These included a creative partnership with China, but at the same time recognition of different but joined responsibilities, the fight against crime (in the period leading up to Patten's arrival there had been a series of vicious armed robberies on jewellery shops involving the participation of illegal immigrants from the Mainland), and his desire for 'as much understanding across the community as possible', but without compromising his executive leadership.[28]

The press conference over, Patten proceeded to the MTR with his wife Lavender for a ride under the harbour to Kowloon side to embark upon a walkabout tour of Mongkok, one of Hong Kong's poorest, most crowded and most vice-infested districts. On arriving at the MTR, no special compartment had been arranged and there was pandemonium as local and international press struggled to board the train with Patten. When he emerged from the MTR station, a crowd of well-wishers and demonstrators was waiting for him. Demonstrators were protesting about a plan for redevelopment of the area, but their shouts were answered by well-wishers crying 'Don't scare them!'

With his first chance to mingle with the crowd, in true politician's fashion Patten zeroed in on a three-year-old baby in the arms of its mother and started to cuddle it. Comments reported in the press on people's reaction to Patten were again overwhelmingly positive. 'Accessible and friendly', 'warm and responsive', 'very handsome', 'sweet and chubby' were some of the comments reported in various English and Chinese language newspapers the next day.

The visit to Mongkok over, the Pattens went by the Kowloon Canton Railway (KCR) to Shatin (one of Hong Kong's high-rise new towns), visited a factory (where a 66-year-old worker was reported to say, 'I like him very much. It's nice he has come to see us'), and then continued to the Diamond Hill squatter area, where the crowd was more disciplined than it had been in Mongkok, as he inspected their living quarters. At the squatter area Patten commented that he wanted to spend as much time out of the office as possible, meeting people, and seeing things for himself and that 'there is a world of difference between reading about things and actually experiencing it for yourself and meeting people on the streets and in their homes'.[29] Even the normally stridently pro-China *Wen Wei Po* reported how a young boy had been surprised when Patten had picked him up and how two children who presented him with flowers forgot what to say.[30]

\* \* \*

Patten's openness, accessibility, and man-of-the-people image had been promoted by his public relations machine even before his arrival. A stable family background is an important aspect of a politician's image and Patten's wife and three daughters were wittingly or unwittingly drafted into the service of promoting Patten's image.

Prior to the arrival, the press were provided with photographs and information on the Patten family, enabling the *South China Morning Post*, for example, to present the following depiction of a happy, healthy, middle-class family, on the day of their arrival.

> The Pattens arrive today. And judging from these photos taken from the family album, Hong Kong will see Government House transformed into a real home...
>
> Mary Lavender St Leger Thornton married Christopher Francis Patten in 1971. By the late 1970s, theirs might have been a typical young family growing up in Britain – except that he was to storm to victory in the 1979 general election with Bath's biggest Conservative turnout in 20 years... Today,... the Pattens need a haven for three teenagers and for parents who love activity, preferably outdoors. There may well be golf clubs and tennis racquets in the corridors, and the happy confusion around the holidays of at least one child – Alice, aged 12, arriving from school. There will be loosened ties and rolled-up sleeves, comfortable tweeds and windblown hairstyles.
>
> And if Mrs Patten can steal any time in the kitchen, the aromas of anything Mediterranean wafting through the private quarters.
>
> There are three daughters – Kate, 19, Laura, 17 and Alice... The man of the house savours the political spotlight and, according to his former constituency, earned the reputation for being diligent and responsive.
>
> But he also makes time for the family. Always has, always will, according to friends... Mr Patten, who is 48 years old, is a staunch Catholic and noted for his easygoing manner.'[31]

\* \* \*

There is no doubt that Patten's style went down very well indeed with the Hong Kong public. After his first walkabout in Mongkok Patten said that the enthusiastic welcome Hong Kong people had for him might not be so great once the initial impact wore off.[32] However, opinion polls conducted in July and August showed his popularity to be increasing. In July, 72 per cent of those polled said that they approved of Patten's performance as Governor, and by late August his popularity had risen to 77 per cent.[33] General public opinion corresponded with the overall evaluation of the liberal press. On 15 September, when Patten was about to make a trip to London to discuss his policies, the *South China Morning Post* commented in an editorial that 'In just a couple of months in office, Mr Patten has demonstrated political skills and acumen that indicate he deserves the full support of London.'[34] In August, when asked about his opinion poll ratings, Patten again played down his popularity, stating that 'all honeymoons come to an end ... I haven't yet had to take any difficult decisions or make any difficult announcements'.[35] Indeed it was not until a full three months after his arrival, when the very strong negative reaction on the part of the Chinese government to his first policy speech, in October, became clear, that his popularity started to waver.[36]

In the three month period between his arrival and his first policy speech, on 7 October, Patten was a listening governor. He spent his time meeting with as many representatives of political parties, of pressure groups, and of businessmen as he could and made a large number of tours to various locations in the territory.

On 27 July, Hong Kong received a visit from the British Foreign Secretary, Douglas Hurd, and Patten took him on one of his walkabouts. It was Patten that the crowds wanted to see and shake hands with, however, not the senior man, Hurd. Under the headline 'Patten Continues to Draw the Crowds', the *South China Morning Post* reported the visit as follows:

> The main attraction in Tsuen Wan yesterday was supposed to be the visiting British Foreign Secretary, Mr Douglas Hurd, but the crowds went for the companion – the Governor, Mr Chris Patten.
>
> The curious residents of the Clague Garden Estate pushed and jostled so hard at one stage that some of them ended up in a heap with press photographers and reporters. No one was hurt.
>
> Most residents did not seem to know who Mr Hurd was. Their main aim was to greet the governor and shake hands with him. The scene was reminiscent of the Mongkok walkabout by Mr Patten on the day after his arrival earlier this month.

Mr Patten was so popular that dozens of children, urged by their parents, approached him trying to hug him or wanted to be held by him.[37]

\* \* \*

Patten's early popularity in Hong Kong must in part be attributed to the public relations team he set up in Government House. Whereas under past governors media reporters had often encountered difficulty in getting anything more than stock comments from the Government Information Service, Patten's team made the governor the willing target of the press.

Leading the information team was Information Co-ordinator and Spokesperson, Mike Hansen, whose office was physically moved from government offices to Government House, the governor's residence, itself. All media enquiries were vetted by Hansen's office. Working with Hansen were John Elliot, Public Affairs Adviser, Richard Hoare, Private Secretary, and Leo Goodstadt, Head of the Central Policy Unit. In addition to these men, whom he inherited from Wilson, Patten brought in two Tory staffers from Britain, Martin Dinham, Deputy Private Secretary, and Edward Llewellyn, Assistant Private Secretary. These latter were usually to be found at Patten's side on official engagements and were soon given the nicknames of Whisky and Soda, after Patten's two Yorkshire terriers. It is ironic that at a time of increasing localisation of the government service in preparation for the 1997 handover Patten's propaganda team should have been made up almost exclusively of expatriates.[38] Perhaps this was one of the reasons why Patten got into such difficulties with China. However, it was a conscious strategy. When interviewed for this book, Patten stressed that while he could have taken advice on linguistic and cultural issues, he preferred not to.[39]

The motivation for all of this pandering to public opinion during the three-month honeymoon period leading up to the October address was two-fold. First, Patten wanted to be able to say that any proposals he made in his policy speech reflected the consensus in Hong Kong as to how far people wanted to go down the road of political reform. Second, Patten wanted to be able to say to the Chinese government that his proposals had the popular support of the public, thus making it more difficult for China to react negatively.

As well as sounding out the various interest groups in face-to-face meetings, government thinking, whether intentionally or by accident, was also 'leaked' to the press. An idea speculated upon in the press allowed Patten to gauge to what degree it was acceptable to the Hong Kong public and to China. Indeed, Patten had already mentioned to the press some of his key ideas on introducing greater democracy even before he arrived in Hong Kong. Leaking also prepared both the Hong Kong public and China for the possible introduction of a given idea, thereby reducing its shock value. In his arrival speech, Patten had mentioned the need to combat inflation as one of his priorities. However, this priority was quickly dropped once Patten realised that the general consensus in Hong Kong was that inflation was primarily a structural problem, due to Hong Kong's rapid transition from a manufacturing to a primarily service-based economy and that a certain level of price rises was something that Hong Kong could live with. In September 1992, Patten wrote to a political group, the Association for Democracy and People's Livelihood (ADPL), in response to their request for an overhaul of the functional constituency system. In his letter, which was reported in the press, Patten stated that he would change the functional constituency system so that it 'can operate in a fair and consistent way'.[40] In this way, the public and China were alerted to this likely reform being introduced.

Another function of the leaking of ideas was that it allowed Patten and his government to demonstrate that they would not be held to ransom by China in negotiations over Hong Kong, although whatever they did would be within the terms of the Joint Declaration and Basic Law. Statements were continually appearing in the press to the effect that whatever reforms Patten might introduce would be within the terms of what Patten was to refer to later as 'the sacred texts', the Joint Declaration and the Basic Law.

Leaking also provided a means for Patten to carry on a public dialogue with China on the one hand, which wanted Patten to keep to the status quo, and with the pro-democracy lobby on the other hand, who wanted a fundamental overhaul of the whole electoral system to bring about total democracy, even if this meant contravening the Basic Law.[41]

The Chinese Government had already received an indication of the sort of things Patten and the British Government had in mind even before the new Hong Kong Governor's arrival in Hong Kong. At a meeting at the Rio de Janeiro environmental conference in June, the British Prime Minister, John Major, informed his Chinese counterpart, Li Peng, of the general thinking of the British side regarding future developments in Hong Kong.

As it became clear that Britain was intent on considering serious reforms of the electoral arrangements, a whole series of warnings began to appear in the Chinese and pro-China Hong Kong press. On 3 August, for example, a signed commentary appeared in the pro-China, Chinese language magazine, *Bauhinia*, claiming that, 'The British-Hong Kong Government should maintain an executive-led administration and ignore any "illegitimate" call to change the Basic Law.'[42] The strongest of these warnings was given by the head of the Hong Kong and Macau Affairs Office, Lu Ping, who said on 25 August that if Patten reformed Legco in such a way that its membership failed to mirror the Basic Law, then new elections would be called immediately after the reversion of sovereignty.[43]

Balanced against this rhetoric on behalf of the Chinese Government and the pro-China faction in Hong Kong were the equally strident claims from the pro-democracy camp. The leader of the UDHK, Martin Lee, for example, claimed that:

> Britain and China should respect the clear wish of the people of Hong Kong for a democratic system of government in line with the promises in the Joint Declaration, by establishing a fully democratically elected legislature as soon as possible, thus implementing the promise of Hong Kong people governing Hong Kong.[44]

* * *

A number of issues dominated the press speculation during the three-month honeymoon period. First, there was the on-going argument between Britain and China over the funding for the new airport. The agreement arrived at by Cradock, it was now clear, had not put an end to this problem. It was widely agreed that China was continuing to stall over any agreement on the airport, as a means of exerting pressure on Patten not to do anything too radical in the way of political reform. In contrast to Wilson and the Foreign Office, under Cradock, who had emphasised the need for patient compromise in all dealings with China, Patten took an opposite tack, arguing in effect that if China failed to agree on financing the airport, then so be it, the airport would not go ahead; after all, it was in China's interests to have a modern airport in Hong Kong after the handover and China which would reap the benefit. On 12 July Patten stated:

> I don't want to spend my time on a lot of hassles on big projects if we can't get agreement. I think we've got to say to our colleagues in the People's Republic of China this is what we intend to do, that we

think this is in the best interests of the people of Hong Kong, but candidly I don't want to get stuck into this if you're going to then pull the plug on it.[45]

In late September, Patten again expressed his frustration over the airport talks, saying that the Chinese side needed to be reminded that they were getting cash reserves from the handover amounting to 'the greatest dowry since Cleopatra'.[46] This kind of talk was not well received by the Chinese side, which, through its mouthpieces in Hong Kong, labelled his remarks as 'unreasonable, rude and childish'[47] and 'improper and acrimonious'.[48]

During this period, China made it clear on many occasions that a visit by Patten to Beijing would be welcome. However, the Governor, perhaps sensing that China would try to put pressure on him, studiously avoided any such commitment, a position which must have further alienated the Chinese side.

An idea not mentioned in Patten's inaugural speech was his interest in making the executive government accountable to Legco. This idea seems to have first appeared in an interview after his first press conference with the *Sunday Morning Post*, when Patten said that an Exco accountable to Legco was provided for in the Joint Declaration and Basic Law. Patten was quoted as stating,

I'm the head of the executive authorities so I'd better be accountable . . . A government is stronger if it is prepared to be more open and accountable. A government is stronger when it is able to mobilise support and consent for what it is doing . . . I'm increasingly interested in what executive-led government accountable to the legislature means and I want to explore that.

Later, Patten floated the idea of standing committees in Legco, which would be able to cross-examine officials in the executive government. This idea was strongly resisted by China. The pro-Beijing, Chinese-language *Bauhinia* warned the governor, for example, on 29 September, to retain the executive-led system and not introduce standing committees to Legco.[49]

Another constitutional issue, one this time that all parties knew was on the agenda from the outset for consideration by Patten, was the make-up of the Exco. Previously, Exco had always been made up of the Governor's direct appointees. By convention, the Chief Executive of the Hong Kong and Shanghai Bank (the largest company in the colony) was guaranteed a place, as was the Commander of British

Forces, and, until the time of Governor Youde, a representative of the Jardine group. Although Governor Wilson had gradually changed Exco's profile from being dominated by business interests to being more representative of academics and lawyers, members of Exco had always been the personal choice of the governor.

Since the first direct elections to Legco, in 1991, the UDHK, under their leader, Martin Lee, had been the largest grouping in Legco. As the largest and most representative political grouping, the UDHK, prior to Patten's arrival, had been demanding representation on Exco, the policy-making body. UDHK representatives had met Patten and John Major in London (and had been well received) before Patten arrived in Hong Kong and they were promoting their case aggressively through the media, as well as to Patten directly. On 29 September, Martin Lee was reported as saying that Patten would become a 'dictator' if he didn't appoint elected Legco members to Exco.[50]

Overriding all other constitutional issues during the period in the lead up to Patten's October policy speech was the question of electoral reform for the 1995 direct elections, reforms which had been agreed by Britain and China. Until the decision to replace Governor Wilson, both China and Britain had stressed the importance of working within the Basic Law model of 20 directly-elected constituencies, 30 functional constituencies and 10 seats chosen by electoral college. After the decision to replace Wilson, the British government started to talk about the possibility of amending the Basic Law, to allow for more directly-elected seats. It became apparent, subsequently, that British enquiries to China on this matter were rebuffed and so Patten concentrated on working within the existing framework. His focus was to be on broadening the functional constituencies, many of which had a very narrow electoral base and could easily be manipulated, and making the electoral committee more democratic.

Patten's thinking on these issues was again leaked in various ways, so that the public and China had a fair idea of the sort of things Patten was thinking of. On 30 August, during a Legco by-election, Patten stated, for example, that 'there is already substantial agreement that we have to take forward the process of democratisation'.[51] Similarly, on 13 September, Patten strongly hinted at his plans to reform the electoral process, when he stated in an interview: 'I don't believe that anybody could reckon that it would be in Hong Kong's interest, or China's interest to have [electoral] arrangements that don't look clean and straightforward and don't have credibility.'[52] On 6 October, the *Hong Kong Standard* commented that, 'It has been speculated that

Mr Patten will abolish the appointment of members to the 19 district boards and two municipal councils. All these directly-elected members would then form an election committee, which would return 10 of the 60 Legco seats in 1995.'[53]

After so many leaks, by 7 October, the day of the policy address, the *Hong Kong Standard* was able to predict the reforms that Patten was likely to propose in his speech.[54] They were that:

(a) Patten would exploit what freedom he had in the area of electoral reform without going outside the Basic Law
(b) appointed local government seats would be replaced by directly elected ones
(c) the election committee for electing ten of the Legco seats would be made up of the elected district board members
(d) the functional constituencies would be broadened
(e) a committee system would be introduced to Legco to make the executive accountable to the legislature
(f) Exco would be made up of non-political figures, thus avoiding the problem of whether or not to appoint members of the UDHK.

The predictions were to prove to be remarkably accurate.

\* \* \*

There is no doubt that Chris Patten took Hong Kong by storm, when he arrived in early July of 1992, until his first policy speech on 7 October. His arrival brought a new feeling of hope and optimism to Hong Kong. Here was a governor who was interested in the man or woman in the street, who had strong views which he was not afraid to express, who was willing to take the initiative in preparing for Hong Kong's future, and who would stand up for Hong Kong in the face of censure from China.

Patten's style marked a radical departure from that of the previous Governor, Wilson. Wilson was a sinologist who had devoted his life to the study of the Chinese language and culture. He tried to reconcile his British background and values with the culture of China and its way of thinking. But the feeling of many in Hong Kong was that instead of enabling him to bridge the cultural gap on behalf of the people of Hong Kong, Wilson's background led to inaction and kow-towing in the face of Chinese threats. Patten, in striking contrast to Wilson, knew nothing of China or the Chinese language. He used the same style as he had used in Britain. He sought to build popular support for his policies, based on direct contact with the public, a powerful rhetoric, and an effective public relations machine.

In a profile of Patten, in the *South China Morning Post*, the writer asked how it was that a man who had been rejected by the voters of Bath could be picked to run the affairs of six million people in a place halfway around the globe and have been so popular.[55] One reason is surely that the Hong Kong people were tired of the secret negotiating and deals made on behalf of Hong Kong by the British Foreign Office – without the direct participation of Hong Kong representatives – which had been the pattern under Wilson. Hong Kong people are proud of their Chinese ethnicity, but as refugees or the children of refugees, they do not harbour positive feelings towards the Chinese Communist Government, all the more so since the events of Tiananmen. A governor like Patten, who was willing to stand up to the Chinese Government, was worthy of their support. This, coupled with Patten's charismatic style – what one newspaper called his 'desanctification of the governorship'[56] – are likely the keys to Patten's initial success. 'Day after day, it seems, Mr Patten has whipped away another silk handkerchief and pulled a new collection of white rabbits out of the administrative hat,' the *Hong Kong Standard* wrote, near the end of Patten's three-month honeymoon period, shortly before his policy speech.[57] By 7 October, the day of the address, what everyone wanted to know was whether Patten could continue to produce the rabbits, and if so, what would be the reaction of China.

# 7 Patten's Political Reform Programme

In spite of the fact that most of the substance of what Patten was to say in his policy speech of 7 October had already been leaked to the press, the *Hong Kong Standard's* reporter was still able to use his magician metaphor in referring to the Hong Kong Governor, after his speech was finally presented. Although the general framework of what Patten planned to announce was already known, the ingenuity with which he exploited this framework had not been anticipated. '"Father Christmas" Patten has pulled more rabbits out of the hat than Merlin the Magician', the *Hong Kong Standard's* report on the policy speech thus began.[1]

Before coming on to specific proposals, in what communication theorists refer to as agenda setting, Patten presented the four dimensions of what were to be the core features of the ideological framework, or the discourse, of his governorship. These were the free market economy, individual freedom (while at the same time helping the less privileged), the rule of law, and democratic participation. As will be detailed in later chapters (especially Chapter 11), these four themes were to be ideologically constructed by Patten as the British legacy to Hong Kong, as an essential component of what is referred to, in the sub-title of this book, as the discourse of colonial withdrawal. The four themes were presented by Patten, as follows:

> The policies of the government I lead will be based on four key principles:
> – first, we must continue to generate the economic success that has made Hong Kong one of the wonders of the world: our approach to business will remain one of minimum interference and maximum support;
> – secondly, we must leave individuals and families free to run their own lives, while providing proper help for those who – often through no fault of their own – are in genuine need;
> – thirdly, we must guarantee the rule of law, with an independent judiciary enforcing laws democratically enacted, and with crime and corruption under unremitting attack;

– fourthly, we must make possible the widest democratic participation by the people of Hong Kong in the running of their own affairs, while reinforcing certainty about Hong Kong's future.

These four features were to re-occur in almost every speech, interview or other public pronouncement Patten was to make during his governorship.

Turning now to the substance of the speech, Patten presented no surprises in stressing the importance of the economy in government thinking and policy-making, and predicting that Hong Kong would be able to sustain a minimum average growth rate of 5 per cent through to the handover in 1997. Patten also announced the establishment of a Governor's Business Council, a measure which gave the appearance of emphasising the role of leading businessmen in government policy-making, but which was also likely to have been used as a sop to the business lobby, which was to lose a considerable amount of the influence it had always had under previous governors.

However, a new emphasis, which would have unsettled China, was the linking of stability and economic development to the need to protect Hong Kong's 'freedoms' and 'way of life': 'My first duty must be to secure stability and prosperity in a way that sustains Hong Kong's freedoms and way of life', Patten stated in his introduction. Such a statement would certainly not have been expected from Governor Wilson, who preferred to stress the economy and executive-led government, rather than 'freedom' or 'Hong Kong's way of life'. In his memoirs, Percy Cradock notes that, on a farewell visit to Beijing in May,[2] he was repeatedly asked what lay behind Patten's use of the word 'freedom', along with 'stability' and 'prosperity'. Cradock argued that this was behind China's renewed demands over the airport.

In addition to the new emphasis on freedoms, a point elaborated upon in the later parts of his speech, Patten revealed plans to enhance various government initiatives in social welfare and the environment, announcing increased social security payments, provision of public housing, and, notably, a major plan to clean up the environment, which had been neglected during Hong Kong's rapid economic development. These measures all involved increased government spending, which Patten justified on the grounds that the territory could afford them because the money would be generated by economic growth, not increased taxation. China, however, in line with its theory that Britain would try to drain Hong Kong's financial reserves before the handover, later claimed that Patten was planning to spend too much on such measures.

The next part of the speech came under the heading of 'Accountable Government'. Here Patten planned to make the government more responsible to the public. Accountability was to be one of the corner-stones of his policy. Although the constraints of the Basic Law and the Joint Declaration precluded the development of full democracy based on universal suffrage, Patten nevertheless aimed to make the government bureaucracy answerable to the public by other means, referring to a 'culture of service' and 'an official attitude of mind which regards the public as "clients" not supplicants'.[3] This was to be done primarily by the adoption by all government departments of 'performance pledges', which would tell members of the public what standards of service they could expect and provide a means by which to monitor actual performance. Officials would be required to identify themselves when dealing with the public, to provide prompt replies to all correspondence, and be monitored by 'Users' Committees', where appropriate. In addition, Patten planned to expand the role of the Commissioner for Administrative Complaints (or Ombudsman).

An important reform announced in the speech, which for many seemed to run counter to Patten's avowed policy of greater accountability, was in the separation of the executive and legislature. Since the first direct elections, in 1991, the Exco and the Legco worked as a cooperative, with some members of Legco sitting also on Exco. Exco, however, operated on a system of collective responsibility, whereas elected Legco members were accountable to their constituencies. In many cases, Patten argued, Legco members, for this reason, were not willing to sit on Exco and abide by its rules of collective responsibility. To solve this problem, Patten proposed that the two councils should be separated, with him, as Governor, directly accountable to Legco, before which he would appear regularly to answer questions. This measure also had the result of eliminating the unjustifiable situation, which had prevailed since the 1991 elections, of excluding from Exco members of the UDHK, the most popular political party, and their leader, Martin Lee, who had been branded as a 'subversive' by China.

The most significant part of Patten's speech concerned his much-awaited plans for constitutional development. As already mentioned, the arrangements for the 1995 legislative council elections, other than stating that there would be 20 directly elected seats, had not been spelled out in any detail in the Basic Law. Patten, while not able to increase the number of directly elected seats,[4] nevertheless had an opportunity to interpret the other general principles which were set out in the Basic Law in the way which most suited his own political goals. It is important to note that what Patten referred to in his speech as 'the constitutional package' was presented as a set of proposals advanced 'for discussion' (presumably with China, with the Legco, and in public debate), and that, as Patten said, the proposals had already been discussed by British Foreign Secretary Douglas Hurd and his Chinese counterpart, Qian Qichen, and that it was the intention that these discussions would continue. This suggests that Patten's ultimate goal was not an across-the-board adoption of his plan, but some sort of compromise, negotiated with the various interest groups in Hong Kong, on the one hand, and with China, on the other.

As stated in the speech, the proposals for the arrangements for the 1995 elections were guided by the aim of developing Hong Kong's representative institutions to 'the maximum extent' within the terms of the Joint Declaration and the Basic Law. Table 7.1 shows the development of the legislature, as envisaged in the Basic Law and agreed upon by Britain, in accordance with the policy of 'convergence'. What Patten sought to do was to exploit this framework to make those elected to the seats agreed upon as representative as possible.

*Table 7.1* The Composition of the Legislative Council, 1984–2003

| | Officials (including the President) | Appointed members | Elected by functional constituencies | Elected by electoral college | Directly elected | Total |
|---|---|---|---|---|---|---|
| 1984 | 17 | 30 | – | – | – | 47 |
| 1985 | 11 | 22 | 12 | 12 | – | 57 |
| 1988 | 11 | 20 | 14 | 12 | – | 57 |
| 1991 | 4 | 18* | 21 | – | 18 | 60 |
| 1995 | – | – | 30 | 10 | 20 | 60 |
| 1999 | – | – | 30 | 6 | 24 | 60 |
| 2003 | – | – | 30 | – | 30 | 60 |

* Including the Deputy President who is appointed by the Governor to officiate when he is absent.
*Source*: Norman Miners, *The Government and Politics of Hong Kong (fifth edition)* (Hong Kong: Oxford University Press, 1995, p.116)

The proposals included the following measures. The voting age would be lowered to 18. A single vote, single seat system would be adopted for geographical constituencies, where, in the 1991 elections, a system of double member constituencies had been used. In addition to the 21 functional constituencies already existing under the previous arrangements, nine new functional constituencies (as envisaged in the Basic Law) would be introduced. At the same time, the franchise for the functional constituencies, which had been based on corporate voting, would be replaced by a system of individual franchise. Taken together, the reforms of the functional constituencies would have the effect of enfranchising the entire working population, as all individuals in employment would be able to register as members of a functional constituency, according to the nature of their work. At the same time, although Patten stated that 'naturally, each voter would only be able to vote in one functional constituency', his proposals would lead to the bizarre situation of the 2.7 million people who made up the working population being able to vote twice, once in their functional constituency and once in their geographical constituency. The last major electoral proposal concerned the election committee, the group that the Basic Law required to be set up in 1995 to elect ten Legislative Councillors. In order to make this committee as democratic as possible, Patten proposed that it should be made up of members of the District Boards who, according to another proposed reform, would, with minor exceptions, be directly elected, whereas in the past a third had been government appointees.

Perhaps equally as worrying as the actual proposals, from China's point of view, was the rhetoric which Patten used to present them. He devoted extensive passages in his speech to the theme of democracy, avowing it to be an essential part of his personal system of belief. Perhaps most threateningly, he proclaimed democracy to be 'an essential element in the pursuit of economic progress'. This is exactly what the Chinese Government did not want to hear. They had spent the last decade or more, in the PRC, promoting economic development, but within an authoritarian political structure. They did not want someone on their doorstep – their own territory, in fact, from their point of view – promoting the cause of democracy. Such calls had led to Tiananmen and a repeat of those events was to be avoided at all costs.

\* \* \*

According to opinion polls, Patten's speech was generally well received by the Hong Kong public. According to one telephone poll, 69 per cent of those willing to give an opinion expressed themselves as satisfied with the contents of the policy speech.[5] The English language press and the more liberal Chinese language press were also generally supportive. The *Hong Kong Standard* called Patten's proposals 'both caring and daring', with reference to the welfare and constitutional proposals, respectively. On the constitutional package, they said 'Patten has found a way through that quagmire, a new road that could and should lead to all parties being entirely satisfied. It is a reasonable and ingenious route that avoids the need for argument and loss of face.'[6] *Ming Pao* described the speech as 'open, straightforward and daring'.[7]

Like the press, local political figures were generally divided in their reaction to the speech, according to whether they were pro-Beijing or not. The leader of the UDHK, Martin Lee, speaking at the Foreign Correspondents' Club a day after the speech, expressed his pleasant surprise that the British would 'do something good' for Hong Kong, although pointing out that he was disappointed that Patten had felt constrained by the Basic Law and failed to increase the number of directly elected Legco seats, when since the announcement of the replacement of Governor Wilson, the British Government had been stressing that the Basic Law was amendable.[8] Outspoken pro-democracy activist and independent legislative councillor Emily Lau, while expressing her dislike for functional constituencies, stated that nevertheless, 'given the circumstances we are in, it is a step in the right direction'.[9] Tsang Yok-sing, chairman of the pro-Beijing Democratic Alliance for the Betterment of Hong Kong (DAB), criticised Patten for going against the spirit of the Basic Law with respect to the election committee and for going against public opinion in scrapping the appointee system for the municipal councils and district boards.[10] Fred Li, spokesperson for Meeting Point, a middle-of-the-road political grouping, was supportive, saying that the measures would strengthen the government's openness and public participation.[11]

Chinese sources were virulently negative towards Patten and his proposals. Chinese criticisms were that Patten's proposals deviated from the Joint Declaration and the Basic Law and that he had not consulted with China before presenting them. Although Patten had stated in his speech that China had been told by Douglas Hurd beforehand about the contents of the speech, China had only been notified and not consulted, an unnamed Chinese source claimed.[12] Patten's action was contrary to repeated assurances by the British side that there would be consultation with China on major issues in the second half of the transitional period. Patten had not even provided the Xinhua with advance copies of the speech, as had been the past practice. All of this indicated to the Chinese that Patten was lacking in 'sincerity', a word which would be much used in the coming months with regard to Sino-British Hong Kong relations. 'Such changes will have a very serious impact on the stability of Hong Kong over the next few years and on the smooth transition of sovereignty in 1997,' the unnamed source stated. Even the separation of the Exco and Legco, a move, as already mentioned, widely thought to have been designed to keep the UDHK (a grouping that China had labelled as subversive) out of policy-making, was criticised. 'No matter what his [Patten's] reason might be, such an arrangement will not converge with the relevant provisions of the Basic Law', commented the unnamed source.

*Wen Wei Po* was typical of the various pro-Beijing Chinese language mouthpieces in Hong Kong. It criticised Patten for '[doing] a show on his own' and for the low weighting given to the China relationship in the speech. Under a headline which read 'Policy Speech no Good for Transition', its editorial said that the dramatic changes proposed for Hong Kong's constitution would diminish executive power, in violation of the spirit of the Joint Declaration. It criticised Patten for not consulting China and for trying to force China to change the Basic Law 'to prolong British rule after 1997'.[13]

Apart from the constitutional measures, the welfare spending proposals also came in for criticism from the Chinese side. Speaking in Beijing, the Hong Kong and Macao Affairs Office Director, Lu Ping, ridiculed Patten's plans for increased welfare spending, stating that, 'As a socialist, I am worrying for the capitalists in Hong Kong, as what the Governor is proposing is just like practising socialism.'[14]

Some of the criticism was directly targeted at Patten. One Chinese newspaper, for example, described the British Governor as 'highly irresponsible and imprudent'.[15] A Vice-director of Xinhua, Zhang Junsheng, accused Patten of masquerading as a 'saviour'.[16] The epithets were to get a lot worse when the ramifications of Patten's proposals had been more fully digested by the Chinese side, however.

\* \* \*

The day after the policy speech, Patten embarked on a hectic round of activities designed to promote his proposals and engage in consultation with the public. Starting at 7:45 a.m. with a radio phone-in programme and finishing at 11:20 at night with a television question and answer session, his day included Hong Kong's first Legco 'Governor's Question Time' and the first of a series of meet-the-people 'Question time with the Governor' public meetings, in City Hall. These mass media appearances and public meetings were all new to Hong Kong and were designed to show the greater government accountability which had been one of the important themes of the policy speech. In the following days and weeks, Patten continued with these public appearances and question and answer sessions.

The 'Question time with the Governor' sessions created a particularly strong impact. Subsequently, a number of local politicians were even to put forward the continued holding of these meetings every year as a test of the openness of the future Chief Executive of the SAR, following the handover.[17] In these meetings Patten was in his element, making full use of his rhetorical skill. At the first of them, for example, he masterfully used the democratic structure of the meeting to demonstrate what he claimed was the maturity of Hong Kong society and its readiness for democratic participation, with people taking turns to put questions to the Governor:

> What it [the meeting] does show is that anyone who's interested, whether here or elsewhere, is that the people of Hong Kong, whatever their views, can be trusted to talk about their future, the future of their families and their community, in a responsible and intelligent and mature and restrained way. And that is how we're going to show to the whole world what a sophisticated and democratic political community this can be.

He used this meeting also to assert the government's accountability:

> Part of that way of life [of Hong Kong] is that we have free and open meetings like this. And I believe that one result of meetings like this is that the decisions that I have to take and others in government have to take are better if we have to go and explain our decision to you. That's what accountability and what greater democracy means. I have to know when I make a decision that at some stage I may have to stand in front of the Legislative Council or stand in front of you and explain myself; and that I can tell you has a great effect on political leaders.[18]

Patten neglected to mention the fact that this part of 'Hong Kong's way of life' and the accompanying 'accountability' was only now being introduced for the first time, after a century and a half of colonial rule during which the government had certainly not been accountable to the Hong Kong public at large. In his 'Question Time' public meetings Patten was in fact 'inventing a tradition', in the sense that the historian Hobsbaum has used the term; that is to say he was introducing a practice which is 'normally governed by overtly or tacitly accepted rules and of a ritual or symbolic nature, which seek[s] to inculcate certain values and norms of behaviour by repetition, which automatically implies continuity with the past'.[19] By doing this, he was contributing to the myth that he was to build up throughout his governorship of the British legacy to Hong Kong, in this case its purported democratic legacy (a theme which will be dealt with in some detail in Chapter 11 of this book).

Returning to the meeting, with heavy use of his trademark repetition and parallelism, Patten further used his powerful rhetoric to sound off against China, and its criticisms of his proposals:

> The proposals that I made yesterday, proposals for discussion with China, were entirely consistent with the Basic Law and the Joint Declaration. They were consistent with the Basic Law and the Joint Declaration in every particular. They were consistent with the Basic Law and the Joint Declaration in what they said about District Boards. They were consistent in what they said about functional constituencies. They were consistent in what they said about the election committee. They were consistent in what they said about lowering the voting age. They were consistent in every part.

In response to one question, concerning China's dissatisfaction with his constitutional proposals, Patten, again using parallelism and repetition, made a display of his frustration that China would not put forward counter-proposals:

> It is for others, if they disagree with me, to point out where my proposals are inconsistent and to put forward their own proposals. It's not enough for people to criticise. People have, if they disagree, to put forward their own proposals for the nineteen ninety five elections. I didn't invent the fact that we have to produce an election committee in nineteen ninety five. I didn't invent the fact that we have to put together new functional constituencies. Those things are all consequences of the Joint Declaration and the Basic Law and those are problems which I have to address on the community's behalf and with the help of the Executive and Legislative Councils.

This frustration with China had already been expressed by Patten at his Legco session earlier in the day (question and answer sessions in Legco were another 'tradition' that Patten 'invented'), where he had again declared his disappointment at Chinese intransigence on his reform proposals. In response to a question as to whether he was confident he would be able to convince the Chinese side to accept his proposals, he answered as follows:

Human history is full of examples of people who were convinced they could do things, and then fell, alas, at the first attempt. So I cannot arrogantly express any such conviction. What I can express is hope that I can demonstrate to our colleagues in Peking[20] that the proposals I have put forward are good for the stability and prosperity of Hong Kong and, therefore, good for the relationship between Hong Kong and China. I can do that as vigorously as possible. What I dare say I can also say is: if not these proposals, then what? I do not make these proposals out of the blue. I do not make these proposals just because it is my initiative. I make these proposals because the Governor of Hong Kong and the Government of Hong Kong have to come forward with proposals about what to do about the election committee in 1995, have to come forward with proposals about functional constituencies in 1995, have to come forward with proposals about electoral arrangements for directly elected seats in 1995. I have to put forward proposals. If others think that I have got those proposals wrong, then they should say what proposals they would offer instead. It is very difficult to have a dialogue if what happens is that the Governor of Hong Kong comes forward with proposals, whether in this matter or on the airport, is then told that those proposals are not any good, returns to base and then is expected presumably to set off with further proposals to see if those are all right. And if there are members of the community, if there are members of this legislature, if there are people elsewhere who think that my proposals are wrong, then I think it is incumbent upon them to say where they would change them and what they would put in their place. That is the way we can have a rational, sensible and open dialogue with officials in China.

In this response, again demonstrating his delight in verbal play, irony, and repetition, Patten repeated the word 'proposals' 15 times. Note also the repetition of the depersonalised, ironic, 'the Governor of Hong Kong' and the use of parallelism, 'I do not make these proposals...', 'I do not make these proposals...', 'have to come forward...', 'have to come forward'. As with Patten's rhetoric in general, this use of language was seen as provocative by the Chinese and one of their frequent criticisms of him was that he was 'lacking in sincerity'. The play on the word 'proposals', here, for example, had a defiant edge, from the Chinese perspective. As far as the Chinese were concerned, Patten had presented them with a *fait accompli*, not proposals; the British Government, as the sovereign authority, should have consulted with them first if they had really wanted discussion, not allowed Patten to unilaterally present them to the Legco, a body which they did not accept as representative of Hong Kong. The emphasis on the expression 'Hong Kong Governor' could also be interpreted as an affront, given China's sensitivity on sovereignty and its frequently reiterated view that any negotiations should be conducted between the sovereign nations. As was clear during the negotiations over the Joint Declaration, the Governor of Hong Kong, as far as China was concerned, had no right to represent the Hong Kong compatriots. When interviewed for this book, Patten suggested that his use of irony and humour might have been one of the factors leading to misunderstanding on the part of the Chinese Government.[21]

* * *

On 20 October, Patten set out on a four day visit to meet with Chinese officials and discuss his proposals. As is the usual case with such diplomatic visits to Beijing, it was not certain exactly who would be the most senior person in the hierarchy with whom Patten would be granted an audience, although previously Governor Wilson had met with the Premier, Li Peng.[22] On this occasion, however, Patten was to be disappointed. The most senior person he met was Foreign Minister Qian Qichen. Before meeting Qian, Patten consulted with the director of the Hong Kong and Macao Affairs Office, Lu Ping.

In an article in *the South China Morning Post,* Geoffrey Crothall described this meeting perceptively, emphasising the cultural differences which separated the two men.[23] First of all, Lu emphasised the importance attached to personal relations in Chinese culture, by alluding to the 'friend of China' concept, and stating: 'Since beginning work on Hong Kong I have dealt with four governors: Lord MacLehose, Sir Edward Youde, Lord Wilson and now you. I have also worked alongside four ambassadors... They are all old friends of China.' According to one school of thought, establishing a personal relationship (known in Chinese as *guan xi*) and becoming a 'friend of China' is the right way to go about negotiating with the Chinese. Officials in the Foreign Office, with their sinologist backgrounds, and under their leader, Percy Cradock, are generally taken to be proponents of this approach. Others, however, including the pro-democracy lobby in Hong Kong (who ironically are themselves ethnic Chinese), see this approach as 'appeasement' and 'kow-towing' to China.[24] After many years of what he saw as unfavourable British compromise with China, it is clear that Patten decided that a more direct, assertive and blunt approach, designed to put China on the defensive, was more likely to be successful.[25]

Following the naming of previous 'old friends of China' in the Hong Kong context, Lu expressed his wish that Patten, too, when he left Hong Kong, would join this illustrious group. Patten, however, seems to have been unwilling to be enticed into Lu's co-optive web, declaring that history would judge him not according to his friendship with China, but by 'how successfully I have helped to implement the Joint Declaration to ensure the stability, the prosperity and the way of life of Hong Kong'. Patten then surprised the Chinese side by the familiarity with which he addressed Lu. 'I've read so much about you', Patten said, leaning over to Lu, 'that I feel I've already known you for five years.' The Chinese were also taken aback by Patten's irreverent quip, when, referring to the situation in Hong Kong in 1997, he said 'whichever airport I leave by', a reference to the on-going airport dispute. While some of the reporters covering the meeting smiled at this, the members of the Chinese team did not. Such familiarity is not a hallmark of Chinese negotiating style, which stresses decorum and reverence for one's interlocutor.

Those familiar with earlier Sino-British negotiations know that such occasions are marked by the quoting of traditional proverbs and phrases from the Chinese classics. As Crothall notes, in his *South China Morning Post* article, the previous governor was a master of this mode of communication, based upon his deep knowledge of the Chinese language and culture. With Patten, in contrast, as one of his aides commented, 'What you see is what you get' and as another unidentified British official later stated, 'Chris Patten is to diplomacy what Fergie [the Duchess of York] is to royalty. He is not a natural.' During the Patten–Lu meeting there was no 'meeting of minds', as Patten admitted at a press conference later in the day. He wanted to negotiate over his proposals, but was met by repeated comments from Lu that 'convergence with the Basic Law' and 'strict adherence to the Joint Declaration' were the only criteria which would satisfy the Chinese side.

Patten's demise seemed to be summed up when the ambassador's Daimler, in which Patten was travelling, broke down with a puncture on the way to the meeting with Foreign Minister Qian, a meeting at which Patten was again reminded of the need for 'co-operation rather than confrontation'. The inauspicious nature of this occurrence reminded a number of observers of the time Margaret Thatcher stumbled on the steps of the Great Hall of the People after her first meeting with Deng, a meeting which ultimately led to the agreement by Britain that Hong Kong should be relinquished, an agreement that Thatcher had at first refused to consider.

\* \* \*

One hour after Patten left Beijing, applying the maxim of media pressure as a negotiating strategy and reminiscent of the negotiations over the Joint Declaration, Lu Ping held a press conference in which he virulently attacked Patten and his constitutional proposals. Whereas until now the Chinese side had rejected the proposals on the grounds that they were contrary to the Joint Declaration and the Basic Law, Lu now introduced another bombshell, claiming that the proposals were also in conflict with a series of secret Sino-British understandings made two years previously on the question of political convergence, and threatening to make public the content of an exchange of letters between the two governments on this matter. Lu then went on to threaten that if Patten persisted with his proposals, China would replace not only the legislature after 1997, but also the executive and the judiciary, thus totally wrecking the whole 'through-train' concept. In addition, if Patten went ahead with construction of the airport without Chinese approval, then China would close its airspace to all aircraft operating through it.

A feature of Chinese discourse is to label various phenomena according to numbers. Thus the programme to modernise industry, agriculture, science and technology was, at one stage during the Mao Zedong period, referred to as the 'four modernisations'; the Red Guards during the Cultural Revolution were called on to destroy the 'four olds' – old thoughts, old cultures, old customs, and old habits;[26] Mao Zedong's wife, Chiang Ching, and her three close associates, who tried to take control of China towards the end of Mao's life but were subsequently disgraced, were referred to as the 'gang of four'. This numbering device makes things memorable and provides a ready shorthand for referring to them. From this moment on, Patten's proposals were referred to by the Chinese as 'the three violations': of the Joint Declaration, of the Basic Law and of the other understandings between the British and Chinese Governments.

As a measure of the effect Lu's comments had, the Hong Kong stock market dropped 3.19 per cent on the first day of trading following his remarks, although most of this was recouped on the following day. In the days and weeks which followed, attacks on Patten and his proposals continued to emanate from Chinese sources. *Outlook Weekly*, a pro-Beijing publication, gave the Chinese account of events leading up to the policy speech.[27] During their meeting in New York on 25 September, according to the *Outlook Weekly* account, British Foreign Minister Douglas Hurd had given his Chinese counterpart, Qian Qichen, a brief account of Patten's policy speech, with Qian objecting and demanding further consultation. On 26 September, Sir Robin MacLaren, British Ambassador to China, passed a message from Patten summarising the speech to a Hong Kong and Macau Affairs Office Deputy Director. On 3 October, Lu Ping, Director of the Hong Kong and Macau Affairs Office, made objections over Patten's message in a meeting with Ambassador McLaren. On the same day, Patten met a Deputy Director of the Hong Kong branch of Xinhua (China's *de facto* embassy in Hong Kong), but gave only a brief account of what he would say in his speech. The complete transcript was delivered only five hours before Patten actually delivered the speech, according to the *Outlook Weekly* account, and none of the objections made by Lu Ping and Qian Qichen had been taken into account.

China's objections to Patten's proposals were ostensibly based on the 'three violations' and the fact that Patten had failed to consult with them. The substantive reason for Chinese objections, however, was that the proposals would make control of the three tiers of representative government less certain.[28] Vice-director of the Xinhua, Zhang Junsheng, who accused Patten of masquerading as a 'saviour', was nearer the mark, when he stated that: 'It looks as if the new airport and democracy are gifts from the saviour. But can we find democracy in Hong Kong throughout the past 150 years.'[29] While Britain was content to rule Hong Kong for 150 years without democracy, why should democracy be introduced in Hong Kong just as Britain was leaving and passing responsibility over to China? Whether or not Patten's proposals contravened the letter of the Joint Declaration and the Basic Law, the spirit of these documents, especially the second of the two, which went into the details of electoral arrangements, was certainly broken. In particular, functional constituencies, a concept introduced by the British in the 1985 White Paper on constitutional reform, had been specifically designed 'to avoid social instability', in the words of that document, by basing themselves on close-knit constituencies of the professional elite. In opening the functional constituencies up to include all working people, Patten was, in effect, trying to introduce universal suffrage by the back door.

\* \* \*

The day following his return from Beijing, Patten reported on his trip to the Legco and answered questions. His emphasis on consulting with the Legco was important as a demonstration of the openness and accountability of the governorship and the growing role of the Legco which, according to his proposals, would become increasingly representative. There is no doubt, either, that in these question and answer sessions Patten delighted in participating in the quintessentially British parliamentary repartee which characterised them.

In an opening statement, Patten told councillors that he had indicated to Lu Ping that if there was no agreement by the end of November, then Hong Kong would proceed as best as it could and build as much of the airport as possible, pending an agreement with China. He had reminded the Chinese side that he would continue to press for more directly elected seats to Legco, but that in the meantime he had made proposals for arrangements for the 1995 elections that were consistent with the Basic Law. The Chinese disagreed strongly, Patten reported, but presented no convincing argument as to how the proposals were indeed in breach of the Hong Kong's future mini-constitution. If the Chinese did not like his proposals, then it was incumbent on them to put forward proposals of their own, Patten had told them. The necessary legislation for putting the constitutional proposals into law would have to be put to Legco in the New Year and Legco members would have the ultimate responsibility for passing it. Patten again stressed that his proposals were not in breach of the Joint Declaration, the Basic Law, or (a reference to the letters referred to by Lu Ping in his press conference) any other agreements between Britain and China:

> I repeat that the proposals I have made, which are my best judgement on the point of balance in Hong Kong thinking on this important issue, do not breach either the Joint Declaration, the Basic Law, or any previous discussions between the present sovereign power and the future sovereign power.

The first question in the meeting came from Allen Lee, leader of the conservative business grouping of Legislative Councillors, who asked if Patten would make the letters referred to by Lu Ping public. Patten stated that if both governments wished to make them public, then he would have no objections. He also affirmed that there was no secret agreement about the 1995 elections that would 'bind the hands of either Britain or China'.

Other conservative members expressed concern that pushing ahead with the proposals might harm co-operation with China on other issues. Patten, however, denied that there could be any question of this and said that 'Chinese officials have repeatedly stated there can be no linkage between one issue and another' (a statement that would be tested over the coming months). Expressing his frustration at China's unwillingness to negotiate, Patten stated that: 'It's not a very easy way of consulting or co-operating to find proposals aren't countered by alternative proposals but get countered by the arguments of a cul-de-sac.' He made short shrift of one pro-Beijing Legislative Councillor who accused him of breaking previous agreements with the Chinese on the 1995 elections, simply answering, 'No'. United Democrat members expressed fears that Patten would back down on his reform proposals, fears which Patten sought to allay, stressing that he would not back down unless others came up with something better. He denied, however, that negotiations with China had totally broken down: 'I haven't broken down, despite a puncture in my car [a reference to the Beijing trip]. I don't think that discussions have broken down. I never think that it's sensible for political leaders to try to close all the doors and all the windows,' he said.

Asked by Martin Lee, leader of the UDHK, whether he would consider a referendum, Patten stated that it wasn't in his plans, but even if there was a referendum it could only be advisory and that Legco had the responsibility of making the final decision on any new legislation. 'On these important matters, Legislative Councillors cannot change their stance or be irresponsible. They cannot sway in their stance or pass the buck,' he said.

This emphasis on the responsibility of Legco was something that some legislators were uneasy with. After the meeting, Allen Lee accused Patten of putting unfair pressure on councillors, saying: 'It's his executive-led government. He has to make a decision. Don't kick the ball into the court of the Legco.'[30]

The radical, pro-democracy legislator, Emily Lau, repeated a question first put to Margaret Thatcher a decade before, asking if it was 'defensible and honourable' to hand millions of British citizens over to Communist rule:

> Governor, having experienced first-hand the way that communist Chinese officials behave, can you tell us, as a representative of Her Majesty's Government running this Colony, and as a staunch Catholic, that the handover of several million British citizens to Chinese communist rule in 1997 is morally defensible and an honourable thing?

Using a favourite trick to deflect awkward questions, Patten responded with humour, retorting: 'Well, that certainly livened up the proceedings.' He then continued with some verbal play and further humour, repeating the phrase 'Governor of Hong Kong', stressing how he was confident that China would honour the Joint Declaration, but that as Governor he needed to give Hong Kong people reassurances to this effect and that they could be best reassured by knowing their Governor was willing to stand up for Hong Kong:

> I think **the Governor of Hong Kong** has far greater credibility in giving the community those reassurances if the community believes that **the Governor of Hong Kong** will stand up for Hong Kong. I feel that very, very strongly. Those reassurances will need to be given again and again and again as we get closer to 1997, and when **the Governor of Hong Kong** gives them, **this Governor of Hong Kong** will, I hope, be able to do so as somebody who has battled for the best interests of this dependent territory.[31]

In this meeting, there were a number of indications that Patten was becoming sensitive to developing criticism that he did not know how to deal with China. (A cartoon depicting Patten had appeared in a newspaper with the caption, 'John Bull in a China shop.') At the outset, in referring to Lu Ping's press conference, he made a point of stating that he had been advised by a number of experienced negotiators that the principal response to his visit would come after leaving Beijing and that so it had proved. He then said that he wanted to comment 'diplomatically' on what had been said in his meetings. Seeking to play down the dispute with China, he stressed that the differences 'have not widened' (although neither had they narrowed.) and that he was willing to discuss these issues 'at any time, anywhere, with anyone'. At the end of the session he stressed that the negotiations in Beijing had not been the first he had had with Chinese officials (although they were the most important) and that they were not the most difficult negotiations he had been involved in, compared with European Community meetings he had participated in, in the past. The encounters in Beijing had been conducted in a 'rational and calm and dignified and non-acrimonious fashion,' he said. He also stressed that he did not have a reputation as a confrontational politician – indeed he had used to be described in Britain – 'a badge', he said, he 'wore with honour' – as an 'arch wet'. 'I am somebody who looks, whenever possible, for agreement, but, to coin a phrase, agreement on a principled position', were his final words to the Legco.

\* \* \*

On 28 October, after much press speculation, the British Government made public the Sino-British correspondence concerning the 1995 elections. The letters had been exchanged during January and February of 1990, when the finishing touches were being put to the Basic Law and when the two foreign ministers, Hurd and Qian, announced that China had agreed to increase the number of directly- elected seats in the 1995 elections from 18 to 20, in return for Britain's acceptance of the principle of 'convergence'. As the *Far Eastern Economic Review* put it, although most analysts agreed that no binding agreement seemed to have been reached in the exchange of letters, the Chinese side may have been led to believe that a political, rather than a legal, understanding may have been come to.[32] Specifically, British Foreign Minister Douglas Hurd had agreed in principle with Chinese proposals on the composition of the 1995 Election Committee, which was to be responsible for selecting the Chief Executive and ten legislators. However, his agreement was accompanied by the proviso that 'precise details of how this should be done can be discussed between our two sides in due course'. In putting forward his precise plan for the constitution of the Election Committee, China may have interpreted this as a failing on the part of Patten and the British Government to discuss 'how this should be done', as undertaken by Hurd. Patten and the British side, on the other hand, in stressing that Patten had only presented 'proposals' in his policy speech, might have argued that this was just the first stage in such discussions. Such an interpretation would have justified Patten's assertion in the Legco meeting reported above that there was no agreement about the 1995 elections that would 'bind the hands of either Britain or China'.

This affair of the exchange of correspondence over the 1995 election proposals is another example of the lack of precision with which Sino-British agreements were sometimes made, allowing each side to put its own interpretation on matters upon which it was difficult to reach specific agreement. A senior British official was reported by the *Far Eastern Economic Review* as stating that the vagueness of the statement on the Election Committee was because 'the only way sometimes to reach a consensus is to maximise the scope of interpretation'.[33] (Similar lack of precision attaches to certain articles of the Joint Declaration, the last minute inclusion of the statement that the Legco 'shall be constituted by elections', being another example of imprecision allowing each side to interpret the statement in its preferred way.) One other notable revelation in the correspondence was that the

British Government did not take into account the consensus that legislators had come to during the Tiananmen period, the OMELCO consensus, that there should be 30 directly elected seats in the Legco by 1997. Britain only pressed for 24 and ended up accepting 20.

\* \* \*

On 9 November 1992, Vincent Lo of the Business and Professionals Federation (BPF) stated that his organisation, representing more than 130 of Hong Kong's largest companies and professional and trade associations, would fight against the implementation of the Patten package. The statement declared that democracy was important, but that it was not the only goal. Echoing the earlier Wilson rhetoric of convergence, the statement added that a smooth transition was more important.[34] William Purves, the head of Hong Kong's largest company, The Hong Kong and Shanghai Banking Corporation, disassociated himself from the statement, on the grounds that he was a member of Patten's Exco. A spokesman for Swire Pacific, another of the British-controlled *hongs*, said that there had already been enough comment from the business community. One of the few business leaders to openly back Patten was Henry Keswick of Jardine-Matheson, who, it was rumoured, had lobbied in London for Wilson's replacement by a political figure. Keswick's support was not to go unnoticed by Beijing. In contrast to the ambivalence of the British-backed *hongs* who were torn between their loyalty to the colonial government and their desire to protect their future prospects in Hong Kong under the SAR Government and their expanding business interests in China, local Chinese companies and trade associations were solid in their support for the BPF statement. 'Not one Chinese-owned organisation opposed our views,' Lo said.

The Chinese businessmen's lobby had already been coopted by Beijing onto the BLDC. Under Wilson, they had been content to bide their time, especially as Wilson did his utmost to cooperate with Beijing. Now that Patten was taking an anti-China line, they came out of the woodwork and aggressively took China's side. Patten must have calculated on this, however. Ever since he and John Major had invited Martin Lee and Yeung Sum of the UDHK to talks in London shortly after the announcement of his appointment as Governor, he must have known that he would alienate the influential Hong Kong Chinese business interests, who were part of China's United Front.

The replacement of business representatives on the Exco by more liberal figures is another indication of this change in direction. The appointment of Patten as Governor and the new, more aggressive line with China has to be seen as a strategic decision of the British administration to align itself with the middle-class and grass roots pro-democracy faction in Hong Kong at the expense of the wealthy conservative business leaders.[35] In this respect, the new line was a rejection of the previously embraced policy of administrative absorption of politics by assimilation of business leaders into the process of elite consensual government.[36] Perhaps this had always been inevitable, once representative democracy, however little, had been introduced for the first time, in 1991, and with the prospect of more directly-elected legislators in 1995. Or perhaps the British Government had come to realise this inevitability for the first time and were therefore merely taking sensible precautionary measures. Certainly, when criticised for his pro-democracy stance subsequently, Patten argued that if he had not taken measures to move towards the pro-democracy position, the British Government, while perhaps ensuring the support of the Chinese Government, might have had the much more difficult task of dealing with a popularly elected majority party which they were denying any political influence, even suggesting there might have been civil disturbances.[37]

On 11 November, Legco voted in support of Patten's proposals, a vote which China immediately condemned. 'This is another obvious proof that the British Hong Kong authorities have abandoned the principles of convergence with the Basic Law, violated the Basic Law and the Sino-British agreements and understandings', a Xinhua statement said.[38]

\* \* \*

One card which Patten played in his high-stakes game of brinkmanship with China was the international one. In spite of John Major's visit to Beijing, China had still not been fully reintegrated into the international community, following Tiananmen. In particular, President Bush was still using the so-called Most Favoured Nation (MFN) trading privilege as a way of putting political pressure on China over its human rights record.[39] Under the economic reform plan instituted by Deng, China's economy was booming. Benefiting from China's cheap, abundant and disciplined work-force, cheap exports of low value-added goods were the driving force for this boom. The largest market for Chinese goods was the United States. The threat of withdrawal of MFN was therefore a powerful one. The human rights movement and the sizeable community of Chinese Americans formed a powerful lobby for putting pressure on China through MFN. Other countries, too, had ethnic Chinese lobbies. Canada and Australia, in particular, had large numbers of immigrants from Hong Kong, many of whom had left because of fear of the transfer of sovereignty in 1997. International interest was created by Patten's confrontational style and the Sino-British dispute was widely reported in the international press. Patten facilitated this coverage through official statements from his public information office and spokesman, by giving interviews and, of course, by his frequent public appearances. As a measure of this international interest, the CNN (Cable Network News) *Larry King Live* show conducted a special edition from Hong Kong, with Patten's participation. To further promote this international concern, in November, Patten made visits to Canada, Britain and Japan.

As an indication of this internationalisation of the Hong Kong issue, on 5 October President Bush signed a United States–Hong Kong policy act, which required the United States Government to report on a regular basis to the Congress on conditions in Hong Kong, including the development of democratic institutions. In addition, there were statements of support for Patten's reforms from various countries. The Canadian Prime Minister, Brian Mulroney, for example, during Patten's visit, said that he thought that the reform proposals were entirely consistent with the Joint Declaration. During a stop-over in Hong Kong on 9 November, Australian Foreign Minister Gareth Evans stated that, 'We think that Governor Patten is right and that he should continue to go for it in terms of his particular package, notwithstanding the nervousness that has been generated at some domestic levels here and the reaction that's in evidence in China.' Even Japan, a country not noted for its confrontational stance, stated through its Consul General in Hong Kong that Tokyo supported Patten's efforts to promote democracy within the confines of the Joint Declaration and Basic Law.[40] Consistent with its view that Hong Kong came under Chinese sovereignty, China's reaction to these tactics of winning international support was to protest that they constituted interference in its internal affairs.

\* \* \*

Patten's constitutional reforms were put forward as proposals 'for discussion'. Most commentators agree that the proposals were the result of a British change in policy over Hong Kong.[41] While Patten presented them as being within the scope of the Joint

Declaration and Basic Law, the fact that he did not consult with China beforehand (a fact interpreted as in itself an affront) suggests that he did not anticipate Chinese agreement. Whether or not they broke the letter of the Joint Declaration and the Basic Law, most would have to agree that they certainly broke the spirit of the latter document in its treatment of functional constituencies. No lesser person that Geoffrey Howe, former British Foreign Secretary, was to comment later:

> It's a legitimate point to be made on the Chinese side that if you seek to transform the functional constituencies so they become wholly unrecognisable as what they were to be, and they become a method of, de facto, outstripping the constraint on directly-elected seats, then that seems to me to be a point that can be legitimately made in the discussions.[42]

Hook maintains that the constitutional reform proposals contained in the 1992 policy speech represented a shift in British policy, a shift which he interprets as due to three factors:

- British disappointment at the Chinese interpretation of the Joint Declaration in the provisions of the Basic Law
- exasperation over the post-1989 wrangles
- a wish to seek improvements, both substantial and cosmetic, in the remainder of the transition, as a basis for a more honourable withdrawal.[43]

In putting forward his proposals 'for discussion', it is not known to what extent Patten was adopting an initial negotiating position and just how far his bottom line was from the previous agreements with China on elections. Consequently, it is not possible to know to what extent the proposals represented a new policy by Britain, from the substantive point of view. Whatever the substantive details might have been, however, the manner in which Patten presented the proposals was certainly a departure from the previous quiet diplomacy of Wilson.

One theory of cross-cultural communication states that, to be successful, both parties engaged in a cross-cultural interaction should show maximum deference to each other.[44] When interviewed for this book, Patten responded as follows to an interpretation of his failure to communicate effectively with China according to this theory, that is, that his failure could be traced back to his decision not to consult them over his political reform programme:

Well, I think the problem with China has not been that the language was insufficiently deferential or that we didn't consult them on our political reform programme... but before we consulted them we told the people of Hong Kong what we were going to consult them about... I mean Hong Kong people had grumbled for years that deals were done, without taking account of their views and interests, behind closed doors. Precisely because of sentiments like that, if you remember, the Court of Final Appeal Agreement in 1991 had been thrown out by the Legislative Council. And I thought that it was impossible to start negotiation about the 94 and 95 electoral arrangements without giving people in Hong Kong some notion of what I wanted to achieve.[45]

It was just this new priority given to the people of Hong Kong, including, of course, the pro-democracy parties and the members of the UDHK, who had been labelled 'subversive', which was so unsettling for China. Meanwhile, Patten's popularity, although falling from 65.5 per cent in a poll taken on 7–8 October, to 53.3 per cent on 15–16 December (in reaction to China's aggressive reaction to his proposals), remained relatively high.[46] To add insult to injury, from the Chinese point of view, another poll of 452 residents of Shenzhen and Guangzhou showed that Patten was better-known and had a higher performance rating over the border than his provincial equivalents.[47]

# 8 The Through Train Derailed

The final months of 1992 and the early part of 1993 were marked by continued dispute between Britain and China over the electoral reform package. Following Patten's meeting with Lu Ping in Beijing, China refused any direct Sino-British discussion on the issue, the dispute taking place in the form of 'megaphone diplomacy' via the media. When the British raised the issue of the reforms in the JLG, on 3 November 1992, China refused to discuss it. On 21 December, over 250 labour and community organisations denounced Patten's reforms in advertisements in the Chinese language newspapers. The Chinese Government's line was that because it was a matter of principle they would not even consider any negotiation or compromise. This view was articulated by the Chinese Premier, Li Peng, when he stated: 'Any counter proposal or any compromise plan on the basis of the Hong Kong Governor's plan is unacceptable. This is a matter of principle...the Chinese Government will never compromise or make any concession on matters of principle.'[1] Similarly, on 31 January, attacking Britain, Director of Xinhua Zhou Nan vowed that China would never 'barter away principles'. This position was reminiscent of the Chinese stance over the Sino-British negotiations, which ultimately led to the Joint Declaration. In those negotiations, as now, China stuck to its basic principles of recovering sovereignty and administration, until Britain gave in.

In addition to arguing that their opposition to Patten's reforms was a matter of principle, the Chinese side used a range of other arguments and conducted a United Front campaign to undermine the Governor's position. One target was Sino-British co-operation on other fronts. JLG team leader Guo Fengmin cast doubt, for example, on there being any value in holding JLG meetings if Patten insisted on going ahead with his plans for political reform.[2] On a visit to London, Chinese Vice-Premier Zhu Rongji even suggested that the whole basis of the Joint Declaration might have been undermined: 'People cannot help but ask,' he said, 'whether we still have to stick to the Joint Declaration between us, whether the important understanding and agreement that we have reached should go with the wind.'[3] The

Chinese also started to talk about setting up an alternative government in waiting, or 'second stove'.[4]

Another major target was Hong Kong business confidence. On 29
November, for example, China threatened to invalidate all current
and future Hong Kong Government contracts and leases which
extended beyond 1 July 1997, if they were not first given Chinese
approval. In late December, the largest of the British controlled *hongs*
or trading companies, Jardine-Matheson, was attacked for supporting
Patten's reform plans. A report issued by Xinhua stated that the
company's success was based on the opium trade in the previous
century and that it had changed its domicile to Bermuda. The report
then went on to claim that the company was trying to undermine
Hong Kong's smooth transition, by supporting Patten (it was widely
rumoured that the Keswick family, who controlled Jardine-Matheson,
had been among those who had lobbied for the replacement of Governor Wilson). In January the legal basis for the allocation of contracts for the construction of a much needed new container terminal,
Terminal 9 (CT9), which included participation by Jardine-Matheson,
was questioned, thus bringing progress on this project to a standstill.

The Hang Seng Index of the Hong Kong stock exchange acted as a
barometer of business confidence during this period. On 1 December
the index fell 309 points, or about 6 per cent, and two days later it fell
433 points, or 8 per cent, to its lowest level since August 1991.[5]
Rumours were rife that the market was being manipulated by Mainland interests selling shares to create an atmosphere of panic. Potential damage to Sino-British trade was also threatened, the first linkage
between the Sino-British disputes and British participation in China's
lucrative market being made on 18 March by China's trade minister,
Li Lanqing; who warned that British business could suffer.[6] It is
widely believed that potential British participation in the construction
of a mass transit railway for Guangzhou was a casualty of this
particular line of invective.

A further target were local Hong Kong Chinese members of the
Patten administration, civil servants whose post-1997 careers
depended upon China. On 26 January, Anson Chan, Secretary for
Economic Services (later to become Chief Secretary) was attacked for
allegedly supporting British violation of the Joint Declaration and
for misleading international investors over Container Terminal 9
(CT9). On 5 February, one of China's Hong Kong Affairs Advisers,
himself a former Secretary for Home Affairs, Donald Liao, said that
civil servants who publicly backed Patten's proposals would be

putting their careers at risk. Later, when negotiations over the reform proposals did start, China was to further criticise Hong Kong Government officials, in particular Michael Sze, Secretary for Constitutional Affairs, who resigned from the government in 1996 to take up a position as head of the Hong Kong Trade Development Council.

China's most virulent attacks, however, were reserved for Patten himself. Premier Li Peng, in an NPC work report, attacked Patten's 'perfidious and unilaterally crafted proposals to violate previous Sino-British Agreements'. On 17 March, Director of the Hong Kong and Macau Affairs Office, Lu Ping, in a press conference in Beijing, said that Patten would be condemned by history as a 'man of guilt'. As time went by, Patten was called a variety of other names by Chinese officials and the pro-Chinese press. Epithets included 'a man to be cursed by history for a thousand years', 'a whore', 'a shyster', 'a snake', 'a robber', 'a thief', 'a prostitute' and 'a tango dancer'.[7] The Chinese language pro-Beijing Hong Kong newspaper *Wen Wei Po* went to the trouble of sending a correspondent to Patten's old constituency in Britain, Bath, devoting a series of three articles on what people thought of Patten there. In the first of these articles, local councillor Mrs Pamela Richards was quoted as saying that, 'Chris Patten is a man who put his own future above people's livelihood. The poll tax issue was a typical example of this. Mr Patten was clearly aware that it was a wrong policy, yet he spared no efforts to serve his master for the sake of his political future,' Mrs Richards said.[8] In the second of the three articles, a Mr Andrews was quoted as describing Patten as 'a sordid politician' who 'had been corrupted by power'. When he had graduated from university, the future Hong Kong Governor had applied simultaneously for jobs in the research department of both the Conservative and Labour Parties, thus demonstrating his opportunism, according to Mr Andrews. Patten had sacrificed the interests of the people, in order to safeguard the Thatcher administration and win himself promotion, he added. 'We tried hard and managed to get rid of Mr Patten. However, the choice of 80 000 people has spelt harm for the six million people in Hong Kong. We're really sorry,' Mr Andrews was also quoted as saying by *Wen Wei Po*.[9]

The former Conservative MP for Bath's reaction to this abuse was typically unflappable, saying that he 'drew strength' from the 'daily doses of diatribe', since it showed that China did not have 'sensible or convincing arguments against his reforms',[10] and describing the Chinese as 'raising the equivalent of Roget's Thesaurus to find new words of abuse'.[11] He may not have remained totally unshaken, however, as in late January he suffered a minor heart attack and had to undergo an operation to widen two of his arteries. The affectionate nick-name 'Fat Pang', given to Patten by the Hong Kong Chinese, was no longer to apply, as he would henceforth follow a strict diet.

Patten also had more heavyweight detractors in Britain. *Wen Wei Po* quoted an article by the Irish politician and commentator, Connor Cruise O'Brien, which had appeared in the *Independent* in Britain. O'Brien had criticised Patten as being confrontational and going against Hong Kong people's interests. Patten was trying to go beyond Beijing's perception of democracy, *Wen Wei Po* quoted O'Brien as saying.[12] Percy Cradock, architect of Britain's Hong Kong policy before the advent of the new policy promoted by Patten and now apparently an 'old friend of China', most unusually for a retired diplomat, spoke out strongly against the constitutional proposals in a letter to *The Times* and on BBC television, claiming that China would rather ruin Hong Kong's economy than accept Patten's reforms.[13]

The Hong Kong Governor was not totally without support, however. The Hong Kong Bar Association, for example, denounced China's threats to set up its own judicial system.[14] And Legco support was solid, a motion to block the introduction of Patten's electoral bill being rejected by 35 votes to 2.[15] Support was solid in the House of Commons in London, too, with all parties backing Patten's proposals. In a pointed statement to the House, Prime Minister John Major said that the British Government was 'four-square' behind the Governor, and that: '[his] proposals for greater democracy are widely supported in Hong Kong, in the United Kingdom and in the international community and I believe have wide support in this House'.[16]

Patten's position during this time was that his reforms were only proposals and that he was ready at any time to consider counter proposals from the Chinese side. Behind the scenes, diplomacy must have been going on also. On four occasions, Patten delayed a scheduled announcement of the introduction of the reform bill to Legco. According to one commentator,[17] on 6 February the British Ambassador passed a copy of Patten's reform bill to the Chinese Foreign Ministry. After some deliberation and discussion over whether or not Hong Kong could be represented at negotiations to try to resolve the reform issue, an agreement was made to start discussions. However, the Chinese refused to agree on a date for the talks to begin and a few hours later Patten went ahead and published his proposals in the Government Gazette, an official indication that they would be presented to Legco. On gazetting the bill, Patten stated that: 'we would have liked the talks to go ahead, but there is a difference between being conciliatory and not having a bottom line'.[18] By gazetting the bill, Patten was not totally closing the door on the possibility of negotiation. It was only an announcement of an intention to introduce the bill; it still had to be presented to Legco. Gazettal was a way of putting further pressure on China to fix the date for talks to start. Indeed, on 13 April, as an indication that Patten's tougher line might be working, Britain and China announced that negotiations would begin nine days later.

The main obstacle to starting what were considered by the Chinese to be only 'talks about talks' was whether or not Hong Kong should be represented. The British side, who wished to emphasise Hong Kong's autonomy, insisted that Hong Kong should be represented at the discussions. For the Chinese, accepting equal representation of Hong Kong would have been to accept the idea of the 'three-legged stool', an idea proposed, unsuccessfully, by the British at the beginning of the talks leading to the Joint Declaration.[19] A compromise was reached whereby the Hong Kong Government would be represented by the Secretary for Constitutional Affairs, but only as an observer, while the actual negotiations would be conducted by the British Ambassador to Beijing and a Chinese Vice-Minister for Foreign Affairs. This was actually a downgrading of the arrangement arrived at during the discussions over the Joint Declaration, when the Hong Kong Governor was at least considered to be a member of the British team.

In the megaphone diplomacy leading up to the agreement on talks, China used similar United Front tactics to those it had deployed earlier during negotiations over the Joint Declaration. These were: public insistence on a non-negotiable principle and foreclosing of the other side's position before agreeing to enter into negotiations (in this case the principle was that Patten's proposals would have to be scrapped); ostracising a key figure (Patten); the use of time pressure; media pressure; use of extreme language; shaming; mobilisation of 'old friends of China'; and putting the opposing side in the position of the supplicant (making Britain beg for China to enter into talks). When an agreement was finally reached to negotiate, as with the Joint Declaration, China chose the venue, Beijing.

Patten gave many indications of not wanting to fall into China's trap and get bogged down in negotiations, his gazettal of the proposals when China delayed over fixing a date for negotiations to start being the most obvious one. The time factor was very significant here, because there was a genuine deadline, which worked to China's advantage. If China could delay Patten long enough in the negotiations, then it could put pressure on him to accommodate to their position or be unable to make the necessary electoral arrangements in time. Patten could see that entering into negotiations would be playing into China's hands, but he was subject to strong pressure from Hong Kong to give them a try at least. While showing the Hong Kong people wanted more democracy, opinion polls during this period also indicated that they wanted smooth relations with China. Patten was left between the devil and the deep blue sea. If he did not negotiate with China, he would be accused of ignoring the Hong Kong people's wish for a smooth transition. If he did enter into the negotiations, he risked getting into a position where he would have to give in to China's demands. On the other hand, given that his reform plans were only 'proposals', he must have been willing to settle for some sort of compromise. If his main long-term objective was British withdrawal from Hong Kong with honour, a negotiated agreement with China which demonstrated that he had done his best for more democracy would go a long way to achieving this aim. Nevertheless, the approach to the talks would have to be more robust than earlier negotiations.

The negotiations were to be led, on the British side, by Malcolm McLaren, Ambassador to Beijing, a sinologist and one of 'Cradock's people'. This did not augur well for Patten or his supporters in the pro-democracy camp. As Margaret Ng, a local lawyer and political commentator put it, in agreeing to negotiations:

> Mr Patten is in danger of being seen to have let the initiative slip to Beijing – and the Whitehall diplomats. Neither Sir Percy Cradock nor Sir Robin McLaren's attitude and methods are unknown to Hong Kong. While going back to the negotiating table is undoubtedly the way to a solution, if negotiations are placed in such hands, as they increasingly appear to be, the outcome could be a foregone conclusion.[20]

On 22 April, the first of what were to be 17 drawn-out rounds of talks began. They were to continue until 27 November. While the talks were proceeding, it was difficult to piece together the way they were going, both sides keeping the contents of the discussions more or less secret. At regular intervals Hong Kong television viewers were treated to pictures of Ambassador McLaren setting out for, or arriving back from, the British Embassy. He was usually on foot and hounded by a pack of mostly young female Hong Kong reporters brandishing tape recorders and microphones in his face.[21] Invariably his comments on the progress of the talks were platitudinous. 'Workmanlike', or 'no progress' were his typical comments.[22] The situation reminded local people of the negotiations ten years earlier, leading to the Joint Declaration. After the talks were over it became possible to have a fair idea of what took place, as both governments published accounts of the discussions in an effort to convince the public that it was not their fault that agreement had not been reached.[23] Although many issues were at stake and the talks did not progress in a logical manner, the following were some of the main points raised for discussion.

The early rounds of talks concentrated on whether attention should first focus on the make-up of the lower tiers of local government (the 'easier' questions), as China wanted, or whether all of Patten's proposals for the 1995 elections should be taken as a package. From the British point of view, the 'package' concept was important, because they wanted the same voting system to apply to all tiers of government. By the sixth and seventh rounds, China made proposals concerning the functional constituencies, namely that the franchise in the existing 21 seats should not be expanded as Patten proposed, and that the nine new functional constituencies should be based on corporate voting rather than the one-person one-vote system proposed by Patten. In addition, the Chinese proposed that the composition of the Election Committee to select ten Legco members should follow the model laid down in the Basic Law,[24] rather than following Patten's model of being constituted by elected District Board members. In response to China's demands, by the ninth round Britain put forward revised proposals on the nine new functional constituencies. By the eleventh round, the British insisted on discussing objective criteria for the through train, but the Chinese refused to comply and negotiations reached a deadlock on this issue.

By the tenth round, the Chinese side reiterated that the British counter-proposals on the various issues still violated the Basic Law, the Joint Declaration and the previous Sino-British agreements. During the eleventh and twelfth rounds Britain insisted that there should be discussion of the criteria for the through train. It was only by the fifteenth round, however, that China responded to this British demand. China's criteria for the through train were that Legco members should 'love Hong Kong and China', should not be opposed to the Basic Law, should not participate in or lead activities aimed at overthrowing Chinese rule or undermining China's socialist system, should be dedicated to bringing about a smooth transition and transfer of power while upholding the resumption of Chinese sovereignty over Hong Kong, and should give full support for the principle of 'one country two systems'. Britain's reaction to these criteria was that they were all already covered in the Basic Law. Their concern, however, was that any application of the criteria should be forward-looking and not be based on past political views or actions. The British were concerned that those legislators who had been branded as subversive by China should be given the opportunity to ride the through train. Highlighting Britain's concern for legal precision and China's preference for broader principles, the British were concerned that the relevant clause on anti-government activities in the Basic Law was ambiguous as regards tense and it was thus unclear if the rules would be applied retrospectively. To this end, during the sixteenth round of talks, the British put forward a draft oath, based on the Chinese criteria, but making clear that it applied to future behaviour. China, however, made no response.

At the seventeenth round the Chinese side proposed that if the voting method for the Legco should not be included, then a Memorandum of Understanding could be published dealing with the local elections in 1994 and that they would accept an 'agreement to disagree' over the question of appointed members for the District Boards and Municipal Councils. Britain would be able to abolish the appointee system for 1994, on the understanding that after 1997 the composition of these bodies would be determined according to the provisions of the Basic Law. Unable to agree to this proposal, the British negotiators suggested a suspension of discussion until December. On 30 November, however, the British Foreign Secretary sent a message to the Chinese Foreign Minister saying that for practical and political reasons the Hong Kong Governor would have to introduce draft legislation covering those issues discussed in the first stage of the talks and that he would announce his intention to do so on 2 December. On 1 December, the Chinese side replied that this would lead to the breakdown of the negotiations.

* * *

In reflecting upon the reasons for the failure of the talks over Patten's political reform programme, one needs to consider the objectives of each side. From the British point of view, they needed to demonstrate to the people of Hong Kong that they had done their utmost to reach an agreement with China, while at the same time insisting they were negotiating with Hong Kong's best interests at heart. For this reason, it was not the British who actually terminated the talks; they merely put the Chinese into a position of having to withdraw. In this way, Patten was able to say that, 'Our team will never be the team that walks away from the negotiating table. Never.'[25] At the same time, however, the British negotiators knew that time was on the side of the Chinese. Legislation had to be submitted for Legco approval, in order that the 1994 local elections and 1995 Legco elections could take place. From the Chinese point of view, the goal was to delay as long as possible and to gradually whittle away Patten's proposals. This is probably why the talks did not seem to progress in a very systematic manner and why deadlock was reached on at least three occasions, with the talks having to be raised to the Foreign Minister level.

In addition to this strategic motive, there is no doubt that China's position was hardened by the role played by Patten. China was shocked that the Hong Kong Governor had refused to negotiate over his reform proposals *before* presenting them to the Hong Kong public and uncomfortable that the British side should give him so much authority. As a mere governor, so Chinese thinking went, Patten should follow the instructions of the government in London, which alone had the authority to discuss bilateral matters between the two sovereigns. But the British Foreign Secretary, Douglas Hurd, had said that there was 'not so much as a tissue paper' between Patten, John Major and himself.[26] There is no doubt, also, that China was unhappy with Patten's uncompromising manner, which contrasted so greatly with the deferential way earlier sinologist governors and diplomats had gone about their business. The political correspondent of *The Guardian*, Hugo Young, summed up how Patten's manner went down with the Chinese, when he reported on a visit by the Governor to London, to attend a House of Commons Foreign Affairs Committee meeting:

Governor Chris Patten is not an old China hand. When he testifies to the Commons Foreign Affairs Committee on Thursday, he may well want to emphasise his message by wagging a finger. China hands don't do that. Nor do they fold their arms in public, something Patten often does in Hong Kong, where the gesture is fraught with repellent meaning. And if his programme for elections weren't bad enough, his body language is held up as inviting bad joss, which a true China man would avoid.[27]

In spite of all the obstacles, both sides did make certain compromises, the British offering more concessions than the Chinese. The British agreed to Chinese demands that the functional constituencies should be based on organisations, rather than one-person one-vote, and that the election committee should be around 600. The Chinese, on the other hand, agreed to lower the voting age from 21 to 18 (not a great concession, given that the voting age in China is 18) and to a reduction in the numbers of appointed members of the District Boards.

Concessions on each side notwithstanding, there was clearly a lot more separating the two sides than bringing them together. One fundamental difference concerned Britain's insistence that any first stage agreement should include the voting method for Legco and its preference for a 'single-seat, single-vote' method of voting. Another fundamental difference concerned Britain's determination that the franchise for the functional constituencies should be broadened. Patten continually insisted that the 1995 elections should be free, fair and open.[28] Perhaps the most important difference separating the two sides were the criteria for the through train. Britain was concerned that these should not be based on past actions, which would mean that leading United Democrats and independent legislators might not be able to stay in office beyond the handover, being considered by China to have participated in activity contrary to the Basic Law.

According to one commentator, the breakdown of the talks was a strategic miscalculation on the part of Britain.[29] Britain would have done better to have accepted a first-stage compromise which avoided mentioning the voting method for Legco direct elections. Then, in a second round of talks, they could have experimented and reached some sort of compromise on the voting method for Legco, perhaps somewhere between the 'single-seat, single-vote', which they preferred, and the proportional representation preferred by China. There is no doubt that Britain was prepared for some sort of compromise. On many occasions, Patten insisted that his reforms were only proposals and that he welcomed counter-proposals from the Chinese side. In subsequent statements, people on the British side have commented that the un-revised package, which is what Hong Kong ended up with, was not what Patten had anticipated. With hindsight, it is clear that Britain provided China with a pretext to go its own way, to disregard the whole package introduced by the British, and to return to its own interpretation of what was foreseen in the Basic Law.

At the end of the day, all of the differences separating the two sides can be reduced to a concern on the part of the British that Hong Kong people, through the ballot box, should be able to select whichever people they chose fit to represent them in Legco, whoever they might be, and a determination as far as China was concerned to maintain control of the political situation in Hong Kong post-1997 and keep out of the political process those members of the pro-democracy camp, such as Martin Lee, whom they adjudged to be subversive. The fact that the two sides were not able to compromise on this issue must at least in part be attributed to the more adversarial approach to dealings with China, as promoted by Patten. Patten was not willing to be as patient as the Foreign Office negotiators who had worked on the Joint Declaration. He was sensitive to criticisms from the pro-democracy camp, who had accused the Foreign Office of kow-towing to China. When interviewed for this book, Patten attributed the failure of the talks to the fact that Britain had a bottom line, thus implying, perhaps, that in previous negotiations the problem had been that British negotiators did not have a bottom line. 'We spent a year pretty well trying to reach agreement on those proposals with the Chinese', Patten said in the interview: 'We failed to do so and the reason why we failed was because we had a bottom line.'[30] China had used all of the tactics it had used in earlier negotiations, but this time they did not work; Britain refused to yield on its own basic principles and presumably was willing to accept the consequences.

At this late stage in the transition, from Britain's point of view, the argument was now a question of honour and Britain's legacy to the last of its significant colonies. This new position had been signalled back in December 1989, when newly appointed Foreign Secretary, Douglas Hurd, had stated in the House of Commons that Hong Kong was 'the last main chapter of the country's empire' and that it 'should not end in a shabby way'.[31] Prime Minister Major, in press interviews following a visit to Hong Kong in March 1996, said that when Patten lost his seat in the 1992 general election, he had offered him either a seat in the House of Lords or the position of the Governor of Hong Kong 'to deal with a very important element of British history'.[32]

Patten's commitment to this perspective of honourable withdrawal was indicated in an interview he gave to the *Far Eastern Economic Review*. Accepting that he had no control over what China would do about Legco in 1997, he said: 'I do not think I would be behaving very honourably if I was to connive at arrangements in 1995 which accepted that [Legco members such as Martin Lee and Szeto Wah] could be thrown out of the Legislative Council in 1997. If there is a through train, why can't everyone travel on it?'[33] Similarly, in January 1994, appearing before the House of Commons Foreign Affairs Select Committee, he stated: 'We have a duty to the people of Hong Kong, a moral responsibility, and a duty to ourselves, to our own notions of decency and honour.'[34] As already noted in Chapter 6, when interviewed for this book, Patten again emphasised the historical dimension of his governorship, with his comment: 'I am conscious that this period and the way we conduct ourselves will go into the history books.'[35]

\* \* \*

From China's point of view, the Joint Declaration had stated that, on reversion to China, Hong Kong's system would remain the same for 50 years. Britain had controlled Hong Kong for a century and a half without democracy and they viewed with suspicion moves by the British to introduce democracy at the eleventh hour, just as they were shedding responsibility and passing the task of maintaining a stable and prosperous Hong Kong over to China. The Joint Declaration and the later Basic Law stated that the 'legislature of the Hong Kong SAR shall be constituted by elections', but this had only been added on British insistence, right at the end of the negotiations leading to the Joint Declaration. As noted in Chapter 3, China refused Britain's wish to define elections as 'democratic elections'. There are great differences in the meaning of 'elections' in the democratic West and in China, where in the National People's Congress (NPC) there is more often than not only one candidate approved by the Communist Party for each seat.

In January of 1994, during an appearance before the House of Commons Select Committee on Foreign Affairs, Patten made a joke at the expense of a well-known Hong Kong figure, ex-Chief Secretary Sir David Akers-Jones, who had been quoted by a British journalist as saying that: 'The Chinese style is not to rig elections. But they do like to know the result before they're held.' As Akers-Jones later explained, his comments came during a long conversation with the journalist and were part of an explanation of Chinese society as he had observed it in Hong Kong over many years.[36] In certain organisations, the former Chief Secretary explained, the chairman will be decided by consultation and discussion among members and an election will only be held once it has been decided who is to take the job.

For Patten, 'elections' meant democratic elections, as in the West. This is made clear in the following citation from a television interview:

Patten: The Joint Declaration makes a couple of things absolutely plain. First that the Legislative Council here in Hong Kong should be formed by elections. Now we all know that that means fair elections not unfair elections.

Interviewer: And of course the Chinese interpretation of what is and what is not a fair election differs substantially from your own and this is why we have these negotiations.

Patten: ... you talk about relative concepts of fairness. Now I think everybody knows the difference between an elephant and a giraffe and you can tell what's fair and you can tell what's unfair.[37]

This view was reiterated in an article written by Patten for *The Spectator*, where he stated:

> The Joint Declaration – the treaty signed by Britain and China – spells out Hong Kong's freedoms and values and the way to secure them. It promised an executive answerable to the legislature, and a legislature wholly composed through election.
>
> Admittedly, it did not say those elections should be open and fair. Could anyone at the negotiating table have thought otherwise?[38]

Patten's motive in asserting that the term 'elections' must mean democratic elections, as he understands the term, and that everyone at the negotiations must have interpreted the term in this way, was to use this as an argument in support of his reform plan. Patten used a manipulative argumentation strategy here, of assuming a view is held by the community at large (including the Chinese) as common sense, as a given and not open to question, and identifying this view with his own. It seems that there are elements of ethnocentricity in this position, on the one hand, and disingenousness, on the other. The position is ethnocentric in that Patten refused to consider that others might have a different conceptualization of elections from his own. It seems highly unlikely, to put it mildly, however, that Patten was unaware of electoral practices in the PRC or in some of Hong Kong's Asian neighbours, where collectivist approaches are also taken to elections. Patten's position is disingenuous in that it seems unlikely that he was not aware that the Chinese side allowed the reference to elections to be included in the Joint Declaration in the knowledge that they would put their own interpretation on that term. In an article in the *South China Morning Post* of 30 September 1996, Percy Cradock, Britain's chief negotiator over the Joint Declaration, in a swingeing attack on Patten, stated categorically that: 'The facts are that there is no reference to democratisation in the Joint Declaration. There is a general statement that the legislature shall be constituted by elections and the

executive shall be accountable to the legislature, nothing more. There
was no bargain or agreement between Britain and China for anything
like the Patten reforms.' It seems highly unlikely, either, that Patten,
well read and well briefed as he was, would not have been familiar
with Deng Xiaoping's speech at a meeting of the BLDC, in 1987,
where he stated as follows:

> So far as democracy is concerned, on the mainland we have
> socialist democracy, which is different in concept from bourgeois
> democracy. Western democracy includes, among other features, the
> separation of the three powers and multi-party elections. We have
> no objection to the Western countries doing it that way, but we on
> the Chinese mainland do not have such elections...
>
> Would it be good for Hong Kong to hold general elections? I
> don't think so. For example, as I have said before, Hong Kong's
> affairs will naturally be administered by Hong Kong people, but
> will it do for the administrators to be elected by a general ballot?
> We say that Hong Kong's administrators should be people of Hong
> Kong who love the motherland and Hong Kong, but will a general
> election necessarily bring out people like that?[39]

When asked about the term 'elections' when interviewed for this
book, Patten cited the debates in the British Parliament and statements made by British ministers at the time of the Joint Declaration
about developing representative democracy in Hong Kong.

> I am sure that when people were talking to Lady Thatcher or
> Geoffrey Howe about the draft that had been agreed in the Joint
> Declaration, they didn't say to them this bit about elections, it
> doesn't mean of course fair elections or democratic elections; it
> means the sort of elections that Chinese officials like when you
> know the result in advance.'[40]

What Patten said here may be perfectly true, but that doesn't mean
that there may not have been a tacit understanding that different
interpretations might be put on the term. Geoffrey Howe is quite
clear in his memoirs that the reference to elections in the Joint
Declaration was only put in at the last minute[41] and Cradock, in his
memoirs, makes it quite clear that the reference to elections was
Britain's 'last shot' and that the Chinese would not have agreed to
the term 'direct elections'.[42] Perhaps the civil servant diplomats, who
had a longer-term commitment to Sino-British affairs, had a different
agenda from the politicians. Perhaps Cradock and his Foreign Office

acolytes knew all along that the Joint Declaration did not really mean there would be democratic elections in Hong Kong, as Cradock's statement about there being no provision for democracy in the Sino-British document suggests. But they may not have felt the need to spell it out to their political masters, being happy for government ministers, who came and went, to think, or at least to talk, as if they did.

In contrast to his earlier assertions, in a 1995 interview Patten himself came near to admitting that Joint Declaration negotiators may have had something else in mind besides democratic Western-style elections, when he stated that: 'If I have a failing, [it has been] that I took the Joint Declaration too literally. I don't see that as a failure, but maybe there are some critics, including some of those who drafted the Joint Declaration, who would regard you as naive, to take literally everything that it says.'[43] It is highly unlikely, however, that many people would accept that Patten, the last colonial Governor of Hong Kong, was naive.

* * *

While the arguments were raging over the reform proposals and the 17 rounds of talks were taking place, China set about making its own arrangements for the resumption of sovereignty, beginning to put into place the 'second stove', or shadow government, which it had threatened when Patten's proposals had first been presented. On 21 March 1993, Zhou Nan, Director of Xinhua (New China News Agency), had already announced that China's 'new stove' would be made up of Hong Kong Affairs Advisers and Chinese experts and that it would dove-tail into the 1996 Preparatory Committee. It would work under the guidance of the Hong Kong and Macau Affairs Office and meet in Beijing. At the end of March, a second batch of 49 Advisers was announced, bringing the number of appointees up to 93, the first batch having been appointed a year earlier. From the Advisers, a majority were drawn from the NPC, the Chinese People's Political Consultative Conference (CPPCC), the Guangdong Provincial Congress, and pro-China Hong Kong business people. The most represented political group was the Democratic Alliance for the Betterment of Hong Kong (DAB), a recently founded pro-Beijing party, followed by the Liberal Party. There was no representation for the United Democrats.[44] As an indication of the change in the British Hong Kong Government's position, one of China's Advisers was Sir David Akers-Jones, the former Chief Secretary mentioned earlier in this chapter, who had also been Acting Governor during the four month interim period between Youde and Wilson. On 22 June, the creation of a Working Committee for the Preparatory Committee (later referred to as the Preliminary Working Committee (PWC)), consisting of 57 members and chaired by the Chinese Foreign Minister, Qian Qichen, was announced and it was endorsed by the NPC on 2 July. The membership consisted of 27 Mainland officials and 30 Hong Kong people. Again there was no place for pro-democracy representatives.

* * *

It is significant that in its arrangements for Hong Kong, China assigned an important role for the pro-business lobby, an indication of the priority it gave to Hong Kong's economic value to China. It is ironic, however, that this same group, as appointed members and functional constituency representatives in Legco, had previously been the main supporters of the colonial British Government. Now that Britain was engaged in the process of decolonising and democratising Hong Kong, members of this group found themselves no longer wanted, at least to such a degree. It was the pro-democracy groups, with their grass roots supporters, who were now more greatly favoured.

As a reaction to this development, in February 1993 the pro-business members of Legco and their supporters formed themselves into a political party for the first time, calling themselves the Liberal Party (a rather odd choice for what was essentially a conservative grouping).[45] If Patten's reforms went through, they would need a party structure in order to contest the direct elections and the new and enlarged functional constituencies foreseen for the 1995 elections. Increasingly, over the past two decades or so, control of Hong Kong business had passed first from the largely British *hongs* or trading companies, to Hong Kong Chinese family-controlled enterprises and, more recently, to Mainland-backed firms. Business in Hong Kong was becoming increasingly dependent on China for cheap labour, for its markets, for its import–export trade and, increasingly, for finance; in the future, it was likely to depend on China for political favours, not only for its operations in China, but also in Hong Kong, after the foundation of the SAR. As an indication of this increasing influence of the pro-China business lobby, on 27 April three pro-China business groups won control of the General Committee of the Hong Kong General Chamber of Commerce, replacing Martin Barrow, chairman and Jardine-Matheson director, with a Chinese businessman.

Although they were slightly less powerful following the 1991 elections, with Democrats elected for the first time, and they were under threat of a further reduction of influence under Patten's proposals for 1995,[46] the Liberals still enjoyed great power in the 1991–5 Legco, easily surpassing their main rivals, the UDHK, in terms of numbers and influence in the Council Chamber and its committees.[47] The Liberal Party and the pro-business lobby in general had as their main aim the protection of their economic interests post-1997. They viewed consensus with China and a smooth handover as more important than the development of democracy, as attested to by their work on the BLDC.[48]

\* \* \*

As Douglas Hurd had warned, on 30 November 1993 Patten duly gazetted his first stage proposals. While indicating his intention of moving forward with only the first stage, Patten could still hold out hope for a second round of negotiations on the second stage, at some later date. This was important in countering those who wanted him to adopt a more conciliatory line and show their desire for a smooth transfer before more democracy. However, if China agreed to a second series of negotiations, it would be presented with a *fait accompli* in so far as the voting method for the 1995 Legco elections would already have been set, with the 'single-seat, single-vote' system adopted for both the 1994 local elections and the 1995 Legco elections.

China's response to the gazettal was swift in activating the United Front. On 3 December 1993, a statement was made that China would 'start a new kitchen after 1997 in accordance with the provisions of the Basic Law'.[49] On 9 December, Xinhua accused Patten of lacking in sincerity and of trying to prolong British influence beyond 1997: 'The real purpose of Patten in unfurling this beautiful banner of democracy,' the Chinese organ said, 'is to try to make British rule last after 1997.'[50] On 11 December, Foreign Minister Qian revived Deng's threat of an early take-over: 'We cannot sit back and watch disorder in Hong Kong,' he said.[51] On 20 December a Chinese commentary accused Britain of attempting to leave the colony in chaos before departure, stating that 'It is well known that whenever the British have had to withdraw from its colonies it has either seized various interests or made trouble in the colonies so as to leave as many problems as possible.' This commentary also targeted Patten directly, stating that: 'Hong Kong Governor Chris Patten has played an infamous role in the British territory.'[52]

The virulent attacks culminated on 27 December, when China finally derailed the through train, with an unsigned statement given out by the Hong Kong and Macao Affairs Office through Xinhua in Beijing, announcing that all three levels of Hong Kong's constitutional system would be disbanded at the handover. A spokesman further stated that the three tiers of government would then be reconstituted according to the Basic Law, adding that it was a pity that no agreement had been reached in the negotiations, due to Britain's deliberate sabotage.[53]

On 23 February 1994, Legco approved the first part of the reform package. This included lowering the voting age to 18, adopting the 'single-seat, single-vote' system for all elections, abolishing appointed members from the district boards and municipal councils and allowing Hong Kong delegates to the NPC to stand for election.

\* \* \*

In contesting Patten's reform plans so vehemently, China had a number of fears. Already, in the 1991–95 Legco, there were signs of confrontation between the executive government and Legco. Directly-elected members, although in the minority, used Legco as a platform to argue for greater democracy, to effectively replace executive-led with legislative-led government.[54] On a number of occasions they thwarted, if only temporarily, attempts by the executive to pass legislation. As mentioned earlier, a proposal to set up the CFA was delayed in 1991, even though it had been agreed in the JLG. In April 1992, budget changes were forced on the government. If Patten's proposals went through, by 1995, with democrats in the majority, who could tell what might happen? Taxes might be increased, negatively impacting on Hong Kong's business community and economy. Even more seriously, pro-democracy legislators might seek to undermine stability on the Mainland, encouraging democratic development there and subverting the 'one country two systems' concept. The example of Taiwan would have come to the mind of Mainland leaders, where democratic reforms had brought to power an anti-Mainland government and where virulent anti-PRC rhetoric was routinely broadcast from the rumbustious Taiwanese parliament. For China, Hong Kong represented a business centre and conduit between the Mainland and the outside world. However, while wanting to take advantage of Hong Kong's unique position in economic terms, China did not want the political influence that might go with it. On many occasions Chinese officials reiterated how Hong Kong must remain a business centre, but not a centre of political activity. In a statement in March 1994, for example, Lu Ping, while promising that China would not meddle in Hong Kong's administration after 1997, warned that the future SAR should remain a 'golden bridge' between two different economic systems, not a 'political bridge'.[55]

As part of their United Front policy, at the same time as arguing against the political reform programme China was attacking on other fronts, most notably the airport and related infrastructure projects. In May, Deng Xiaoping himself was reported in the *People's Daily* and in the Hong Kong press as saying that the airport project was a conspiracy by the British to drain money out of Hong Kong.[56] In Chinese politics, if the leader of the Communist Party makes a statement, there is a tendency for that statement to be treated as official policy until he says otherwise. Consequently, following Deng's reported statement, attacks on the airport project were increased. According to the report in the *People's Daily*, the contract for the airport terminal went to the highest bidder, the Mott Consortium, comprising one British and two British Hong Kong firms. The bid was reported to be $70 million higher than the losing bidder's. As part of the general attack on the infrastructure project, by September the Chinese attacks were also directed at the port development side of the scheme and tendering for the CT9 container terminal. The contract to construct the terminal was awarded by private tender to a consortium which included Jardine-Matheson, a company with a black history, as far as China was concerned. Beijing demanded that a re-tendering should be carried out before they would approve the project, under conditions that would be impossible for Jardine-Matheson to meet. On a different front again, in August Zhou Nan, Director of Xinhua, accused Britain of training agents to be left in Hong Kong after 1997, in a bid to retain control of the territory.[57]

But the most virulent campaign was still directed at Patten himself. This took the form of ostracism, on the one hand, and continuing verbal attacks on the other. Chinese officials in Hong Kong were meticulous in avoiding any encounters at official functions which they would normally attend with the Hong Kong Governor and Patten was not invited to Chinese Government backed functions, where Governor Wilson had been a regular guest. Patten's absence was most noticeable at a ceremony to celebrate the first note issued by the Bank of China of Hong Kong currency.[58] On one notorious occasion, by accident, Patten did come face to face with Xinhua Director Zhou Nan, at the inauguration of a giant Buddha at the Po Lin Monastery on the island of Lantau. As the two men crossed each others' paths, Patten held out his hand to Zhou, who refused to take it, preferring instead the Buddhist greeting of touching the fists of both hands with a slight bow, even though he had until then shaken hands with everyone else he had met. In an allusion to the Buddhist scriptures, Zhou referred to those who violated the 'three principles' as 'sinners lost in the boundless sea of bitterness'.[59] As the perpetrator of the 'three violations', the remarks were, of course, directed at Patten. The British Hong Kong Governor's comment on the event was: 'I shake hands with everyone everywhere. If others do not do so, that is something for them to explain.'[60] In May 1994, Lu Ping, Director of the Hong Kong and Macau Affairs Office, visited the territory. But he kept a very low profile, refused to meet Patten and spoke only to local China advisers.

* * *

After being the target of these tactics for more than a year, in October 1993, Patten presented his second annual policy speech. His personal adviser, Edward Llewelyn, described the situation to the author, in 1996, as follows: 'We were in the middle of very difficult, particularly very difficult talks with the Chinese. The adjectives were still raining down. The community needed, Legco needed, inspiration,' Llewelyn said.[61] Patten decided to provide this inspiration through some high-flown rhetoric on the theme of democracy and freedom. Heavy with parallelism, antithesis and metaphor,[62] and forgetting that the Joint Declaration had not in fact promised democracy and that, with its executive-led government, the laws of Hong Kong would be made by a narrow elite and not the grass roots community, the speech concluded as follows:

> The democratic ideal clearly enshrined in the Joint Declaration means that the community, through its elected legislature, makes the laws that govern it. You are both the rulers and the ruled. That is why democracy is both a high privilege and a heavy responsibility.
>
> I say all this because I believe it to be true. And I say it as well because I am growing to love Hong Kong as you who have created it from rock and scrub love Hong Kong. And I want, as you want, to see Hong Kong as it confidently enters the next millennium under Chinese sovereignty, a blazing beacon of good fortune, a dazzling example of what free men and women, putting adversity and

hardship behind them – can together achieve. That is what we want. And that is what we can achieve. All we require is to keep our confidence in the values that bind us into a thriving community. With the courage that has brought success in the past, and the confidence that success has earned, everything is possible. And I believe that you believe it, too.

Following the speech, Patten's official spokesperson, Kerry McGlinn, met one of the journalists who had heard it. He described the encounter to the author, as follows:

I remember coming up in Government Information Service, and Teresa Poole, who's the *Independent* correspondent in Beijing, was rushing excitedly to his press conference from Legco. And she said to me: 'On a day like today', she said, 'I feel proud to be English.' And I understood exactly what she meant. It was a very moving oration, or peroration.[63]

How the speech went down with the Chinese Government is another matter.

# 9 A Lame Duck Government?

Following the approval of the first stage political reforms, the more controversial second stage was presented to Legco in late June of 1994. After Seventeen and a half hours of discussion, the whole package, as put forward by Patten, was endorsed. This was only after an amendment proposed by the Liberal Party, to approximate to what they thought China would have wanted, had been defeated by just one vote and a private member's bill submitted by independent legislator, Emily Lau, proposing a fully elected legislature was voted down, again by just one vote. The debate was so emotive that one legislator broke into tears while making his speech. The *Hong Kong Standard* published a selection of views expressed during the debate, in favour of and against the reforms, as follows:[1]

Why is the Liberal Party so afraid of democracy? Why seek to appease China with a pale and anaemic copy of the type of election China would want to set up in 1997? We must reject the undemocratic monstrosity before us.

*Independent legislator Jimmy McGregor*

The abolition (by China) of representative institutions which are carefully constituted, properly elected, and which command the support of our people cannot be conducive to a smooth transition.

*Chief Secretary Anson Chan*

No one on earth would believe that there would be continuity as a result of the passing of the (government's) 1992 package. Only an idiot would believe that.

*Liberal Party leader Allen Lee*

The hopes of 1997 have been crushed by Mr Patten who believed he knew how to deal with China.

*Independent legislator Elsie Tu*

No matter which package is passed today it cannot achieve the through-train, and Hong Kong people will suffer profound damage.

*Independent legislator Eric Li*

Are we crawling towards 1997 or are we walking tall?

*United Democrats legislator Szeto Wah*

The wish of the Hong Kong people is that we have a high degree of autonomy from Beijing. They want you to do what they can't do themselves.

*United Democrats leader Martin Lee*

It is perhaps ironic that Patten's reform plan should have been passed '*in toto*'. Back in October 1992, the proposals had been presented 'for discussion', presumably with China, but also in Legco. It is highly likely that Patten anticipated some watering down of what he had put forward as a result of these discussions. During a House of Commons debate on Hong Kong in April 1995, Conservative MP Timothy Renton described how he was at Government House in 1992 and how, as he put it, Patten 'served the tennis ball, but the Chinese didn't play it back'. Indeed, the British side did agree to alter some of the proposals during the 17 rounds of discussion. However, the talks having broken down, Patten decided to stand by his original plan when submitting it to Legco. There would have been too much loss of face to introduce a less radical version at this stage. As regards Legco, this body was too polarised to arrive at any compromise between the pro-China package put forward by the Liberals and Emily Lau's private member's bill for a fully elected legislature. And Patten held the balance of power with the appointed legislators. As it was, the package having been approved, elections would take place in October 1995 with a greatly enlarged franchise, but with the rather strange arrangement of some people being able to vote twice: once in their geographical constituency and once in their functional constituency.

While the media reported fully on the debate, and in spite of its cliff-hanging excitement and the fact that it demonstrated for the first time that Legco could have real power and not be just a rubber-stamp operation, as it had been in the past, the attitude of the public could be said to have been one of anti-climax. When proposed, some three months after Patten's arrival and with his popularity at a peak, the reform programme was received with excitement and admiration. When finally approved, some twenty months later, after all sorts of threats from China, people had become tired of political reform and fearsome of China's promised retaliation. Prior to the debate, the *Sunday Morning Post* published the results of a survey which showed only 15 per cent of those polled were interested in the outcome of the vote.[2]

It was appearing increasingly likely that the scenario depicted by Percy Cradock would prevail, with China repeatedly saying that the reforms would be dismantled. Speaking at a businessmen's lunch in the territory, in April, Cradock urged Legco to vote down the second stage of the reform bill, arguing that: 'They [Legco] are being pushed and driven into a legislative Charge of the Light Brigade, of which the British contingent will be quietly withdrawn in 1997.' In passing the bill, Legco would be signing its own 'death warrant', Cradock warned, because China had reiterated that it would dismantle Legco after 1997. 'When the Chinese are making solemn statements repeatedly and formally, which in fact they have been making since 1989 to me, and when I remember that track record and realise they are talking about something near to their hearts, on which you have very strong feelings, then I incline to believe what they say,' he said.[3]

Patten had not totally lost the confidence of the public, however, as an article – no doubt facilitated by the Governor's publicity machine – describing how he spent the day of the Legco debate, shows:[4]

### THE HEAT IS ON BUT GOVERNOR KEEPS COOL
*By Bonnie Chiu*

Governor Chris Patten was in a sweat yesterday. But the fate of his reform proposal in the Legco wasn't the reason – it was just the summer weather.

Rather than listen to the historic debate at Legco, Mr Patten chose to spend the day visiting the people of Kwai Tsing.

Although the sweltering heat was no hotter than the atmosphere in the council chamber where vehement debate went on deep into the night, Mr Patten sweated profusely throughout his visit.

Wearing a light brown shirt and drab trousers, Mr Patten took to the streets for an encounter with the locals.

An experienced political campaigner, he was calm and unruffled.

After visiting an oil depot on Tsing Yi Island, he reached On Yam Estate at 3.20 PM. There hundreds of smiling primary school students, residents and shouting petitioners met him.

He smiled back, shook hands, accepted bouquets, kissed little children, received petitions, listened to residents' interpreters translating their demands, asked information officers questions about the area, and visited a public housing flat.

His charisma proved itself again as the public warmed to him.

'What a friendly governor!' a security guard said.

At the same time, in the Legco chamber, less complimentary descriptions of the Governor were heard from legislators opposing his reforms.

\* \* \*

Three months after the endorsement of the second stage of Patten's electoral reform bill, enactment of the first stage, concerning the arrangements for the District Board elections, which had been approved back in February, took place. Using one of his favourite rhetorical tricks, 'creating a scene', Patten praised the way the elections were carried out as 'the mark of a civilised community like this to see husbands and wives coming out with their children to cast their votes'.[5] Out of the 2.09 million registered voters, 33.1 per cent turned out to vote, not a tremendous number considering all the controversy that had been created in setting-up the elections, and that this was the first time that the public in general had been given the opportunity to vote in the first totally elected District Board elections. However, compared with local elections in other more mature jurisdictions, the turnout was quite reasonable. These elections for the first time involved the participation of political parties: the UDHK, the Liberals and various pro-Beijing factions were represented, although exit polls suggested voters had taken local considerations into account in deciding who to vote for, rather than party affiliation. The overall outcome was less satisfactory for the pro-democracy candidates than the previous 1991 polls had been, with the pro-Beijing DAB doing well and winning 37 of the 83 seats it contested.[6]

The same *Sunday Morning Post* poll cited above also showed that now that Patten had achieved what was widely perceived to be the main objective of his governorship, the establishment of the constitutional reforms, over half of those polled said Patten no longer had a useful role to play in Hong Kong.[7] Patten had consistently been called a one-issue governor. Various commentators had long speculated that he might be replaced at some point, either to appease the Chinese or because of his own political ambitions back home in Britain. Now that his main task had been achieved, speculation about his future resurfaced. The Governor, however, repeatedly denied such speculation and insisted that he would remain in Hong Kong right up until the handover. To recall Patten at this stage would not only have meant great loss of face for the British, but would also have sent out the wrong signal to those in Hong Kong who saw themselves as fighting for greater democracy. Having decided to continue as Governor right through to the handover, now that his reforms had been passed, Patten had to find a role for himself.

In his October 1994 policy speech, the emphasis was put on mending relations with China. Britain was as committed to ensuring a smooth transition for Hong Kong as China was, Patten said:

I have heard Chinese officials say that ensuring the prosperity and future well-being of Hong Kong is for them a tremendous and historic task. I fully understand their commitment, not least for reasons of history and patriotism, to the success of that task. Whatever our disagreements, whatever our differences of perception and background, whatever the misunderstandings and the mistrust, I urge them to understand that we, too, are similarly committed.

However, he could not refrain from pointing a finger at China's previous attitude, implying that it was China that had not been co-operative in the past. Britain would 'do everything that is honourable and sensible to co-operate with China for the remaining thousand days of British rule', he said, but:

Co-operation, however, is not a one-way street; nor is sincerity to be judged by whether one party always agrees with the other. That is not what the real world is like. Co-operation must mean exactly what it says, working together: in this case, working together in Hong Kong's interests, putting behind us past differences and focusing, instead, on how to build a better future for the men and women of Hong Kong.

This rather ambivalent appeal for co-operation was not to be answered, as ensuing events would demonstrate. China would continue to ostracise Patten and make its own arrangements for 1997. Too much face was at stake, for both sides, for rapprochement.

The policy speech concluded with the following sentences: 'We have a stake here – yes, a stake in the commercial sense, but also a stake in people and a stake in honour. This is part of our history, too'. The remaining period of Patten's governorship was not to be conducted in a spirit of co-operation. This was not to be Patten's role for the rest of his time in Hong Kong. His time was to be spent instead, primarily, in asserting what Patten considered to be Britain's legacy to the future SAR.

* * *

The labelling of Patten as a one-issue governor was always rejected by the Governor himself. The constitutional reforms drew so much attention that they had the effect of overshadowing other issues. The 1992 policy speech emphasised continued development of the economy, increased social welfare provision, environmental protection and the maintenance of law and order as other key areas of policy, in addition to the elusive co-operation with China. How could Patten's performance be rated in this sense?

Regarding the economy, given Hong Kong's avowed policy of 'positive non-intervention' there was not much really that Patten's government needed to do. Nevertheless, Hong Kong continued to grow at around the 5 per cent mark during the years of Patten's governorship and on just about every possible occasion he praised the success of Hong Kong's free market economy. While the 5 per cent annual increase was somewhat lower than the double digit average annual growth for the seventies and eighties, it was certainly still much better than the larger OECD countries, including the sovereign, Britain, which just about managed a 1 to 2 per cent annual growth rate during the same period (a negative growth rate in the case of Japan).

One important factor in this lower growth rate was the continued shift of manufacturing operations out of Hong Kong and over the border into the Pearl River Delta hinterland, with its abundant supplies of cheap labour. Hong Kong had been undergoing a qualitative shift from a manufacturing to a service-oriented economy. Companies still maintained their headquarters in Hong Kong, but the actual manufacturing was now carried out in China. In addition, there was great growth in other service industries, especially in the information, financial services, and tourism sectors and in the import and re-export trade for China.

Throughout the period, many overseas organisations rated Hong Kong's economy as one of the most competitive in the world. In 1995, for example, on 8 May, the Asia Pacific Economic Group said Hong Kong was about to begin a decade of 'remarkable growth', and would soon become the 'Manhattan of East Asia', with per capita income close to the world's highest. On 5 September, the World Competitiveness Report put Hong Kong in third position, behind the US and Singapore. Ironically, in November of that year, Hong Kong's growth fell to a four-year low, with the highest rate of unemployment for 11 years, but still only just above 3 per cent.

These developments, however, can be put down to cyclical factors and praise or blame should not go to Patten. Hong Kong's buoyant economy, however, did mean that Patten could depend on a certain 'feel-good' factor on the part of the public, which certainly would have done his image and popularity no harm. In March 1994, Patten was in the enviable position (for a government leader) of being able to 'give back' $7 billion to the public in the annual budget and to forecast that by the time of the handover, in 1997, treasury funds would stand at $269 billion, whereas they had previously been forecast at only $32 billion, thus fully justifying an earlier remark by Patten that the SAR government would receive from the Hong Kong colonial government what he termed 'the largest dowry since Cleopatra'.[8]

A negative aspect of Hong Kong's continued economic expansion was high inflation. In March 1994, going against its avowed non-interventionist philosophy, the government announced what it termed 'exceptional measures' to cool the residential property market, which was spiralling out of control. Following these measures, there was a considerable slackening of property prices. It is not clear if this can be attributed to the government-imposed controls or whether it was a natural market correction, the price of apartments having risen way beyond the affordability levels of most families. By 1997, prices had started to shoot up again.

Early in 1994 the stock market had reached an all-time high, rising in January to a figure of 12 201. The rally had been stimulated by an American fund manager saying that he was 'maximum bullish' on the Hong Kong market, following a visit to China where he had seen with his own eyes the tremendous economic growth that was taking place there. Shortly afterwards, however, the bubble burst, and throughout 1994 there was a slump of nearly 50 per cent, with the market falling to 6967 by 5 January 1995. This slump may well have had something to do with the moderation in property prices. Partly as a safeguard against the endemic relatively high inflation, and perhaps also because of the Hong Kong people's love of gambling, the territory has a very high level of participation in the stock market on the part of the general public. The Hang Seng Index is monitored regularly by a large section of the population and is seen as a sign of the territory's well-being.

The health of the government's finances did not come without any cost. Provision for those 'fellow citizens who fall by the wayside', as Patten had described Hong Kong's less fortunate in his 1992 policy speech, whilst increasing exponentially in real terms during his period of office, was still well below the provision of other advanced countries. In spite of having some of the world's wealthiest tycoons, Hong Kong has one of the widest disparities between the rich and the poor.[9] This did not stop one Chinese Government representative on the JLG budget committee from denouncing, in late 1995, Hong Kong's welfare spending as too extravagant, likening it to a Formula 1 racing car which was out of control and likely to crash and kill all six million Hong Kong people.[10] However, a poll commissioned by the Chinese language *Apple Daily,* shortly after these remarks, showed that the general public was not in agreement with this Mainland official, 78 per cent of respondents in the poll feeling social welfare provision in Hong Kong to be inadequate.[11] This was in spite of increased allowances of up to 54 per cent for single parents, the sick and the elderly in the October budget. As another indication of poor social provision, a report by Oxfam in September had shown that the real income of poor households had dropped over the last ten years, in spite of Hong Kong's tremendous economic growth.

Also in September 1995, Patten experienced probably the worst public relations disaster of his governorship when, on a visit to a temporary housing area, a mob of angry residents mounted a protest about their crowded, rat-infested, flooded living conditions. Pictures were splashed across the newspapers of the Governor's Daimler, its Union Jack prominently displayed on the bonnet, surrounded by protesters, one proffering a live rat in a cage. Reports also claimed that dead rats were thrown at the British colonial Governor.

To further highlight the government's apparently uncaring attitude, in October, the welfare secretary, Katherine Fok, suggested that elderly people should be able to live on the $1800 per month allowances they were provided with, a sum which was a hundred times less than her salary. The huge discrepancies in income were highlighted again the following year, when *Forbes* magazine listed Hong Kong as having the highest per capita percentage of billionaires in the world.[12]

In such a small, densely populated, economically productive territory as Hong Kong, environmental protection is an important issue, deserving of a high priority on the government's list of concerns.[13] With so many people packed into such a small space, with gigantic infrastructure projects going on, the air, land and water in Hong Kong have become severely polluted. For this reason Patten included the issue of environmental protection in his 1992 policy speech, along with proposals to improve matters. One of the government's major plans for the environment, initiated under Governor Wilson, was the Strategic Sewage Disposal Scheme. This was a tremendously expensive project, payment for which would extend over several years, beyond 1997. Not surprisingly, the scheme became the subject of dispute in the JLG, the Chinese side being suspicious that it was a plot to saddle the future SAR Government with another financial mill-stone, in addition to that of the airport. The scheme was also the subject of criticism within Hong Kong over whether it was the most cost-effective and environmentally-sound programme. Given the *de facto* integration of much of Hong Kong's manufacturing industry with the Guangdong area of the Mainland, across the border, many environmental issues require co-operation with Mainland authorities. Given the breakdown in Sino-British relations and the log-jam in the JLG, there was little progress in this area, in spite of the urgent need.

At the time of the 1992 policy speech, law and order was a growing concern in Hong Kong, as the preceding summer had been marked by a spate of violent robberies on jewellery shops and mah-jong parlours. The robberies were perpetrated by illegal immigrants from the Mainland, although it was believed they were under the control of local Hong Kong 'snake-heads', or triad gang leaders. A variety of deadly weapons was used in the robberies, including hand grenades and sub-machine guns, mostly obtained from the People's Liberation Army (PLA). On 6 May 1992, for example, two men were shot dead and nineteen other people were injured as a gang of six or seven masked men raided a mah-jong parlour, spraying bullets indiscriminately and setting off grenades as they fled into the street. These robberies having been curtailed, the crime figures in Hong Kong reverted to their normally low levels.

Not recorded as part of the crime figures, however, during Patten's tenure as Governor, was continuing violence associated with the Vietnamese boat people. On 7 April 1994, for example, a group of Vietnamese asylum seekers was transferred by the police and Correctional Services Department officers from one detention camp to another, without warning. Extreme force was used and 330 injuries to Vietnamese were recorded. On 20 May 1995, in a raid on a Vietnamese detention camp, 3250 tear-gas canisters were fired at a group of asylum seekers, about half of which were women and children. The Police and Correctional Services officers involved in the raid were praised by Patten for 'carrying out their duty in an exemplary fashion.'[14]

Patten suffered a number of other setbacks in 1995. In January, he was forced to withdraw a proposal to introduce a compulsory old age pension scheme because of opposition from the business sector, who would have been expected to pay for it in large part, and from China. The more reform-minded complained that Patten had not done enough to lobby for his plan, too easily settling for a much less comprehensive provident fund which would provide nothing for those who were already too old to contribute to the scheme or who were not in employment. Patten's failure in this area was attributed to the strong opposition from China and the business community, both of whom were concerned about the cost of the full-blown old age pension scheme. Accusations were made that Patten was able to exert tremendous efforts to have his constitutional reform bill passed, with the publicity this would create in the international press of Patten standing up for democracy in the face of China, while he was not willing to go out of his way to fight for the welfare of the elderly, a less attractive issue for the international media.[15]

In May 1995, the government decided to shelve a long-awaited broadcasting bill, letting slip that the decision was taken on the grounds that it would be viewed as a sensitive issue by China. 'If we raise the bill now, we have to discuss it with China,' Fred Ting Fook-cheung, the acting responsible official, stated in Legco: 'It might take another year or so. It's 1997 by then,' he said. 'Under the present circumstances, a smooth political transition is very important, even more than prosperity,' he further stated.[16] Describing, the past two years of drafting work as a 'half-baked chestnut cake', he said the 'ingredients' would not be wasted and the contents could be incorporated into other existing legislation.

In 1995 unemployment continued to increase, rising to its highest level for 11 years. It was accompanied by the weakest private consumption for twenty years and a further slump in the residential property market. Added to the earlier slump in the stock market, all these negative factors probably contributed to people's thinking when nearly half of those questioned in an opinion poll conducted in May 1995 said that they would like to see Patten leave and be replaced by a local person.[17]

Perhaps in order to redress some of this negative feeling and accusations of being a 'lame duck' governor, Patten adopted a number of high-profile activities which projected him as showing leadership. He conducted what he called Governor's Summits on important issues concerning the public: drugs, the disabled and unemployment. There was a perception by many, however, that these round-table discussions were really not much more than talking shops and did not really lead to effective policy initiatives. Also the name, Governor's Summit, smacked of paternalistic colonialism, as if the Governor alone had the power to resolve these social problems. This, of course, was but one of a range of incongruities deriving from Patten's position as colonial Governor, but at the same time champion of democracy and accountability.

Another defence against criticism which Patten used during this period, with some justification, was that, as he put it, 'at the moment, the Governor is the target for everybody. And I think one of my roles is actually to take some of the flack and try to protect my officials on issues that may be unpopular or difficult.'[18] As it was, senior civil servants found themselves in the difficult position of having to promote policies which their future masters were strongly opposed to. Under Hong Kong's executive-led system of government, the head of the government, the Governor, did not have a cabinet of elected ministers.[19] He had his Exco, but this was merely advisory. Apart from the Governor, the civil servant policy secretaries were, therefore, the only people in a position to answer for the government's policies; and under Patten's regime of 'accountable government' there was strong pressure for them to appear in public and in Legco.

\* \* \*

As noted in Chapter 5 Britain and China had come to an agreement, back in 1991, over the composition of the future Court of Final Appeal (CFA), a body foreseen in the Joint Declaration and Basic Law as replacing the Privy Council in London which had, during the colonial period, acted as the court of last resort. A court of final appeal was an important part of Britain's decolonisation programme for Hong Kong, as it represents the pinnacle of the judicial branch of the political structure. The British wanted it up and running a number of years before the handover, for it to establish itself. As noted in Chapter 5, because of concerns over the number of overseas judges who could be invited to sit on the court and problems with how to define the term 'act of state', the bill was rejected when it was put to Legco in 1991.

In May 1995 the bill was again introduced, in spite of the fact that China had by this time had second thoughts and decided that the court should not be set up before the handover. In 1991, in coming to the agreement with Britain and before the advent of Patten, China probably did not think that there would be any possibility of Legco rejecting it. Now, in 1994, why should China risk the possibility of any further agreement with Britain being rejected by a body which it had deemed to be in contravention of the Joint Declaration and Basic Law? Britain, presumably, on the other hand, was keen to have arrangements for the court in place before the change of sovereignty, even if China would not agree to it actually operating until after the handover, in order to avoid possible Chinese interference in its terms of reference if the court was established after 1997. Even if the bill was again turned down by Legco, Britain would be able to argue that they had done their best to set up the court before the handover, but it was Legco which had blocked them. In the event, the bill was again rejected. Somewhat surprisingly, however, on 9 June 1994, Britain and China announced a fresh agreement to set up the court, but not until 1 July 1997. Britain had thus now given in on its demand that the CFA should be up and running before the handover. With the support of China, Patten's government now lobbied harder for the support of Legco and the bill went through.

Patten came in for a lot of criticism as a result of his about-face. His support of the agreement was in direct contradiction to his earlier insistence that the court should be in place before 1997 and his more general emphasis on the importance of the rule of law as an essential bulwark of Hong Kong's post-1997 autonomy. Under the heading 'The safeguards for the rule of law in Hong Kong are imperfect', the London *Times* concluded that because of his role in the CFA affair Patten was 'unlikely to regain the authority and trust he has won by defending Hong Kong's rights to true autonomy'.[20] It was striking that those who supported Patten in Legco over the CFA were those who usually voted against him – the pro-Beijing legislators and the business lobby – while those who voted against him were his more natural allies – the Democrats and pro-democracy independents who had supported him over political reform.

As a result of his political climb-down, on 12 July Patten was the target of a vote of no-confidence, the first time a British colonial Governor had been the target of such a move. There were a number of ironies in this vote. First, it was instigated by Legco members, many of whom had been voted into office as a result of reforms instigated by Patten, their target. Second, it was Patten who had encouraged a more confrontational style of politics, where previously such an aggressive and disrespectful move would not have been considered. Third, even if the vote had gone through – which it did not – Patten would not have been removed from office, as would be the case in a normal democratic parliament; in spite of his so-called democratic reforms and promotion of accountable government, Patten, as colonial Governor, was still strictly speaking only accountable to the Queen. And in spite of Patten's protestations concerning the importance of Legco, when all is told, it still remained a toothless tiger.

\* \* \*

While the Hong Kong Government was preoccupied with three sets of elections in 1994–5, China was busy making its own plans and preparations for the dismantling of the three tiers of government which the Hong Kong Government was so busily setting up. On many occasions, representatives of the Chinese camp made it clear that Patten's legislative machinery would be scrapped and that there was no chance of the through train travelling beyond the handover. The British and Hong Kong Governments' line on this was to bury their heads in the sand and express the hope that China would reconsider and still let the Legco 'through train' run. In a radio interview in June of 1995, for example, Patten stated:

> Well, if the Chinese side in 1997 seek to dismantle a Legislative Council which would have enjoyed the support of the people of Hong Kong, a Legislative Council which I hope would have done its job very responsibly, they will have to justify that decision to the people of Hong Kong and to the international community. And I think they would have some difficulty doing that.[21]

As far as Patten was concerned, the only reason for dismantling Legco could be that China wanted to, as he put it during one of his district walkabouts, 'tear out the roots of democracy in Hong Kong'. Any other arguments for a provisional legislature were unjustified, because, according to Patten, the elections held in 1995 were completely in line with the Joint Declaration and the Basic Law. 'I am sure all of us in Hong Kong will go on asking those questions [about how the elections were in contravention of the Joint Declaration and Basic Law] until somebody does answer them', he said in March of 1996.[22] However, he must have known by then that answers to these questions would not be forthcoming. In spite of this, he continued to urge Hong Kong people not to give up the fight for democracy. The principle of democratic development was never 'some Hong Kong people running Hong Kong' or 'people in Hong Kong who agreed with the Hong Kong and Macau Affairs Office running Hong Kong', he stated on another, later occasion.[23] When interviewed for this book, Patten emphasised that one of the most important communicative strategies of his governorship was 'to encourage people in Hong Kong to have the self confidence to stand up for the things they believe in and not to unnecessarily give away their autonomy or those things that make this decent society'.[24]

Meanwhile, Patten and his government refused to co-operate with China's Preliminary Working Committee (PWC), on the grounds that the body was not foreseen in the Basic Law and that the JLG was the appropriate channel for the discussion of transitional matters.[25] Patten, in fact, was most scathing in his criticism of the PWC. In October 1995, he described advice given by them as 'very bad' and 'very damaging to Hong Kong and people's confidence in Hong Kong as an open and plural society';[26] and he referred to proposals to replace or amend the Bill of Rights – the legislation which had been introduced to reassure people of their political freedoms, following Tiananmen – as 'the recent proposal, ill-advised proposal, by the PWC legal sub-group, to gut the Bill of Rights'.[27] In November 1995, he referred to a 'sad and sorry business' of what he called 'the extraordinary spectacle of members of the PWC and Chinese officials themselves making proposals which would be in breach of the Basic Law'.[28]

In spite of this denigration of the work of the PWC, in actual practice some assistance was gradually given, if only to allow the British side to have some input to their decision-making.[29] As early as September 1994, Patten had acknowledged that government officials were already in individual contacts with PWC members. By May 1995, he was adopting proposals from the body he so reviled in drawing up the revised bill for the setting up of the CFA, on the grounds this would be likely to make it acceptable to Beijing.[30]

* * *

China's decision to abandon the through train and its resultant change of policy, as a result of Patten's proposals, created a problem for Mainland policy-makers. They had to be careful not to come into conflict with provisions made in the Basic Law, which had been promulgated back in 1990 when it had been anticipated that Britain and China would together follow the 'through train'. China could not condemn Britain for contravening the Basic Law with Patten's reforms, and then herself contravene the provisions of this same document. The Basic Law, for example, did not anticipate the Pre-paratory Committee (PC) being set up until 1996, but now China needed to set about making plans much earlier than that date, if alternative arrangements for the legislature were to be in place by the time of the handover. In order not to contravene the provisions of the Basic Law, therefore, instead of calling the body created to get on with this work before the due date of 1996 the Preparatory Committee (PC), China named it the Preliminary Working Committee of the Preparatory Committee (PWC). Similarly, the other body China planned to set up which was not provided for in the Basic Law, the Provisional Legislature, was so-named in order to avoid contravening the provisions in the Basic Law which specified in some detail how the SAR's first legislature would be elected. By naming the interim body the Provisional Legislature, China would not be in contravention of the Basic Law because that document only refers to the first legislature of the SAR, not the Provisional Legislature. The Provisional Legislature would not therefore be tied by the provisions in the Basic Law concerning how it was to be constituted.

Certain members of the anti-Beijing faction, of course, highlighted what they saw as a subterfuge in this naming process. One commentator, for example, cited the Chinese proverb, 'Pointing to a deer and calling it a horse', as aptly describing the situation, referring also to 'verbal gymnastics' on the part of the Chinese and an attempt to persuade the public that 'words can have any meaning the government chooses to give them at any particular time, depending on its own convenience'.[31] Even Patten himself and the British government were not able to claim categorically that the arrangements for the provisional legislature were in contravention of the Basic Law, although they did refuse (at least in their public statements) to co-operate with them, on the grounds that they had not been provided for in the document which was to be China's mini-constitution for the future SAR.

The work of the PWC was carried out in a number of sub-committees: political, economic, legal, culture and education, security, external economic relations, and trade relations with China. The 60-member body was made up of Mainland officials, long-time pro-China Hong Kong representatives, and more recent converts from the pro-British camp from among the Hong Kong Advisers, including one executive councillor, Rita Fan, who had been discarded by Patten in his reshuffle of Exco in 1992.[32] The anomalous situation of the previous pro-British supporters shifting their allegiance was not lost on the press or the general public. Many of them held foreign (often British) passports and had received various awards and honours from the colonial government. Some, who had served the British Hong Kong government in various capacities, had sworn allegiance to the Crown, a state of affairs which contrasted strongly with their new-found allegiance to Beijing. Rita Fan, for example, the convenor of the sub-group dealing with nationality and right-of-abode issues, herself held a British passport. The presence of these out-of-favour former British protégés irritated some of the longer serving pro-Beijing group. Dorothy Liu Yiu-chu, for example, a Hong Kong lawyer and National People's Congress (NPC) representative, referred to them as 'old', or 'used' batteries, discarded by the British.[33]

There were suggestions in some quarters that members of the PWC and its sub-committees took a harder line than the Chinese Government might have wanted, in order to ingratiate themselves with their future masters. There were sometimes announcements, during press briefings following PWC meetings or by individual members, which created consternation in Hong Kong. Because the work of the PWC was only advisory, there was no way of knowing which of the comments emanating from it had the authority of Beijing and which were merely the opinion of the committee or of its individual members. For example, the PWC started to talk about the appointment or confirmation of judges, who, it had been assumed in most quarters, would be able to ride the 'through train'. Sir Sze-Yuen Chung, a leading PWC member and ex-senior member of the Exco, from 1980–8, under Governors MacLehose, Youde and Wilson,[34] warned at one point of a shadow government being set up in the lead-up to the handover, but China later stated that this was merely his individual opinion. Of course, some of these statements might have been intended as 'kites' to find out what the reaction of the Hong Kong media and public would be if plans for certain measures were in fact put in place. Indeed, there is evidence that the PWC and other bodies set up by China were sensitive to public opinion and an important role of the Governor could be said to have been in articulating this opinion (where it suited him, that is).

\* \* \*

Rejecting the possible alternative of assigning interim power to the Chief Executive or China's NPC, it was the PWC which first made the recommendation (later adopted) that a provisional legislature should be set up to fill the legislative vacuum that would be created when the British constitutional arrangements were dismantled and new arrangements, in accordance with China's interpretation of the Basic Law, were being made. An influential member of the PWC, Hong Kong academic Professor Lau Siu-Kai, justified this arrangement in December 1994 by stating that critics of the plan had overlooked the fact that Hong Kong's legislature had never been a powerful organ in government under the British and that the provisional legislature would take no more than the passive role currently played by the Legco under British rule.[35]

It was also the PWC which recommended, in October 1995, the scrapping of the overriding power of Hong Kong's Bill of Rights and the reinstatement of six colonial laws restricting personal liberty which had been annulled or amended to fall in line with this overriding rights legislation. The rationale for these recommendations was that the Bill of Rights was in contravention of the Basic Law. This proposal created such consternation in Hong Kong that China took the unprecedented step of sending down a group of Chinese lawyers to explain matters. However, the mission was unsuccessful, as these Mainland representatives only spoke Putonghua and merely reiterated the official line.

A further issue considered by the PWC, in its culture and education sub-group, concerned the contents of school textbooks post-1997. The Hong Kong Government's Director of Education, Dominic Wong, seemed to be going in the direction of self-censorship when, in June 1994, he recommended that history books not deal with the contemporary period, on the grounds that interpretation of this period has not been fully worked out by historians. His warning was widely interpreted as a signal to avoid mention of the 1989 Tiananmen events. Following a public outcry, Wong retracted his recommendation.

* * *

The most important outcome of the political reform programme took place with the Legco elections of 16 September 1995. An active campaign resulted in 920 567 people voting, representing a turnout of 35.8 per cent in the geographical and 39.2 per cent in the new functional constituencies, from a pool of the approximately 60 per cent of those on the electoral register. This was a slightly lower percentage of those voting than in 1991, perhaps understandably in the light of a statement issued by the Xinhua at 7:30 on the morning of the elections that the Chinese Government and the Standing Committee of China's NPC had made it clear that Legco and all other bodies 'elected under Patten's package' would stop functioning in 1997, with China's resumption of sovereignty. The dismissive nature of this statement contrasted strongly with the positive tone of the early-morning message put out by Patten to the press: 'I think that everyone in Hong Kong and out of Hong Kong will have to take account of what the voice of Hong Kong has said today', Patten said. More explicitly, he asked China to 'think again' about giving 'the thumbs down' to what he claimed were the most democratic elections ever held in Hong Kong. He further went on: 'I'm sure that in the way they vote today, people are thinking not just of the short term .... I'm sure they are expressing a view about the sort of place they want Hong Kong to be. And I think most people want Hong Kong to be an open, plural society and want both the present sovereign and the future sovereign powers to live up to the promises that have been given to the people of Hong Kong in good faith, that there would be a steady process of democratisation in the territory.'[36]

The electoral result was a categorical victory for the pro-democracy camp, with the Democrats winning 19 of the 60 seats, in addition to seats won by other strong anti-China independents, such as Emily Lau and Christine Lo and newly-elected former civil servant Elizabeth Wong. The democratic forces had first come to prominence following Tiananmen, in 1989, and in the 1991 elections. Their victory in 1995, however, affirmed that they were not just a protest party, but had a considerable faithful majority of supporters among the people of Hong Kong. The pro-China party, the DAB, won just six seats, but their leader Tsang Yok-Sing who, it had earlier been revealed, had applied for a Canadian passport following Tiananmen, was defeated.[37] Other notable pro-Beijing candidates such as the redoubtable Elsie Tu, and ex-pillar of the British establishment Peggy Lam, were also defeated by pro-democracy candidates. The pro-business grouping, the Liberals, made a respectable showing, with ten seats, although most of these were won in the non-directly elected constituencies.

* * *

The 1995 October policy speech was the last given by Patten in which he would be able to announce plans for the whole of the coming year. By October 1996, there would only be nine months before the change of sovereignty and so it would not be realistic to introduce new policies, with a new government due to take over in less than a year's time. The day of the 1995 policy speech was the first sitting of the new Legco membership which had been voted in on 16 September. The result of his 1992 reform proposals, this Legco was one of Patten's own making. Whatever critics might say about it, it was nevertheless the most democratic Legco in Hong Kong's colonial history. Although still only a third of its members were directly elected, it was the first time in the history of Legco that representatives of the grass-roots of society, not only appointees of the business, legal and academic elite, would be significantly represented. Patten began his 1995 policy speech by reiterating his view that his constitutional reforms had been legitimate. 'Your existence represents the fulfilment of the promises made to the people of Hong Kong in the Joint Declaration and is wholly in line with the community's future constitution, the Basic Law,' he told legislators. Playing the international card and at the same time indirectly rebuking China for saying it would disband the legislative body at the change of sovereignty, he continued, 'I believe that it is the view not just of the Hong Kong people and the Hong Kong Government and not just of the British Government, but of most of our friends around the world, that you should be allowed to do your job for the full term for which you were elected.'

Patten took the opportunity to use the 1995 speech to evaluate the extent to which he had managed to achieve the objectives he had set for his government in his first policy speech in 1992, stressing the goals of economic growth and rights and freedoms under the law. He was able to reel off some impressive statistics concerning economic growth; for example, Gross Domestic Product (GDP) had grown by 18 per cent in real terms, new investment had grown by 31 per cent and the fiscal reserves had grown by 57 per cent, with public spending remaining below 20 per cent of GDP. He also claimed progress in education, help for the needy, and improvements in the provision of housing. Turning to rights and freedoms, he stressed the electoral arrangements he had introduced as being fair and open, and referred to amendments of 31 items of legislation which had been made to bring them in line with the Bill of Rights.

On managing the transition, he listed JLG agreements on defence lands, airport financing and the CFA. He also listed a range of issues which still needed to be resolved, including who would have the right of abode in Hong Kong after the handover.

In presenting the policy address, in line with his policy of greater accountability, Patten's government at the same time had issued progress reports in the form of an audit of the performance of the various government departments. Ever humorous, but also betraying the cosmetic nature of the process, Patten stated that the 'fair-minded' would appreciate the 94 per cent achievement rate claimed by the Government, while the 'perfectionists' would have noted that the government was behind with was six per cent of its targets.

As far as new initiatives went, the speech was modest. There were to be increased welfare benefits and further limits were to be put on the importation of labour (an issue which had received a lot of attention, given Hong Kong's rising unemployment rate). An equal opportunities office was to be set up.

A section of the speech dealt with liaison with China. Following meetings between the Foreign Ministers of Britain and China it had been agreed that a liaison office would be set up to work with the PC and that Hong Kong and Chinese civil servants would liaise with each other.

Before coming to the conclusion of his speech, Patten emphasised his wish that his government and Legco would be able to co-operate. He then issued what was considered by most commentators to be a threat, warning that he would not hesitate to use his power of veto on any private member's Bill which he did not judge to be in Hong Kong's best interests. This was a somewhat surprising statement, to say the least, from someone who had gone to such efforts to create a more democratic Hong Kong.[38] As the *Eastern Express* commented in an editorial, it also seemed very arrogant: 'What makes Patten so sure he knows what is best for Hong Kong? Better than a chamber of legislators chosen by the people? Better than a council with a diversity of political views, who will have given a majority endorsement to a bill before it reaches his desk?'[39]

The day following the policy speech, in a question-time session with the Legislative Council, Patten stressed that he had agreed to co-operate with the PC because, as he put it (in a reference to the Basic Law and Joint Declaration), it had 'emerged from the sacred texts'. He refused to have anything to do with the Provisional Legislature, however, stating that: 'There can be no question of us assisting in the production of some alternative whose genesis in relation to the Joint Declaration and the Basic Law is decidedly unclear'. At this meeting, Patten also reiterated his warning regarding the use of the veto, provoking the following response from Martin Lee, leader of the Democrats:

> We are fully aware of the constitutional powers of a colonial governor, including his veto power. But it is grossly inappropriate for the appointed Governor of Hong Kong to suggest that he knows better than representatives elected only last month as to what is in the best interest of Hong Kong.[40]

\* \* \*

At the end of the 1995 policy speech, Patten invoked his preoccupation with the ceremonial aspect of the actual handover, thereby lending support to the contention of this book that the British colonial Governor's discourse was preoccupied with the idea of the historical significance of Hong Kong's retrocession and with withdrawal with honour.

> There are just over 600 days to the lowering of one flag and the raising of another, just over 600 days to the bands, the speeches and I dare say the fireworks. It is not long now, and every day will count. We should dedicate ourselves – Britain, China and Hong Kong – to using each of those days to help make this community's future secure. That is what we owe the people of Hong Kong. That

is what they expect of us. We must not fail them. My government, for its part, is determined to succeed.

As with other extracts of Patten's more high-flown rhetoric cited in this book, this closing section of the 1995 policy speech is heavy with repetition, parallelism, antithesis and metaphor. Evoking the historical nature of the reversion (and Patten's role in it) in this extract is the emphasis on the inexorable progress of time. In his first policy speech, in 1992, Patten used the metaphor of the chapters of a book to evoke the historical nature of the change of sovereignty. Here, the metaphor for the change-over is of one flag coming down and another going up. This evocation is not wholly metaphorical, however, as Patten paints a picture of the actual scene he envisages at the moment of the transfer. Accompanying the changing flags, in this evocation, are also 'the bands, the speeches and the fireworks', essential features of earlier scenes of British colonial withdrawal.

# 10 The Die is Cast

The heightened rhetoric with which the previous chapter concluded is just one manifestation of a concern running right through Patten's governorship, the desire for an honourable withdrawal. The goal of withdrawal with honour was also demonstrated by a preoccupation with the actual handover arrangements for 1 July 1997. Already, in his first policy speech, Patten had speculated on how he would leave Hong Kong – by the new airport, the old airport, or by boat. In his second policy speech, with nearly four years still to go, Patten stated that, 'We shall also be happy to begin discussions whenever China wishes to do so on the arrangements for the ceremonies to mark in an appropriately dignified way the transfer of sovereignty in 1997.' In January 1994, arrangements for Britain's official departure from Hong Kong were said to figure highly on the agenda of discussions between Patten and Prime Minister Major during consultations in London.[1] At a meeting of the British and Chinese foreign ministers, in October 1995, on the initiative of the British, an agreement was reached to set up an expert group to plan for the handover ceremonies and to make sure that they were 'solemn, grand, and decent'.[2]

China's view on the handover was, of course, different from Britain's. Obviously aware of the British concern to make a dignified final withdrawal, China's policy seems to have been to keep the British guessing about whether it would co-operate, and thereby obtain leverage over other transitional matters. For example, prior to newly-appointed Foreign Minister Rifkind's first visit to Beijing in January 1996, following speculation that the handover ceremony would be high on his agenda, a warning was disseminated through the press that China would only co-operate in the ceremonies if the Hong Kong Governor became less confrontational. If Patten 'misbehaved' during the 18 months leading up to the handover, then China would alter what it referred to as its 'appraisal' of British rule over the previous 150 years.[3] The 'appraisal' would be delivered in a speech at the handover ceremony and would incorporate derogatory remarks specifically about Patten.[4] China was indeed still arguing for Patten's removal at this time. The 3 January edition of the pro-China *Wen Wei Po* reported that the Chinese Government had already delivered a message concerning Patten's replacement, prior to Rifkind's Beijing visit, but that the British had not responded.[5]

Following his Beijing meetings, Rifkind publicly stated that the handover should not only be 'dignified and appropriate' but that it must also 'send the right message to the world'. Rifkind was playing the international card here, the argument being that co-operation at the actual handover would be in China's best interests, as it would inspire confidence in the international business community upon which the success of the SAR would depend. Rifkind also rejected Chinese suggestions that Patten should not be present at the handover: 'The Governor is very much part of any handover ceremony and in any event it is for the British Government to decide who will represent the United Kingdom's position with regard to that ceremony,' he said.[6]

From China's point of view, the argument about international confidence was a valid one but, on the other hand, China wanted to play down any idea that Hong Kong might become what it called an international 'political' city, with the possible destabilising interference of Western states in support of pro-democracy forces both in Hong Kong and ultimately the Mainland, following their take-over. A low-key ceremony to mark the actual handover, followed by much larger celebrations, once the British had left, might be a better way to go, according to Chinese thinking.[7]

Regarding Patten's attendance, China was also ambivalent. Another report at the time of Rifkind's visit to Beijing quoted a Chinese official as saying: 'We meant what we said when we described Patten as the person of guilt of a thousand generations. Can one really imagine Chinese leaders shaking hands or standing shoulder by shoulder with somebody guilty for a thousand generations?'[8] On the one hand, the Chinese accepted that co-operation might be to both countries' good. Lu Ping, for example, in an interview with the *Financial Times*, stated: 'Maybe some politicians in Britain hope the handover ceremony can symbolise the glorious or honourable withdrawal of Britain from Hong Kong. We have no objection to that because that means we can take over in a dignified and honourable manner.'[9] On the other hand, China did not want Britain to gain face at the ceremonies at its expense. As a pro-Beijing columnist in the *Hong Kong Standard*, Alan Castro, proclaimed: 'British honour at the expense of Chinese national dignity (as in 1842) – and this time with the whole world looking on – is an event China cannot allow into history again.'[10] China was particularly concerned by Britain's plans for naval participation, with a landing near the ex-colonial naval headquarters adjoining the handover venue. The pro-Beijing *Mirror* monthly magazine of May 1996 expressed reservations on this matter, as follows: 'The take-over of Hong Kong is to wash away the humiliation in the past 150 years of history. How can we allow the British navy to revive memories of its victory?'[11]

Such concerns may have been behind another plan being put about that the ceremony would not be in Hong Kong at all, but in Beijing. This idea also fitted in with China's view of the handover as an agreement by two sovereign states. Hong Kong having all along been a part of China (as China did not recognise the 'unequal' treaties), there was no reason to effect the handover in the future SAR, rather than in the nation's capital. All the other important signings, such as the Joint Declaration and the Basic Law, had taken place, after all, in Beijing. In addition, this argument went, the event had great significance for all of China and not just for the people of Hong Kong. Furthermore, this proposal had the merit of downplaying any future role for Britain over Hong Kong after 1997, emphasising, as it did, that Hong Kong was just another part of China. Finally, in putting Britain in the position of the supplicant, in having to come to Beijing, further mileage would be gained in recovering from the national shame of 150 years of colonial subjugation of Chinese territory.

Perhaps this idea of the ceremony taking place in Beijing was put forward merely as a bargaining chip, as it would have represented too much loss of face for Britain ever to agree to it. Perhaps to counter such an idea, talk started to develop on the British side of two separate ceremonies, one for Britain and one for China.[12] Not all of the cards were stacked in China's favour. China did not really have much control over what Britain did, unilaterally, up to the stroke of midnight of the night of 30 June 1997. For a long time before the actual transfer of sovereignty, the Hong Kong Government had booked all the possible venues for handover ceremonies on the night of 30 June, ensuring that they could not be used by anyone else. Unless they co-operated, to all practical intents and purposes the Chinese side would not be able to hold any ceremonies in public venues in Hong Kong until 1 July, after they had been vacated by the British.

To pro-democracy Legco member Emily Lau, writing in the *South China Morning Post*, 'these trivial matters' (concerning the handover arrangements) were 'a million miles removed from the more weighty concerns of the Hong Kong people'.[13] From an international point of view, the ceremony did have an important symbolic value, however. As Qian Qichen said in May 1995 at the closing of a PWC meeting, during one of Beijing's more conciliatory phases, and echoing a statement made by Deng at the time of the signing of the Joint Declaration, 'The solemn handover ceremony at midnight on 30 June 1997 should be held jointly by China and Britain. We should show the world that problems left over by history can be resolved through peaceful negotiations.'

\* \* \*

Once it became clear that China was deadly serious in dismantling the legislative apparatus created by the Patten reforms and that a provisional legislature was to be put in place, a new pattern of Sino-British Hong Kong relations developed. The Chinese had in effect called Britain's bluff, in derailing the through train. Once they had decided on this course of action, there was nothing the British could really do about it. There was no way that Patten could climb down now and co-operate fully with the Chinese, for to do so would have been a tacit acceptance of the provisional legislature and unilateral action on the part of the Chinese to dismantle his reforms. The British Government could have decided to replace Patten, of course, but Prime Minister John Major had promoted the Governor as his protégé and friend and had been one of the instigators of the so-called Patten policy. Patten's replacement would therefore have been a loss of face for him too. Patten continued to criticise China's plans, therefore, and in fact, if anything, he became more outspoken in his censure, provoking the usual reaction in the pro-Beijing Hong Kong press. The 15 January 1996 edition of *Wen Wei Po,* for example, claimed he was still being confrontational and that he did not regret impeding a smooth transition. An invitation to Chinese Foreign Minister Qian Qichen to visit Hong Kong that Patten had issued in one of his radio talks was described as 'very cheap political propaganda by an insecure politician without any diplomatic manner'. The fact that the invitation violated the normal diplomatic channels was proof that Patten was merely 'putting on a show', according to *Wen Wei Po.*[14]

\* \* \*

At the same time as the sniping between Patten and his detractors was going on, however, direct Sino-British relations had moved back into gear. By April 1995, Patten's reforms had been approved by Legco, but China had decided that they should be dismantled at the handover. As far as Britain and China were concerned, therefore, the die was cast. Britain would continue to express its opposition to the provisional legislature, but China would ignore it. China and Britain could now get back to business, leaving Patten on the sideline while nominally standing up for Hong Kong's autonomy.

Even before the 1995 Legco elections, which were the actual fruit of Patten's reforms, Sino-British relations had become warmer. In May 1995, Michael Heseltine, Minister for Trade, became the first British cabinet minister to visit China for two years. In late September, Foreign Minister Qian Qichen visited London and agreed on a package of links in the months up to 1997.

The renewed contact and co-operation may have had something to do with the new Foreign Minister, Malcolm Rifkind. Rifkind had replaced Douglas Hurd, who had decided the time had come to resign from a post which he had held for nearly six years. From the Chinese perspective, the new man, Rifkind, was not tainted, as Hurd had been, by a close association with the Patten reforms. Rifkind was more willing to play down the role of Patten and more amenable to direct contacts between capitals. In addition, Michael Heseltine, a strong supporter of British business and trade, had growing influence, as he had become Deputy Prime Minister. Indeed, Heseltine was one of the first people that Qian met during his London visit. Heseltine's pro-trade line was to be summed up by Martin Lee, following a meeting with the British Deputy Prime Minister, in March 1996, during which, Lee claimed, Heseltine's position could be summed up as: 'China trade, China trade, and China trade – and then maybe Hong Kong.'[15]

With the emphasis moving away from the more contentious Hong Kong issues to other bi-lateral affairs, especially trade, relations were thus getting back to a more acceptable footing as far as Qian was concerned. The agreements reached in London which concerned Hong Kong included a programme of ministerial visits, meetings between Hong Kong and Chinese civil servants, the setting-up of an expert group to arrange the actual handover ceremony (which, the two sides agreed, would be 'solemn and grand'), and a promise of greater efforts to resolve the CT9 controversy. Most noticeably, Foreign Minister Rifkind did not repeat Britain's opposition to the provisional legislature to Qian, only reiterating his disapproval of it when prompted by journalists. Qian, on the other hand, when questioned about the provisional legislature, said: 'this is a question that has already been resolved'; and when asked if the current Legco would cease in 1997, answered emphatically, 'yes'.[16]

As Sino-British relations continued on their more positive tack, in Bangkok, in March 1996, during a conference of Asian and European leaders, British Prime Minister Major had a meeting with his Chinese counterpart, Li Peng: a meeting which Major exuberantly described as 'one of the best meetings' he had ever had,[17] adding that, 'The relationship undoubtedly has improved between the United Kingdom and China over the last year, economically and in terms of co-operation about matters of such vital importance to Hong Kong.' Britain was still officially disapproving of the provisional legislature, but this was not being allowed to disrupt other bi-lateral relations. Indeed, at a meeting between the British and Chinese foreign ministers in The Hague, in April 1996, while Rifkind refused to co-operate with a request by China to assist in the setting up of the provisional body, Qian was still able to say that his talks with Foreign Secretary Rifkind in The Hague had shown there was no bar to a smooth transition. 'I believe all Hong Kong problems can be said to have been settled. The smooth transition of Hong Kong can be a reality,' he said in one interview, using the more colourful phrase 'The rice is cooked' in another.[18]

\* \* \*

John Major's attendance at the summit in Bangkok was a prelude to a two-day visit to Hong Kong, the last to be made by a British Prime Minister before the handover. Major used the visit to reaffirm his support for his protégé, Patten. The two were photographed in intimate tête-à-têtes, sending out a signal, via the press, of Major's confidence in the Hong Kong Governor. When questioned by journalists about whether the issues of the provisional legislature and possible changes to the Hong Kong Bill of Rights had come up in his Bangkok meeting with Li Peng, in contrast to his up-beat message given in Bangkok, Major stressed how he had expressed his opposition to the Chinese position on these issues. 'We didn't agree to disagree [on the provisional legislature and the Bill of Rights]', he said, 'We disagreed.'[19] In a further emphatic indication of his support for Patten, on his return flight to Britain, Major even announced in a BBC interview his great admiration for his friend the Hong Kong Governor and how he would be a likely successor to him as leader of the Conservative Party, should he, at some point, step down.

In addition to expressing his support for Patten, Major used his visit to Hong Kong to announce some positive measures for the territory. He revealed that his government had finally decided to issue full British passports to the small group of Hong Kong war widows who had until then been denied them. He stated that although his government was not prepared to offer passports to Hong Kong's ethnic minorities, who had for a long time been campaigning for them, he stressed that Britain would provide a refuge for them, should anything go wrong after the handover. Finally, he announced that holders of future SAR passports would be allowed visa-free access to Britain after 1997.

\* \* \*

In spite of the improvement in Sino-British ties, as already suggested, Patten's war of words with Chinese officials during the final stages of the transitional period continued. Throughout 1995, there was an argument over whether the personal files of civil servants should be handed over to the Chinese Government. Patten said that they should go to the head of the SAR Government, not China. China insisted that, in accordance with the Joint Declaration, all civil service files had to be handed over to the incoming sovereign. It was generally understood that China wanted to obtain the files so as to find out which civil servants had foreign passports, it being stipulated in the Basic Law that holders of overseas nationality would not be permitted to occupy the most senior posts in the civil service.[20] In September, Patten lobbied the British Government for full British passports for all of the 3.3 million Hong Kong holders of British Dependent Territories Passports (travel documents which did not allow the right of abode in Britain). This was claimed by China to be the equivalent of 'openly tearing up' the Joint Declaration. A Mainland member of the JLG, Chen Zuo'er, claimed that Patten was 'dishonest' and 'lying to the people of Hong Kong', for trying to do something he knew he could not achieve.[21] He may have been close to the mark here, as Patten must have known that there was no way he was going to change the minds of any of the political parties in Britain, all of whom had strong anti-immigration policies, in spite of the fact that many of the leading newspapers in Britain supported Patten's request.[22]

The attacks on Patten seemed to reach a high point in October 1995. An article in the *Eastern Express* of 14–15 October described how China was convinced Patten was trying to 'stir up trouble' in Sino-British ties and, in a reference to his attempts to get British passports for Hong Kong people, even going so far as 'to challenge his own government in London' on some issues. 'Issues involving Hong Kong will be discussed by officials from Beijing and Hong Kong directly and by-pass Patten', one source was quoted as saying. 'Any decisions reached will be announced through the mass media in order to maintain pressure on Patten', another source said. These sources also confirmed that China had requested that Patten be recalled by London and that British businessmen had also been approached with the request. Direct contact had already been made with the Chief Secretary, Anson Chan, who had secretly stopped-over in Beijing on her way back from London for a visit with Hong Kong and Macau Affairs Office Director, Lu Ping. These attempts at undermining Patten's position may have been the reason for John Major's show of support for the Hong Kong Governor during his March 1996 visit.

Further adding to the pressure on Patten, in the lead-up to the 1995 October budget, the Hong Kong Governor was again attacked by China. It was at this time that Chinese JLG official Chen Zuo'er came out with his statement that since Patten's arrival Hong Kong welfare spending had become like an out-of-control Formula 1 racing car, as reported in Chapter 9. Patten's response to this accusation was characteristically robust. 'People should leave us to drive our own car' he said, 'and I'm sure that they'll be able to get some good tips from us as we continue to cruise along the road'.[23] At this time also, Patten was accused by Chen of being 'a big dictator', and not qualified to speak on budget issues, because he had been appointed by the Queen (that is, that he was therefore not in a position to represent the people of Hong Kong, who were Chinese compatriots). This led to an official complaint lodged by the Foreign Office with Beijing's London embassy, on the grounds that the statements by Chen concerning the Hong Kong budget represented an infringement of the high degree of autonomy promised to Hong Kong.[24]

On a visit to London in October 1995, Patten expressed his frustration over his dealings with China. 'The whole saga has been a demeaning one. But I'm very relaxed about it. It's a matter for them to decide,' he told reporters. He made a plea, however, for a 'sensible grown-up relationship' with China, adding that he didn't think that 'any other government in the world... would behave in this way. It's not behaviour that anyone would begin to comprehend,' he said.[25] By Christmas, however, the Hong Kong Governor could not resist a further dig at Chinese officials himself, when, at the launch of a new radio programme on RTHK, he dedicated a recording of Fidelio – a Beethoven opera about a political dissident – to Director of the Hong Kong and Macau Affairs Office Lu Ping.[26]

By the spring of 1996, China's United Front campaign against Patten was put into perspective, when a rather frightening campaign was launched against the Taiwanese President, Lee Teng-hui, during Taiwan's first ever presidential election. In order to dissuade Taiwanese voters from supporting Lee, whom they accused of abandoning the one-China policy and taking Taiwan down the road of independence, Chinese officials and army generals made violent threats against Taiwan, held military manoeuvres and fired off live missiles over Taiwanese territory, in a rehearsal of a possible invasion. When the United States sent aircraft carriers into the Straits of Taiwan, Los Angeles was threatened with nuclear bombs if the United States dared to defend Taiwan.[27]

Although it might have been comforting to Patten to know that he was not the only target of United Front tactics, these events were a further unsettling signal for Hong Kong's future. Hong Kong was supposed to be a model for future reunification with Taiwan. But even before Hong Kong had the opportunity to demonstrate how the 'one country two systems' model could work, the future SAR was already learning its own lesson about the potential violence of the Mainland regime.[28]

Patten's strongest invective was reserved for the provisional legislature. In a speech in New York, in May 1996, he referred to the proposed body as a 'lunatic idea'[29] and in June he reasserted his total opposition: 'I've made it clear again and again. We will do absolutely nothing whatsoever to compromise the authority of the Legco or to assist in its dismantling and there can be no other Legco as far as we are concerned, none whatsoever, before the 30 June 1997.' Describing the decision to set up the provisional legislature as 'reprehensible and unjustifiable', he followed up with an emphatic four-part parallel list: 'That's our policy. It has been our policy. It's our policy today. It will be our policy till the 30 June 1997. Full stop.'[30]

Patten also spoke out strongly against Director of Hong and Macau Affairs Office Lu Ping, who, in June 1996, came out with some comments concerning future press freedom in Hong Kong. Lu made a distinction between 'criticism and disagreement', on the one hand, and 'advocacy', on the other. The Hong Kong press would, of course, be free to criticise and disagree, after 1997, even with the central PRC government, Lu explained, but advocating a policy, such as independence for Taiwan or Hong Kong, constituted 'action' and this would not be tolerated. According to Patten, such interpretations concerning the limits of press freedom would be determined according to the Basic Law and as such were within the autonomy promised for Hong Kong.[31] He was overlooking the fact, however, that interpretation of the Basic Law would rest with the National People's Congress of

China. In a reference to pro-Beijing newspapers in Hong Kong, using his much favoured understatement, Patten also stated that he found it difficult to distinguish between advocacy and reporting. 'I'm sure it's the case that in leading articles in *Ta Kung Pao* and *Wen Wei Po* they sometimes advocate as well as report,' he said.[32,33]

In October 1996, fears were again created in Hong Kong, when Qian Qichen, Vice Premier, Foreign Minister and Chairman of the Preparatory Committee, came out with further strictures limiting freedom of expression. He said that personal attacks on Chinese leaders would not be tolerated, that the press would be allowed to print 'criticism', but not 'rumours or lies', and, in an apparent reference to demonstrations commemorating the 4 June Tiananmen crackdown, that 'political activities which directly interfere in the affairs of the mainland' would be banned.[34] In spite of the fact that, later, a spokesperson for Qian said that he had been mis-reported, these remarks again created consternation among pro-democracy supporters in Hong Kong, especially as Deng Xiaoping, had, many years before, specifically stated that criticism of Chinese leaders would be tolerated.[35] This time it was left to Kerry McGlynn, the governor's spokesperson, to react on behalf of Patten: 'If personal attacks against the Governor were not allowed, there would hardly be any journalists not in jail', he said, 'that's a free press and that's what Hong Kong has been promised.'[36]

Patten's invective was not limited to people in Beijing. He also criticised those Hong Kong people who were involved in China's provisional bodies, especially the rich businessmen who made up the majority of their membership. During his American visit, in May 1996, an interview with Patten appeared in *Newsweek* under the headline 'Betraying Hong Kong'.[37] In the interview, in a reference to the business people supporting the provisional legislature, Patten asked, rhetorically: 'Why is it that privileged people are prepared to sign up to arrangements whose sole intention is to choke off the voice of those who by every measure represent the majority of public opinion?' His answer was, 'Well, I'll say this. They wouldn't be doing it if most of them didn't have foreign passports in their back pockets.' The statement incited the anger of the Hong Kong businessmen, who sent off a letter to John Major complaining that Patten had misrepresented them as not working for the best interests of Hong Kong.[38] They received little sympathy from Major, however, who in reply suggested that the businessmen 'rather owe him [Governor Patten] gratitude for working so hard to make your case [in promoting Hong Kong during his US visit]'.[39]

Patten's position did not find total support from the British government, however. Under the headline 'The Winner Loses – Patten gets a slap on the back and in the face', the *Far Eastern Economic Review* reported how, at the same time as Prime Minister Major was supporting Patten in the debate with the tycoons, Deputy Prime Minister Michael Heseltine was travelling with a group of British businessmen on a trade mission to Beijing. On his way home, on 24 May, Heseltine called in at Hong Kong. His support for the Governor was ambivalent. 'The Governor is a man of absolute integrity; he will do what he believes to be right,' he said, when asked about the dispute with the businessmen. However, he also seemed to support the businessmen, in calling for more positive news coverage of Sino-British Hong Kong relations, which, of course, went right against Patten's policy of encouraging Hong Kong people to speak out against China. The difference between the two men reached its most telling moment when Heseltine, trying to play down fears for Hong Kong's future, stressed how the people of Hong Kong were not unique in being unable to predict their exact future. Even he didn't know where he would be in half an hour's time, he said. At this point, Patten had heard enough, interjecting, 'I hope you'll be on a helicopter to the airport.'[40]

* * *

When the PC itself was set up at the beginning of 1996, following the ground-laying work of the PWC, initially a news blackout was observed, presumably to guard against the negative sort of publicity attracted by its precursor. This led to even more consternation, however. The ethos that the Patten regime had been trying to promote within Hong Kong was concerned with accountability and transparency (although, of course Exco had always met in closed session). Secret meetings went contrary to this. As a result of the outcry, the press was given some access to PC deliberations, but this was limited.

The PC was chaired by Chinese Foreign Minister Qian Qichen and its Secretary-General was Hong Kong and Macau Affairs Office Director Lu Ping. There was further criticism of the PC concerning its lack of representativeness. Of the 150 members, 95 were from Hong Kong and the rest from the Mainland. Of the 95 Hong Kong members, 64 were from the business and professional sectors, an indication of the pre-eminence given by China to economic issues regarding Hong Kong. There was no place for any members of the Democratic Party, the most representative party in Hong Kong, based on democratic elections.[41]

In March 1996, the PC voted on a proposal for the setting up of the provisional legislature. Frederick Fung, the only pro-democracy member of the committee (selected for the mildness of his views), was the only member to vote against the proposal. Fung's action enraged the Director of the Hong Kong and Macau Affairs Office, Lu Ping, who immediately declared that as a result of his negative vote, Fung would not be eligible to sit on the provisional legislature or on the selection committee for the Chief Executive. Although the ban was later withdrawn, Lu's statement showed just how little freedom the members of the PC were to be allowed and seemed to confirm the worst fears of the pro-democracy camp in Hong Kong. Fung's reaction to Lu's statements was to say that China had not yet reached a stage of development at which it would be willing to accept dissenting views. Chinese Foreign Minister and PC Chairman Qian Qichen's reaction, on the other hand, was to declare that it was 'inadequate' for people to judge democracy simply by looking at the form and procedure of elections. 'To mechanically ape the Western democratic model does not accord with Hong Kong's actual conditions or accommodate the interests of all social strata', he said.[42] As a measure of Patten's standing vis-à-vis China, when he came out with a statement on behalf of Fung the latter's reaction was to say that 'If he wants to help us he should stand aside.'[43] Intervention by the outspoken British Hong Kong Governor was regarded as a liability.

While Fung was the only dissenting voice inside the PC, many voices were raised against it outside. Already, on 10 December 1995, the Democratic Party had launched a united campaign to fight against it. On 13 March 1996, Legco passed a motion objecting to its formation. On 14 April, opposition to it was brought to the world's attention when pictures appeared in the international press showing violent demonstrators burning tyres in protest at public consultations being held by the PC in Hong Kong to collect opinions about it. The PC was selective in the opinions it sought, excluding representatives of those groups which had expressed opposition to the provisional legislature. Two representatives of the Federation of Students who had been invited to attend were ejected when they removed their jackets to reveal anti-provisional-legislature T-shirts. As one commentator noted, the ejection of the students was based more on their disruptive behaviour than their objection to the provisional body per se.[44] Chinese officials disliked the confrontational style of the students, a style which had been tolerated under Patten's regime in Hong Kong, and, indeed, even encouraged, with such demonstrations being quite common.[45] On 18 April, the Coalition to Oppose the Provisional Legislature was formed, following the street demonstrations and a 59-hour hunger strike by legislators. On 1 July, opposition to the provisional legislature again made the international press, when eight members of the Coalition on a mission to Beijing to present a petition to the Chinese Government were prevented by the Chinese authorities from leaving their aircraft. In October, however, a Law Society delegation was able to visit Beijing to express its opposition to the provisional body. In spite of all this opposition, on 2 November, in Beijing, the Selection Committee for the provisional legislature was formed, with the naming of 400 selectors.

* * *

The Selection Committee had originally been anticipated in the Basic Law, as a means of choosing the first SAR Chief Executive. Indeed it was the election of the first Chief Executive which was its first priority. For a long time, only one person had let it be known that he was interested in the position. This was T.S. Lo, a controversial figure who, back in 1984, had resigned from the Exco and Legco to throw in his lot with the Beijing Government when it became clear that Britain was going to give up Hong Kong. In a press conference following his resignation, Lo had expressed his dislike for democracy and his view that Hong Kong should continue to operate as it had done under the British, but with the governor replaced by a local person acceptable to China.[46] Since the signing of the Joint Declaration Lo had assiduously courted China. He had been a member of the various committees created by the Mainland government, had financed a pro-Beijing English-language magazine, *Window*, to provide an antidote to the other pro-British English language press, and had even managed to obtain a Chinese passport, something which Hong Kong citizens were not supposed to have.

In December 1995, Lu Ping created speculation about who would in fact become the first Chief Executive, when he said that a 'dark horse' might be the winner of the Chief Executive Race.[47] When, at a meeting of the newly formed PC shortly after Lu's statement, the Chinese leader Jiang Zemin went out of his way to make a great display of personally shaking hands with and congratulating a hitherto little-known figure among China's Hong Kong advisers, the newly appointed Vice Chairman, Tung Chee-hwa, it became widely assumed that this could be the dark horse to whom Lu had been referring. Until his appointment to the PC, Tung, a billionaire shipping tycoon, had been a low-profile member of Patten's Exco, representing the business sector. Patten had welcomed Tung's membership of both his own Exco and the PC, as Tung's participation in the Beijing-backed committee provided the British governor with a means of keeping abreast of what was going on on that body.

Some speculated that only Tung, China's preferred candidate, would be nominated for the position of Chief Executive and then selected 'by consultation', in line with Chinese Communist practice,[48] but word had it that Jiang Zemin himself wanted a real race and that China wanted to be sure that the person chosen would be acceptable to the people of Hong Kong.[49] It is likely that China always favoured Tung as their preferred candidate, but wanted to use the opportunity of a competition to demonstrate, on the one hand, the openness of the selection process, and to make sure, on the other, that the chosen candidate was indeed acceptable to the Hong Kong people. As it turned out, initially, apart from Tung there were three other serious candidates for the position of Chief Executive. They were T.S. Lo, already mentioned, T.L. Yang, the Chief Justice, who resigned his position and gave up his knighthood to stand, and Peter Woo, a youngish, American-style businessman who had given up his business interests some time previously to devote himself to public service, having become Chairman of the Hospital Authority.

As the four contenders announced their candidature, a two-tier election campaign developed. On one level, the important lobbying that had to be done was of the 400-member Selection Committee, who would be doing the voting. On another level, however, the Hong Kong media, by treating the candidates as if they were in a Western-style election, ensured that another campaign had to be mounted to demonstrate the candidates' openness and acceptability to the public in general. China had said that the future Chief Executive had to be acceptable to the people of Hong Kong and this was a good way of finding out which of the candidates were acceptable and which were not. Indeed, opinion polls published in the press quickly made it clear that T.S. Lo commanded very little trust among the public at large. As a result, he soon withdrew his candidature, in favour of his friend Simon Li, a retired judge, who entered the contest.[50]

In the early days of the campaign, there was a rather bizarre situation of the most popular candidate with the public, according to the polls, being someone who was not even standing in the race. This was Anson Chan, the Chief Secretary in Patten's government. In a poll published by the *South China Morning Post* on 5 June 1996, for example, Chan received 56.5 per cent support, Martin Lee (also not standing) 10.6 per cent, T.L. Yang 7.2 per cent, Tung Chee-hwa 5.2 per cent and T.S. Lo only 1.2 per cent.[51] As a result of her popularity, there was much speculation that Chan might decide to stand. She presumably judged that she would not be acceptable to China, given her close association with Patten and the British, however, and decided to stay out of the race. Once Chan had announced that she would not be standing, the most popular candidate was Yang, who held the most moderate views with regard to such controversial issues as the Bill of Rights, laws affecting personal liberty, and the scope of the provisional legislature. Also in Yang's favour, as far as the public was concerned, was his independent stance compared to Tung and Woo, who both had extensive business interests. As it became clear that Tung had by far the most support among the members of the Selection Committee, however, his overall popularity with the public rose and he overtook Yang in the opinion polls. By the time the final vote was carried out in the Selection Committee, the result was a landslide victory for Tung.

The feel of the actual election was effectively evoked in an article in the *Hong Kong Standard*, as follows:

CHEERS ALL ROUND AS RICH MAKE MARK
*By Jackie Sam*
IT was a run-up to the election of the chief executive with Chinese characteristics. Austere, sombre, disciplined. And it went like clockwork.

Outside the Hong Kong Convention and Exhibition Centre the election campaign had been clipping along in American president-ial-election style. But here, inside the centre, it was strictly National People's Congress, with row after row of electors filing out to put their secret ballots into the maroon box and then filing back to their seats.

But if all the trappings were strictly Beijing, from the maroon backdrop with the Chinese state crest and the use of Putonghua, the gathering was strictly Hong Kong.

Moneyed Hong Kong. From 10 am to 5 pm the collective wealth represented in that gathering came to well over $2000 billion. The bosses of 20 of the 33 blue chip companies were there or 60 per cent of the total wealth of all the listed companies in the territory.

If China can be accused of manipulating the election, then it is in allowing the moneyed class to dominate. But this was exactly the way the British manipulated Hong Kong these many years. It was testimony to how successful Beijing has been in anchoring its future to the people who really matter.

The men who once supped with governors and contributed to the Conservative Party were there to vote for shipping tycoon Tung Chee-hwa.

Inside the hall the first vote went to Wheelock boss Peter Woo Kwong-ching. From then on it was Mr Tung all the way.

The applause and the groans would have been unseemly in Beijing's Great Hall of the People. But this was Hong Kong.[52]

In spite of the very controlled way in which the election for the Chief Executive had been carried out, Chinese President Jiang Zemin was able to claim that the election of Tung was 'a symbol of the beginning of a new era for Hong Kong'. Speaking at a reception for Tung in Beijing, Jiang said that the views of Hong Kong people had never been taken into account when the Queen had appointed governors. 'Mr Tung is the first Chinese to become the Chief Executive', Jiang said: 'This is the genuine realisation of the policy of "Hong Kong people ruling Hong Kong".' Hong Kong people could be assured of the sincerity and determination of the Chinese government to fully implement the policy of Hong Kong people ruling Hong Kong and its high degree of autonomy, he reiterated. China would abide strictly by the Basic Law and would definitely not interfere with matters that were within the high degree of autonomy promised for the SAR.[53]

\* \* \*

In his background and approach, the selected candidate, Tung Chee-hwa, in many ways represents the sort of leader that could serve Hong Kong well. Indeed, an opinion poll published on the day of his election credited him with 70.1 per cent public support.[54] He was brought up in a bi-lingual and bi-cultural environment, having been educated in Britain and having worked for several years in the United States. His father, Tung Hao-ung, was a famous Shanghai shipping tycoon who moved to Hong Kong following the Communist take-over in 1949. He over-expanded his company and by the time his son had taken over, in the early eighties, the company was some US $350 million dollars in debt. From the mid-1980s, Tung devoted his efforts to restructuring the company and making it solvent again, so that by the 1990s his family had regained its controlling stake. Tung is

well-connected and is personally known to international figures such
as Margaret Thatcher and George Bush, as well as the PRC leadership. On the negative side, he is regarded with suspicion by some for
his business dealings and interests. In the 1980s, he was only able to
save his family's company by securing generous loans from PRC
interests. He also has extensive business interests in the Mainland, in
collaboration with another well-known Hong Kong tycoon, Li Ka-
shing. Some fear that these commitments will make Tung too behol-
den to the PRC Government and that he will not be willing to stand
up for Hong Kong.[55]

Tung's approach is conciliatory, although he professes to be a firm
leader. Some fear that he may be too conciliatory, as regards China.
He remained on Chris Patten's Exco at the time of the constitutional
reforms and during the period when Patten was condemning the
setting up of the provisional legislature, but since his candidature for
the Chief Executive position, he has stated firmly that Patten's
reforms were wrong and that the provisional legislature is necessary.[56]
In his election manifesto and speeches he has proclaimed the traditional Chinese virtues of humility, respect for the elderly, persistence
and hard-work, stressing the importance of obligations to the community in preference to individual rights and a preference for consultation rather than open confrontation.[57] Some commentators have
interpreted this as a strategic use of these values to impose a more
authoritarian form of government.[58] On the other hand, Tung sought
to come to some sort of accommodation with the Democratic Party
and, in a contradiction of statements made by Chinese officials
regarding political demonstrations, said that they are 'part of Hong
Kong's way of life'.[59] In addition, he invited Anson Chan, a woman
closely identified with Patten, for whom she acted as a loyal Chief
Secretary and head of the civil service, to stay on in her position.

\* \* \*

Following quickly on the heels of the election of the Chief Executive,
the Selection Committee took up its second task, the appointment of
members of the provisional legislature. This selection procedure came
in for a lot more criticism than did that for the Chief Executive. While
Tung Chee-hwa was widely regarded as a good choice for the future
Chief Executive and the way he was elected was entirely in accordance
with the provisions of the Basic Law, neither the idea of a provisional
legislature, nor those people chosen, nor the way they were chosen,
enjoyed much popular support.[60] Of the 60 seats on the provisional

legislature, only four went to people who had themselves been members of neither the Selection Committee nor the preparatory committee, which was itself responsible for appointing the Selection Committee. Such an outcome was possible because people were able to nominate each other and vote for themselves or each other. In an apparent attempt to give the body more credibility, Chinese Vice Premier and Foreign Minister Qian Qichen recommended that committee members vote for those (pro-Beijing) candidates who were already legislative councillors. Although this intervention by Qian again provoked criticism, on the grounds that it was undemocratic, it ensured that 33 of the 34 incumbent legislators who stood for election to the provisional legislature were successful.[61] Reducing the credibility of the body still further, however, five of those elected had earlier been defeated in the 1995 Legco elections.[62]

Patten described the selection process for the provisional legislature as 'stomach churning' and 'a bizarre farce'.[63] 'If a questionable institution is established on questionable foundations doing questionable things' he said, 'then it stands to reason that its actions are going to be questioned.'[64] Martin Lee referred to 'The iron fist of Beijing' which could never extinguish the 'flame of democracy'. British Foreign Secretary Malcolm Rifkind said that 'Common sense suggests that a body chosen by a hand-picked "electorate" of 400 is not in any reasonable sense a "legislature constituted by elections", as required by paragraph 49 of the Joint Declaration.' In a challenge that he must have known China would decline to take up, he demanded that China and Britain go to the International Court of Justice to decide the legality of the provisional body.[65] In further weak words, Rifkind promised that Britain would 'work closely with the United States, the European Union and the other international partners in monitoring observance of provisions of the Joint Declaration in Hong Kong after the handover'.[66]

Aware of the general negative feeling towards the provisional legislature, Chief Executive designate Tung promised that it would last no longer than 30 June 1998, and that the elections for the legislature which would replace the provisional body would take place as soon as possible, probably during the first half of 1988.[67] The only positive outcome of the selection process for the provisional legislature, for those who supported more democracy, was that members of the provisional body, if they intended to participate in the 1988 elections, would run the risk of alienating their future electors if they were too hawkish with regard to the introduction of laws against subversion and sedition, or if they supported a dilution of the Bill of Rights: proposals which were on the provisional legislature's agenda.[68]

\* \* \*

By the end of 1996, the die had been firmly cast for the handover in six months time. The first Chief Executive had been chosen and the provisional legislature established. There was effectively nothing now that the British could do to try to shape the course of the transition. In spite of this, Patten remained defiant. While agreeing to co-operate with the Chief Executive designate, he was adamant that he would have nothing to do with the provisional legislature, in spite of an attempt by Chief Executive designate Tung to make him change his mind when the two men met for the first time following Tung's appointment. Even more than in the past, Patten's role was rhetorical, affirming Hong Kong's autonomy after 1997 and responding to statements or actions by China which he regarded as any sort of threat to what was promised to Hong Kong in the Joint Declaration and Basic Law. Already, in fact, in his final valedictory policy speech in October 1995, he came up with the clever idea of setting out what he referred to as 'benchmarks' by which the extent to which Hong Kong retained its autonomy would be judged. Playing the international card, he said that 'The world should want China to succeed as it continues its brave economic revolution. It will want to be reassured that two systems are surviving and cohabiting in one country. We all hope that the world will get reassuring answers.' The benchmarks included the following (there were sixteen altogether):

- a meritocratic civil service
- public finances free from pressure from Beijing
- a legislature responsive to the aspirations of the Hong Kong community and SAR Government, and free from pressure from Beijing
- independent courts
- a free press and freedom for foreign journalists and news agencies to act without controls
- continued freedom of assembly
- fair and open legislative elections
- freedom from harassment of people for their social, political, or religious views
- a chief executive exercising genuine autonomy.

Predictably, the benchmarks were criticised by China as interference in what, after 1997, would be its internal affairs, a pointer to China's likely reaction to any future intervention by the international community on Hong Kong's behalf after 1997.

In concluding his October 1995 policy speech, Patten said that on his retirement to his 'grey and green island', like other governors before him, he would watch with interest as Hong Kong's history unfolded. He would leave 'carrying one frustration, gnawed by one anxiety, comforted by one certainty,' he said. The frustration was that he had not been able to legitimise his personal vision of Hong Kong through the ballot box (although Hong Kong had been promised that its government would develop so that one day that could happen, he added). The anxiety was that Hong Kong's autonomy might be taken away, not by people in Beijing, but by people in Hong Kong (and here he alluded to the businessmen). The certainty was that the qualities, beliefs and ideals that had made Hong Kong's present would remain to shape its future.

Citing a socialist writer (he could never resist an ironic twist), Patten concluded his policy speech, the last by a British Governor of Hong Kong, by reaffirming his optimism. Hong Kong, he said, had always lived by the author Jack London's credo:

'I would rather be ashes than dust,
I would rather my spark should burn out in a brilliant blaze,
Than it should be stifled in dry rot.
I would rather be a superb meteor,
With every atom of me in magnificent glow,
Than a sleepy and permanent planet.'

Whatever the challenges ahead, 'nothing should bring this meteor crashing down to earth', Patten said, 'nothing should snuff out its glow. I hope that Hong Kong will take tomorrow by storm. And when it does, history will stand and cheer', he concluded.

Stirring stuff from the neo-colonialist perspective, perhaps, but inappropriate as far as a Chinese audience is concerned. As one commentator pointed out, a meteor, in Chinese, is a 'broom-stick star', an ill-omen. Meteors burn themselves out or crash to earth. No Chinese would draw such a parallel for Hong Kong. Forced to choose between a 'superb meteor' and a 'sleepy and permanent planet', every pragmatic Chinese, according to this commentator, knew what to choose. As the Chinese proverb says: 'Better the broken jade than the whole porcelain piece.'[69]

# 11 Ideology and Values

This chapter will step back from the 'story' of Patten's governorship, to examine some of the theoretical issues concerning ideology and values which it raised. Ideology has been defined as 'essentially a set of beliefs which cannot and must not be questioned. It is buttressed by dogmas, and, indeed, depends on them for its existence and survival.'[1] Political leaders strive to present a single coherent unified ideology capable of grouping together a range of potentially different individual positions in a single constituency or social base.[2] This is essentially what was referred to in the Introduction to this book as a 'discourse', where discourse was defined as 'a domain of language use which is underpinned by a set of common presuppositions'. Where a new political party is being formed, a leader needs to weld together a collection of previously disparate discourses in order to accommodate individuals from varying positions.[3] Similarly, where a new leader who wants to bring about a change in the ideology of a party takes over, new discourses need to be brought together. The discourse analyst, Fairclough, describes the way Margaret Thatcher brought about a shift in British Conservative Party ideology, in the 1980s, to what he labels an ideology of 'authoritarian populism', as follows: 'What is involved is essentially a matter of projecting onto the audience a configuration of assumptions, beliefs, and values which accord with the mix of political elements which constitutes what I referred to above as the 'authoritarian populism' of Thatcherite politics.'[4]

There are many parallels between the way Margaret Thatcher brought about this shift in Conservative ideology in Britain and the change Patten (who was closely associated with Thatcher during her period in office, writing, for example, many of her speeches[5]) tried to bring about in Hong Kong. Under Patten's predecessor as Governor (Wilson, a career diplomat) what in Western-style democracies would constitute public discourse was paradoxically mostly conducted behind closed doors. A lot of secret negotiating over Hong Kong went on between Britain and China, with Hong Kong people playing little or no part. The message put out by the British Hong Kong administration was that the best policy for Hong Kong (and Britain) was to adapt its policies so as to tie in with China's plans for Hong Kong after the handover, the policy labelled 'convergence'.

In their discourse directed to and about China, Hong Kong and British Government statements were essentially positive and conciliatory, even when disagreement occurred (as it did over funding for the infrastructure projects for example). This positive attitude to the Mainland was reinforced by the fact that Sir David Wilson was a life-long sinologist and Chinese speaker. As noted earlier, when he was replaced by Patten, he was invited to take a holiday in China by the head of the Hong Kong and Macau Affairs Office, the department responsible for China's dealings over Hong Kong, and was dubbed 'an old friend of China'.

In dealings with the Hong Kong public, British policy operated through a very narrow, elitist constituency made up of executive councillors appointed from the business, legal and university sectors. Government was 'executive-led', that is, controlled by the Governor and his appointed advisers, with minimal direct public participation. The Legco, which after 1991 did have a few directly elected members, was still dominated by government appointees and representatives of particular professional groups. The legislature had no power to initiate policies, only to vet them. Because it was largely controlled by the government, it was effectively a 'rubber-stamp' institution. Symbolising the paternalistic nature of government, Legco sessions were presided over by the Governor, from a raised throne-like chair. The United Democrats (later 'Democratic Party'), the largest and most popular political party from 1991, was tolerated, but its influence was held in check due to the very limited role assigned to elected representatives.

\* \* \*

When Patten took over, there was a complete change of attitude. His aim was to introduce as much democracy into Hong Kong before the handover as the previous agreements with China allowed, even if this meant going beyond the spirit of these agreements, if not the letter. In order to promote this democratic agenda, he projected himself as a man of the people. His style was totally different to that of Wilson. While Wilson was somewhat aloof, Patten adopted a very high public profile, taking every opportunity to be photographed by the press and be seen meeting ordinary Hong Kong people on so-called 'walkabouts'. Indicative of the more confrontational attitude to China, as earlier chapters have shown, Patten refused to confer with the Mainland government before submitting his reform proposals.

According to the discourse analyst, Kress, discourses are 'systematically organised sets of statements which give expression to the meanings and values of an institution'.[6] In the shift in the British position over Hong Kong as it was instantiated by the replacement of the previous governor, Wilson, with Patten, we can see the replacement of one discourse, that of 'convergence' and 'transition', by another, that of 'confrontation' and 'collision'. In terms of rhetoric, Wilson and the Foreign Office believed in 'present[ing] our point of view patiently and carefully'[7], while Patten was willing to argue in public via the media with Mainland officials, in what the press dubbed 'megaphone diplomacy', or a 'war of words'.

While Wilson and Cradock would exchange quotations from the Chinese classics with Chinese officials, Patten (who, following his abortive meeting with Lu Ping, in 1992, never officially met with any Chinese official) dedicated a recording of Fidelio, a Beethoven opera about a political dissident, to his Chinese counterpart, Lu Ping.[8]

Representing the British Foreign Office view, Wilson saw Britain as being in a very weak negotiating position in the face of, in the words of Cradock, 'a regime enjoying vastly superior power, imbued with nationalist sentiment, determined to recover lost territory, and impatient to issue its decrees to that end.'[9] Patten, on the other hand, was determined that Britain should be seen to be standing by what he called its 'moral obligation' towards Hong Kong and should not give in to China's demands. Wilson's era was characterised by drawn-out negotiations with China, especially over the finance of the infrastructure plans. Patten was impatient with this style of dealing with China. After reluctantly conceding to 'talks about talks' over his political reform programme, after 17 rounds of discussion Patten broke off and unilaterally went ahead with his proposals.

From the time of his 1992 political reform proposals, the Chinese refused to have anything to do with Patten, on the grounds that he had broken previous agreements between Britain and China. The Chinese seemed to be acting according to the Confucian proverb, 'There is no point in people taking counsel together who follow different ways.' Instead of face-to-face meetings, bitter rhetorical exchanges were conducted through the media, with Patten promoting the democratic cause, against China's claims that he was trying to destabilise Hong Kong and create chaos in the lead-up to the transfer of sovereignty. In this way, Patten positioned himself as the champion of democracy and positive moral values, in the face of China and the negative forces of authoritarianism.

\* \* \*

In addition to the role played by his political and social reforms in creating a positive image of British withdrawal, Patten also used his powerful rhetoric, often directed at China, to pronounce on Western liberal values. Through an efficient public relations team, Patten ensured that his message got over not only to the people of Hong Kong, but also to the international media. As noted in earlier chapters, he made high profile visits overseas, meeting with the United States' President, the German Chancellor, the Japanese Prime Minister and other Western leaders, enlisting their overt, or at least tacit, support. He appeared on the influential CNN Larry King television show. As the local pro-democracy legislator, Emily Lau, commented in the press, this essentially rhetorical action had the effect of erasing Britain's earlier image of compromise and powerlessness against China over Hong Kong and replacing it with a dynamic image of a Britain fighting for democracy:

> Mr Patten's robust governorship and Beijing's attacks have made him a hero in the international news media, which lionised him as a fighter for democracy. Almost single-handedly, Mr Patten the shrewd operator has managed to erase Britain's image of appeasing and kow-towing to China in the Western media.[10]

Apart from his approach to dealing with China, Patten's discourse directed at the people of Hong Kong was radically different from that of his predecessor, Wilson, and the Foreign Office. And, as already mentioned, it was directed at the international media, as well as the people of Hong Kong. In examining Patten's public pronouncements, a number of themes continually recur. The major themes are woven together into a coherent ideology, made up essentially of Western liberal values, emphasising laissez-faire economics, the freedom of the individual (although not at the expense of the welfare of the less privileged), the rule of law, and democracy.

Although these values are essentially those of Western liberalism, they were not presented as being imposed on the people of Hong Kong (whose values have their basis in Confucianism as much, if not more, than in any Western ideology),[11] but as universals which had always been a part of Hong Kong's way of life. As noted in Chapter 7, in this Patten undertook what Hobsbawm described as the 'invention of tradition'. Patten did not make the connection that these values are essentially the same as those promoted by the left-of-centre tendency within the British Conservative Party to which he belonged. Kress refers to how discourses can 'colonise the social world imperialistically'.[12] This is what Patten sought to do in Hong Kong. It is ironic, however, that he should have undertaken the discursive colonisation of Hong Kong, while at the same time ostensibly managing the process of political decolonisation.

\* \* \*

In his first policy speech in 1992, in what communication theorists refer to as 'agenda setting', Patten emphasised the four elements which were to be the core features of his ideology throughout his governorship. The four features were to re-occur in almost every speech, interview or other public pronouncement Patten was to make during his governorship.

## THE FREE MARKET ECONOMY

Hong Kong, as one of the Asian 'tiger' economies, is a very wealthy metropolis. It has a low-tax, free-market approach to trade. Its per capita income exceeds that of the sovereign, Britain, although this income in very unequally distributed.[13] In many ways, Hong Kong is, on the surface, a successful example of the sort of system espoused by the British Conservative Party, most notably under Margaret Thatcher. Those cognisant with British Conservative ideology will be familiar with the sort of rhetoric exemplified in the following extract from Patten's 1992 policy speech, which elaborated further on the ideology of market economics:

> The success of the economy is central to all our hopes. We must do nothing to jeopardise it. Our prescription for prosperity is straightforward. We believe that businessmen not politicians or officials make the best commercial decisions. We believe that low and predictable taxes are the best form of investment incentive. We believe that government spending must follow, not outpace, economic growth. We believe in competition within a sound, fair framework of regulation and law. (1992 policy speech)

Returning to the theme of free market economics three years later, in the 1995 policy speech, Patten's emphasis on the need to balance the books is again reminiscent of the rhetoric of Margaret Thatcher, for whom, as already mentioned, he had written many speeches.

The programme I launched in 1992 was built on two bedrock principles. These principles are so ingrained in Hong Kong's systems, so much a part of our consensus, that they are usually taken as self-evident and universal truths. The first concerns the economy. Hong Kong knows better than other communities that we must first create the wealth before spending a share of it on improving our public services. We must never lose sight of this fundamental economic reality, and we must accept its implications. There are no short-cuts, no soft options. Social progress is linked directly to economic progress. If we want better services, we must fund them by creating new wealth. (1995 policy speech)

Backing up his claims about the importance of free-market economics, on almost every possible occasion Patten proclaimed the success of the Hong Kong economic system. In his inaugural speech, he described Hong Kong as 'the best example in the post-war world of an open market economy'. He regularly cited outside sources who had described Hong Kong as, for example, the 'most business-friendly', the 'freest', and the 'most competitive' economy in the world.[14] On numerous occasions he emphasised the fact that Hong Kong represented nearly a quarter of China's Gross National Product (GNP) and was the world's eighth largest trading economy.[15] He even proposed Hong Kong's economic system as a role model for the sovereign, Britain, and as likely to become the world's richest city.[16]

## INDIVIDUAL FREEDOM AND HELP FOR THE DISADVANTAGED

The freedom of the individual is one of the fundamental beliefs of Western liberalism. It is also one of the lynch-pins of British Toryism. British Conservative Party rhetoric reverberates with references to the negative influence of 'state interference' and 'the need for individuals to be free to run their own lives'. Similar emphasis is put on the role of the family in British Conservative politics, with emphasis on 'family values' as a stabilising force within society. These ideas on the role of the individual and the family in society also run through Patten's pronouncements on his picture of Hong Kong. The following lists of references to the individual and the family, for example, are drawn just from Patten's four policy speeches:

**The Individual:**

- We will be able to find the correct balance between the freedom of the **individual** in a modern society and the practical requirements of police officers in upholding the law in a civilised society. (1992 policy speech)
- Decency and fairness **individuality** and enterprise are at the very centre of our Hong Kong way of life. (1994 policy speech)
- We will introduce a comprehensive package to strengthen the rights of the **individual** and to eliminate discrimination. (1994 policy speech)
- All our efforts to make the government more open and accountable, to develop our civic institutions in line with our economic and social progress, have been based on the firm belief that **individuals** can make a difference. (1995 policy speech)
- In the last resort, confidence in the future depends on **individuals** being convinced that 1997 will not mean an undermining of the personal liberties which they enjoy and which are a vital ingredient in our separate system, our special way of life. (1993 policy speech)
- We insist that respect for **individual** rights should extend to everyone. There can be no exceptions. (1994 policy speech)
- When we talk about the rights of the **individual**, we mean everyone: the poor as well as the rich, the disabled as well as the able-bodied. (1994 policy speech)

**The Family:**

- More and more **families** want to progress from being rent-paying tenants to owner-occupiers. (1992 policy speech)
- The powerful network of **family** which remains such a valuable feature of Hong Kong society. (1995 policy speech)
- I hope we will be able to... reaffirm the **family's** role as the basic building block for a stable society. (1993 policy speech)
- ...the freedom of **families** to manage their affairs without fear of arbitrary interference by the government or the improper influence of the rich and powerful. (1994 policy speech)
- All our efforts... have been based on the firm belief that **families** can make a difference... For **families** to shape their own lives, to achieve their own goals, to realise their own dreams as members of the most vibrant and dynamic city in this region. (1995 policy speech)

At the same time as allowing individuals and families to get on with their lives without outside interference, Patten was concerned to stress also that the needy should be looked after. In his first policy speech, this balance between non-government interference and help for the less-privileged was expressed by means of the antithetical sentence, 'Hong Kong is not a welfare state, but we are a society that cares deeply about the state of welfare'. In making social welfare the focus of policy, Patten was making up for neglect by past governments which had been content to leave Hong Kong without any form of old age pension scheme or unemployment benefit, at a time when the government was racking up huge financial reserves. At the same time, as earlier chapters have shown, he provoked criticism from China, backed up by the business lobby, for welfarism.

## THE RULE OF LAW

In spite of the lack of democratic development in Hong Kong, Patten promoted the idea that Hong Kong nevertheless had many facets of a Western-style democracy, including a relatively free press and, most importantly, an independent judiciary.[17] The role of the judiciary was presented as crucial to preserving Hong Kong's way of life and economic system under the 'one country two systems' policy. It is the rule of law, Patten claimed, which provided a framework for Hong Kong's freedom and prosperity – past, present, and future:

- What makes Hong Kong special, what makes it unique, is the **rule of law** and the freedoms of a plural society. Hong Kong's **rule of law** is the bedrock of its prosperity, the ultimate protection for the rights and freedoms of our society. (Maiden speech, 9 July 1992)
- In my first address to this council last October, I set out an agenda for Hong Kong for the five years from 1992 to 1997. It covered social, educational, environmental and economic priorities. It sought to show how we would work to secure Hong Kong's way of life , a market economy operating within the **rule of law**, enjoying all the values of a free society. (1993 policy speech)

The rule of law was at risk, however, according to Patten, if China failed to honour its commitments to 'one country two systems' according to the terms of the Joint Declaration:

- Will business be done in the same way after 1997, people ask. How can I be sure that the **rule of law** will prevail? (*Sunday Morning Post*, 14 May 1995)
- Everyone wants reassurances about the future **rule of law**. That's why businessmen from Hong Kong and from other countries press Mr Lu (the head of the Chinese Hong Kong and Macau Affairs office) so hard on the Court of Final Appeal. (*Sunday Morning Post*, 14 May 1995)
- Some may doubt it, that China too is fully committed to preserving Hong Kong's way of life and **rule of law**. (*Sunday Morning Post*, 14 May 1995)

## DEMOCRACY

Equal with the rule of law, in terms of the emphasis placed upon it in Patten's discourse, is democracy. (The Hong Kong public became so familiar with Patten's references to the rule of law and democracy that a cartoon appeared in one newspaper, picturing Patten standing next to a parrot repeating the two terms, 'democracy, rule of law, democracy, rule of law'.) Although by objective measures Patten's political reform programmes only offered what one local legislator has called 'a drop of democracy',[18] China's rejection of his proposals and the resulting war of words with Chinese officials and the Chinese-backed press put Patten in the position of a champion of democracy.

In claiming the need for democratic reform, Patten took up a range of positions. First, he claimed the moral high ground, by citing the political philosopher Isaiah Berlin:

> I have always been moved by Isaiah Berlin's description of democracy as 'the view that the promotion of social justice and individual liberty does not necessarily mean the end of all efficient government; that power and order are not identical with a straitjacket of doctrine, whether economic or political; that it is possible to reconcile individual liberty – a loose texture of society – with the indispensable minimum of organising and authority' (1992 policy speech)

Second, he argued that democracy is essential to Hong Kong, in order to cement the other features of a democratic polity which are already in place:

- We believe that the people of Hong Kong deserve a credible legislature, fairly and openly elected. Anything less than that would surely undermine the rule of law, and that rule of law is essential to the maintenance of Hong Kong's prosperity and freedom. (1993 policy speech)
- There is an intimate relationship between the integrity of the elections and the integrity of the rule of law in Hong Kong, the rule of law on which Hong Kong's prosperity depends. Compromise on the first and you jeopardise the second. (*Sunday Times*, 3 July 1994)

Furthermore, he claimed democracy to be essential for economic progress:

Democracy is more than just a philosophical ideal. It is, for instance, an essential element in the pursuit of economic progress. (1992 policy speech)

Finally, he promoted democracy as an essential part of his personal system of belief:

This discussion about democracy in Hong Kong is one on which I wish to make my own beliefs and objectives clear . . . I have spent my entire career engaged in a political system based on representative democracy. It would be surprising if it had not marked me. (1992 policy speech)

## INTEGRATION OF THE FOUR DIMENSIONS OF PATTEN'S IDEOLOGY

Part of Patten's political stance was to show how the four themes of a market economy, rule of law, freedom of the individual, and democratic participation are inter-related, how it is not possible to have one without the other. This is an important aspect of Patten's ideology, because other East Asian statesmen have argued that it is possible to have strong economic growth without some of the other attributes of the developed Western democracies, such as party politics and high levels of social welfare provision, some arguing that this 'Asian' model is more appropriate for Hong Kong and thus undermining Patten's political and social reform programme.

At times, Patten overtly stated this purported relationship. In the following extract, for example, three of these concepts are integrated, starting with the rule of law, moving on to the freedom of the individual, and concluding with the free market economy:

The rule of law is essential for Hong Kong's future. It begins with individuals and their right to seek the protection of the Courts, in which justice is administered by impartial judges. It protects the freedom of individuals to manage their affairs without fear of arbitrary interference by the government or the improper influence of the rich and powerful. Its starting point is the individual but it encompasses the whole of society. For the business community in particular, the rule of law is crucial. Without it, there is no protection against corruption, nepotism or expropriation. (1994 policy speech)

In the next example, which continues a quotation from the previous page, democracy (not mentioned in the previous extract) is integrated with the market economy and the rule of law, respectively:

Democracy is more than just a philosophical ideal. It is, for instance, an essential element in the pursuit of economic progress. Let me give an example of what I mean. Without the rule of law buttressed by democratic institutions, investors are left unprotected. Without an independent judiciary enforcing laws democratically enacted, businesses will be vulnerable to arbitrary political decisions taken on a whim – a sure recipe for a collapse in confidence and a powerful deterrent to investors from overseas. So democracy brings benefits as well as representing values. It helps to create the sort of society, as well as the business opportunities that first attract talent and capital. (1992 policy speech)

## THE MYTHOLOGISING DIMENSION OF PATTEN'S DISCOURSE

Considered critically, Patten's discourse carries an important element of mythologising (where myth is defined as a belief given uncritical acceptance by a group, whether or not it is true). According to the French philosopher, Barthes, a function of myth is to '[transform] history into nature'.[19] That is to say a situation is created where a particular state of affairs is judged to be perfectly normal and acceptable. Citing an example from French imperialism/colonialism, Barthes demonstrates, in perhaps his best-known analysis of contemporary myth, how a photograph of a black soldier in French army uniform, saluting the French flag, might be interpreted as either a symbol of imperialism or as what he referred to as an 'alibi of coloniality'. In both cases, if one of these interpretations occurs, however, there would be no myth. It is when the viewer feels that the picture seems quite 'natural' and no particular symbolic interpretation is suggested that the myth comes into being and, as Barthes puts it, that 'French imperiality achieves its natural state'.[20] Or, as other writers such as Fairclough have conceptualised this process, the discourse (if we accept visual information as part of discourse) becomes 'naturalised';[21] the ideological element in the relation between the French flag and the black soldier is no longer apparent.

One way that politicians seek to put over their ideology is through just such a process of naturalisation. By continually repeating their message, which, like a myth, is usually put in simplistic terms, politicians seek to make their view of society the generally accepted one.[22] In constantly reiterating, both overtly and covertly, his conception of Hong Kong society, Patten can be seen to be attempting to create a myth. Through constant repetition, he attempted to bring his conception of Hong Kong to a state of naturalness, to paraphrase Barthes. The four components of Patten's model were presented as axiomatic – Patten frequently referred to them as 'bedrock principles' and as 'self-evident and universal truths' – that is to say there is no requirement to justify them, provide evidence in their support, or question them in any way. This in spite of the fact that the four components of Patten's ideology have long and complex philosophical histories, and that their applicability within the context of British colonial rule in Hong Kong may be doubted.

Just a few of the counter-arguments which might be brought to bear to at least cast doubt on Patten's claims might be as follows. Taking first the free market economy, the assumption that Patten promoted is that a laissez-faire regime provides the best possible environment for economic growth. One needs to look no further than some of Hong Kong's neighbours, such as Japan, South Korea, Taiwan, Singapore and Malaysia, to find countries where strong economic growth has been brought about within highly regulated, interventionist systems.[23]

Another assumption of Patten's discourse is that Hong Kong has a totally free economic environment. A recent article in the Business section of the *South China Morning Post*, however, described Hong Kong as 'a cartel economy, where big firms earn monopoly profits'.[24] While it is true that in many areas Hong Kong does allow for free competition, other sectors are in the hands of powerful cartels or monopolies (the ports, the banks, the utilities, the airlines, transport, property development, retailing, to name but a few areas)[25] and traditionally these have been British-controlled enterprises.[26] To take the property market as an example of this monopolistic practice, a recent report pointed out that the residential property market is in the hands of just seven large companies. Colluding in this monopolistic practice, the government keeps tight control of the release of land for development, thus ensuring that prices remain artificially high. The result of this policy is that property ownership is beyond the reach of most people, over 40 per cent of whom rely on public housing, another contradiction in the supposedly free market system.

A further assumption promoted by Patten is that strong economic growth leads to greater prosperity. While Hong Kong has experienced a huge increase in GNP in recent years, the fruits of this growth have remained largely in the hands of the wealthy few, Hong Kong having one of the world's greatest disparities between rich and poor.[27]

Turning now to individualism, while in theory individuals are able to run their lives without undue government interference or undue influence from the rich or powerful in Hong Kong, the reality is somewhat different. During the colonial era, as earlier chapters have pointed out, racial discrimination was institutionalised in Hong Kong government and society. It was only with the signing of the Joint Declaration that ethnic Chinese, for example, were offered the chance to work at the senior levels in the civil service and even here localisation was very slow. Right up until 1990, all the most senior posts – Governor, Chief Secretary, Financial Secretary, Attorney General and Commander British Forces (all also ex-officio members of the Exco) and 40 per cent of the directorate officers, the next level down – in the Hong Kong administration were expatriates,[28] and expatriates were still offered superior conditions of service. During the colonial era, also, reform-minded, pro-democracy political activists routinely came under police surveillance. (Ironically, some of these people, who were later elected or appointed to the Legco, were upheld by Patten as shining examples of responsible democratic representatives of the people.)[29]

Another restriction on access to positions of power and influence, and one which is still maintained, is the government policy of bilingualism.[30] Proficiency in English is a requirement for just about any position of responsibility in Hong Kong, but for the great majority of the Cantonese-speaking population the opportunity to acquire native-like English skills is limited. While most government schools have an official policy of English-medium instruction, it is only a few elite government schools and the private international schools which are actually able to carry this policy out. In most government schools, teaching is conducted in Cantonese, a practice which may be educationally sound (given that this is the mother tongue of the pupils), but which means that students are not acquiring the native-like fluency in English that success at the prestigious universities and in the job market requires.

As regards social welfare, the British, and Patten's, record, is open to criticism. After democracy, an improvement in social welfare, which had been glaringly deficient under previous Hong Kong governments, was Patten's most ambitious policy initiative. However, the main plank in this policy, the introduction of an old age pension scheme, was voted down by an unholy alliance of liberal legislators, who wanted a more generous provision, and conservatives, who wanted less. Patten was willing to make every effort to push through his political reform programme, critics have argued, but was not willing to make a similar effort when it came to social welfare. In addition, as mentioned in Chapter 9, Patten's record on housing came in for violent criticism on the part of the residents of temporary housing, who mobbed him on one occasion to complain about the slow pace of initiatives to improve their living conditions. Furthermore, work-related death and injury levels remained scandalously high among the Hong Kong work force during Patten's governorship. Finally, lax fire regulations were to blame for a series of tragic fires which claimed 40 lives, in the final year of Patten's period of time.

*The Oxford Companion to Law* defines the term 'rule of law' as follows:

> Rule of Law. A concept of the utmost importance but having no defined, nor readily definable, content. It implies the subordination of all authorities, legislative, executive, judicial, and other to certain principles which would generally be accepted as characteristic of law, such as the ideas of the fundamental principles of justice, moral principles, fairness and due process. It implies respect for the supreme value and dignity of the individual.
>
> In any legal system it implies limitations on legislative power, safeguards against abuse of executive power, adequate and equal opportunities of access to legal advice and assistance and protection, proper protection of individual and group rights and liberties, and equality before the law.[31]

A number of aspects of this definition do not apply in Hong Kong, in spite of Patten's rhetoric. Perhaps the most striking of these concerns safeguards against the abuse of executive power. As previously mentioned, the Governor had practically absolute power to do what he wanted. Although there is a general consensus that this power was used benevolently, at least since the signing of the Joint Declaration, until recently there remained on the statute books a number of draconian laws which restrict freedom of speech and give the government the power to arrest and detain people without charging them. Even after Patten became Governor, the Hong Kong Government was consistently criticised by the United Nations on human rights and Patten thwarted efforts to create a Human Rights Commission in Hong Kong, even though this was recommended by the House of Commons Foreign Affairs Committee in Britain.[32]

One glaring restriction on the application of the rule of law in Hong Kong concerns the question of language rights. English is still the predominant language of legal proceedings, a state of affairs which means that in the great majority of cases, a Hong Kong person accused of a crime in Hong Kong is only made aware of what is going on in court through an interpreter.[33]

Corruption adds a further blemish to the record of the British colonial Hong Kong administration. As indicated in Chapter 3, during the sixties and early seventies corruption was rife in many areas of society, particularly the police, a situation which was acknowledged in the setting up of the Independent Commission Against Corruption (ICAC). Although corruption in more recent years has been less prevalent (but, by no means, eradicated), the ICAC still maintains its draconian powers today.

Finally, concerning democracy, while it is true that Patten tried to increase the level of participation in the Legco by increasing the number of directly elected seats, Britain's record on democracy can be summed up as 'too little too late'. As already noted, until the signing of the Joint Declaration the British made little or no effort to introduce democracy in Hong Kong, and Patten's reforms only provided 'a drop of democracy', in the words of the legislator cited above. Only a percentage of the seats in the Legco are directly elected and the Legco still does not have the power to make legislation of its own, under the policy of 'executive-led' government. As Patten noted during his 1994 policy speech, in a memorable paraphrase of the Christian philosopher, Thomas a Kempis, under the Hong Kong system 'the administration proposes and the legislature disposes'.

Patten's eulogising of the role of democracy in society was thus largely hypothetical in the context of Hong Kong. Democracy may well offer at least some of the benefits Patten claimed for it, but these benefits do not and will not apply in Hong Kong, where the British never felt the need to seriously introduce it. In spite of this, when it suited him, Patten still refereed to a 'wholly elected' or 'fully elected' Legco,[34] thus allowing the impression that his reforms created true democracy. The vulnerability of Patten's position on this issue was brought out by China and the pro-Beijing camp in Hong Kong when they were able to say, correctly, that their selection procedure for the first Chief Executive was far more democratic than the selection of any British Governor had ever been.

Unable to do much on the democracy front at the constitutional level, Patten laid great emphasis on 'open' and 'accountable' government as another dimension of democracy. Here again, however, there was an important manipulative dimension to his agenda. As Governor, he appeared before Legco on a monthly basis to answer questions and, after each policy speech, he appeared at public meetings. In each of these situations, however, he was able to control the debate. In the Legco sessions, he invariably began with a prepared statement of his own, and used his skill as a debater to score points off his questioners. As was noted in Chapter 7, in the public meetings which, to use Hobsbawm's terminology, were a 'tradition' which Patten 'invented', by proclaiming them (or meetings like them), to be 'a part of Hong Kong's way of life' (in spite of the fact that they had never occurred before), he used them more as a display of accountability than a real attempt to deal with grass-roots problems.

Patten also tried to make his officials appear accountable. He required government departments to make performance pledges to the public and to provide annual reports as to how successful they had been. Given that the same departments did the reporting as made the pledges, there was obviously considerable scope for manipulation here. Patten also required officials to appear before Legco. Where this occurred, however, press reports of these sessions were more notable for what the officials were able not to say, rather than for what they revealed.

At the end of 1996 one incident, in particular, highlighted the cosmetic nature of 'accountability'. The Director of Immigration, Lawrence Leung, had abruptly retired, for 'personal reasons', according to the government. For a long time, the press and legislative councillors tried to find out if there was more to his retirement than appeared on the surface, given that the official was in such a sensitive position. When required to testify under oath, government officials finally revealed that the Director of Immigration had not in fact retired for personal reasons, but because he had been given an ultimatum to resign or be dismissed, following the discovery of financial improprieties on his part. In choosing retirement over dismissal the official would ensure that he kept his pension and other benefits. The government, according to this quid pro quo, would ensure that misconduct in its ranks was kept secret. This case revealed what one commentator called the 'shiftiness' of the Patten administration. 'We have a leader who, after preaching the virtues of open government, conspired with a civil servant – whom he had accused of wrongdoing – to hide details of the misconduct', according to this commentator.[35] Confirmation of the cosmetic nature of Patten's 'open' government came at the same time as the Lawrence Leung affair was going on, when the State Department of the United States released its annual report on international human rights, describing media and general public access to government information in Hong Kong as 'strictly controlled'.[36]

\* \* \*

In Patten's discourse there was little evidence of any sort of critical evaluation of his 'bedrock principles' of the above sort. It was up to the Chinese to develop an alternative view.[37] Certainly, the Chinese position on Hong Kong was radically different from that of Patten. For the Chinese, Hong Kong was seized by Britain following various wars and unequal treaties. Britain has exploited the local Chinese people in the pursuit of financial gain. Viewed from this perspective, Britain's occupation of Hong Kong is a source of national shame.

Just as Britain should take no pride in its occupation of Hong Kong, according to this Chinese view, neither is it justified in claiming credit for Hong Kong's economic success. In contrast to Patten's view, which attributes Hong Kong's success to British administration combined with the Chinese work ethic and entrepreneurial skill,[38] for the Chinese, Hong Kong's success is not due to any British contribution, but solely to the efforts of the great majority of Chinese people who make up its population. China's position was put very succinctly by Li Ruihuan, a senior Chinese official, as follows: 'What Hong Kong has achieved has been mainly achieved by its own people, not the British. The British haven't done a good job at home. Its status in Europe, its finance and trade, are not that good.'[39]

Mythic discourse (and other simplistic types of discourse), according to one discourse analyst, can forge consensus and bring the members of a community together, making them aware of their shared values, views and histories (even if these shared values, views and histories are themselves actually myths).[40] This was clearly Patten's purpose, to establish a unified constituency of support among the people of Hong Kong, based upon his so-called 'bedrock principles'. At the same time, however, such rhetorical strategies can 'intoxicate' or 'mystify' the community, over-simplifying political situations and obscuring important differences. This would also seem to be the case with Patten. It is notable that his approval rating was high, as measured by public opinion polls, for the period immediately following his appointment and that it went even higher when he announced his plans for constitutional reform. Once China launched its violent attack on the Hong Kong Governor and his proposals, when the community became aware of the risks involved in provoking China and the complexity of the true political situation became clearer, his approval rating went down considerably.[41] As the transitional period came to an end and there were arguments over laws restricting human rights, it can also be argued that Patten's mythologising again misled the Hong Kong people into confronting China and standing up for the so-called freedoms that Patten had persuaded them, or that they had allowed themselves to be persuaded, they had enjoyed under British rule. From this perspective, perhaps, Plato was right to exclude the poet from the Republic.


PATTEN'S ORIENTALISM

In his famous book, *Orientalism*,[42] Edward Said demonstrates how, through the ages, Western conceptions of the Orient have been used as a way of defining the West, as its 'contrasting image'. By viewing the Orient (the Other), one is able to see a reflection of the West (the Self), although in the case of Orientalism, most often the reflection of the West (the Self) is shown up as superior to the East (the Other); by describing the often barbaric and heathen values and practices of the Orient, the superior values and practices of the West are highlighted. The definition of the West/Self in this process may be explicit or (more often) implicit; it may be conscious or unconscious. Because, at heart, they were often more concerned with defining the West as superior rather than coming to a true understanding of the Orient, many Orientalists, according to Said, preferred to base their thoughts on stereotypes found in texts (often produced by Westerners), rather than confronting the Oriental reality itself. Because the study of the Orient may be a mere pretext to dwell upon superior Western values, it is also often the case that the Orient is hardly mentioned at all in Orientalist studies, or its presence may be there by mere implication.

It seems that a good case can be made for Patten as an Orientalist; not as one of those who makes a careful study of the Orient – indeed, Patten, on many occasions, professed his ignorance of China and Chinese history and culture and he never made any attempt to learn the language – but as one of those who bases their thoughts on negative Oriental stereotypes, whose main purpose is to project a positive image of the West, and in whose pronouncements the presence of the Oriental Other is often merely implicit. Just as the Orientalists studied by Said may select those Oriental values, practices and experiences to consider on the basis of their negativity – because they may be considered to be inferior to their own values, practices and experiences – so did Patten, in selecting as the 'bedrock principles' of the ideology he projected onto the Hong Kong people – free trade, individual freedom (and welfare), the rule of law, democracy – choose those values, practices and experiences which most strikingly contrast with the situation prevailing in the PRC. This process of using what Nobel-prize-winning author Toni Morrison has called the 'Serviceable Other' is, of course, demeaning and may be recognised as so when perceived by the Other; it may go some way towards explaining why Patten was attacked so virulently and ostracised by China.

If the components of Patten's ideology are taken one by one, the negative implications as far as China is concerned are clear:

**The Free Market Economy:**
Every time Patten pronounced on the free market economy – a notion originally promoted by the British economist, Adam Smith, as Patten on many occasions pointed out – there is a potential contrast with the collectivist system of the Mainland and its inferior record of economic growth and levels of prosperity.[43] In addition, and more galling from the point of view of the PRC, when free trade is mentioned there is also a potential reminder of the seizure of Hong Kong by Britain from China and other British imperialist rapacity on Chinese soil, as described in Chapter 1 of this book, in the name of free trade.

**Freedom of the individual and the rule of law:**
Individual freedom in Hong Kong, claimed by Patten to be a gift of the British rule of law, may be contrasted with China's lack of individual freedom. China's emphasis on the good of the collective coming before the good of the individual and the need to ensure freedom to eat and to work before individual freedom is not mentioned, or dismissed as inferior. Nor are the difficulties of creating a polity which allows

optimal individual freedom in a country of 1.3 billion people of diverse backgrounds and which has only recently thrown off the shackles of imperialism referred to. Mention of the rule of law highlights what, for the West, is the primitive state of China's legal system. While China has been gradually introducing a Western-style legal system, especially in the economic area regarding contracts and such like, this was not mentioned by Patten. Patten frequently warned of the dangers of corruption creeping in to Hong Kong from the Mainland, but did not draw attention to the British colonial record of rampant corruption in Hong Kong in the sixties and early seventies.

**Democracy:**
Again, the emphasis on democracy draws attention to the contrasting authoritarian constitutional system of the Mainland. Of course, there was no democracy in Hong Kong until the signing of the Joint Declaration, and the Basic Law, a document drawn up by China, allows for far greater democracy than ever permitted by the British; but this is an issue not dwelt upon by Patten. Neither did Patten acknowledge the difficulties of governing a country with the largest population in the world and sizeable ethnic and religious minorities. The mention of democracy may also give rise to thoughts of Tiananmen, an incident over which China was condemned by the Western nations for its barbaric actions (another example of China being used as a 'Serviceable Other'). Most worrying, from China's point of view, a recurrent theme of Patten's discourse is the relation he consistently claimed between economic development and democracy, with its possible implication that democracy will inevitably overtake China. 'I was brought up to believe that there is almost a mechanistic connection between economic freedom and political liberty' Patten said, shortly after revealing his 1992 political reform plan.[44] The idea was elaborated in one of his broadcast 'Letters to Hong Kong'.

> The way we run our affairs has started to catch up with the sort of people we've become. Better educated. Better travelled. Better off. It's not a question of politics being imposed on Hong Kong. What has happened here is what happens, sooner or later, wherever there's economic development and social progress.[45]

There are many other references to this idea in Patten's speeches and other pronouncements.

In all of the above areas, there is no suggestion in Patten's discourse that the perceived inadequacies on the part of China may be at least to some extent due to imperialist intervention in China since Britain's first incursion at the time of the first Opium War.

It should be emphasised that the intention here is not to condone the position of the Chinese Government on all of these issues. The purpose is to highlight an alternative discourse which might be put forward by China in response to Patten's negative construction of the Other.

\* \* \*

Another ideological issue Patten engaged himself in is the question of Asian values. There is a school of thought in Asia that the tremendous economic and social progress of the Asian countries in recent years may be due to certain values which have their roots in Confucianism or other traditional philosophies. Very briefly, these values include a respect for authority, emphasis on collective obligations above individual rights, a belief in order and stability, a strong belief in the value of education, and strong family ties. These values, it is argued, have produced high levels of economic growth, minimal dependence on social welfare, great social stability, high levels of educational achievement, low crime rates, and low rates of marital breakdown.[46]

Patten entered into this debate, frequently making speeches and lectures denouncing these arguments and again taking a negative position vis-à-vis the Asian Other. In line with his Orientalist approach, Patten either denied the existence of Asian values or claimed them not to be particularly Asian, but universal (although the 'universal' values he proclaimed, it turned out, invariably had a Western or British origin). One of Patten's speeches, made at the International Institute of Strategic Studies in London in 1996, may serve as an example. After listing the purported Asian values, Patten then gave his own explanation for Asia's economic success: a belief in progress, economic liberty and free trade. These values, as Patten pointed out, are, of course, values held in 19th century Britain. The following quotations from his speech illustrate this appropriation of supposed Asian values by Patten and how he claims them to be universal/Western /British:

- 'What is the difference between the Asian values of hard work and thrift on the one hand and the Protestant work ethic on the other?'
- 'Free trade was an idea born in Britain. An idea put into practice throughout the British Empire over a hundred years ago. And it is an idea, call it a value, which is sustaining economic expansion and trade throughout the world today.'

- 'Hong Kong has... had the effect of reinforcing my belief in what a recent reviewer of Roy Jenkins' biography of Gladstone called the best Victorian values – liberty, representative government, free trade and international co-operation.'
- '[faith in progress, economic liberty and free trade] are as much part of the history of Europe's industrial revolutions as they are part of Asia's current success story. They are quite simply universal.'

Interpreting Patten's approach in Orientalist terms, what he did was to find something positive and successful in Asia, but rather than examining it in its own terms, as Asians themselves have interpreted it, he denied that it is in fact Asian, claiming it to be universal, and, as already suggested, the origins of what is universal may often be traced back to Britain. So while Patten did claim that Britain and the West can learn from the Asian experience – he claimed that Britain and Europe need to regain their faith in progress and pursue free markets more rigorously – the Asian experience is nothing in fact but a replication of the earlier European experience.

* * *

Given Patten's negative discourse on Asia, two questions arise. First, how did he manage to retain his relative popularity in Hong Kong, given that those he governed were Asians?[47] Second, what might make a governor of a territory take such a line in public? Taking these questions in turn, concerning his popularity, there is no doubt that Patten is a very charismatic character. He has been touted by a whole range of people, including the incumbent, John Major, as indicated earlier, as a possible future Prime Minister. Even his detractors in Hong Kong recognise his powerful personality and energy.[48] The experience of this author, observing Patten in public engagements and interviewing him, is in agreement with this perspective. Combined with his personality, while critical of China, Patten was extremely deferential and polite in his dealings with the people of Hong Kong, and full of praise for their achievements. When interviewed for this book, he agreed that important strategies he used in communicating with the people of Hong Kong were 'praising the people of Hong Kong for their character and achievements' and 'showing deference and politeness to the people of Hong Kong', features of his discourse which I had consistently noted.[49] Given that most Hong Kong people, although Chinese, have a low regard for the Chinese Government (a large percentage of them being refugees from Mainland China or the children of refugees), Patten's 'cocking a snook' at the Chinese Government may not be viewed negatively. Finally, Hong Kong Chinese people's traditional respect for authority should also not be discounted, a respect which was fostered during the colonial period, when the teaching of politics was frowned upon in the schools and respect for authority encouraged.

Turning now to the second of the questions, his motivation, the response that Patten would probably give here would be that he was standing up for the 'one country' side of the 'one country two systems' formula. When interviewed for this book, while agreeing with the strategies that I had identified him as using in his communication with the people of Hong Kong, he added an additional strategy, encouraging people to stand up for their autonomy. In this respect, in confronting China, he would be leading by example. There are other possible explanations for Patten's motivation, however, relating to his personal ambition. Some have argued that the confrontation with China raised Patten's profile as an international statesman and prepared the way for his possible return to British politics, either in London or Brussels. His high profile meetings with leaders such as the United States' President, the German Chancellor, and the Japanese Prime Minister certainly did him no harm in this respect. In addition, his discourse on the success of Hong Kong and the other Asian economies, interpreting it in terms of traditional British (Tory) values, provided him with a way of presenting a refreshing affirmation of what the British Conservative Party stands for, at a time when, after a long period in government, it seemed jaded and lacking in new initiatives.

# 12 Conclusion

This book has documented the British experience in Hong Kong. Starting with Britain's rapacious colonial behaviour and seizure of the colony in the mid-19th century, Part 1 described the territory's early development, the post-war economic success story, the Sino-British agreement to return Hong Kong to China, the drafting of the Basic Law, the tragic events of Tiananmen, Britain's subsequent attempts to restore confidence, and the conciliatory attitude to Sino-British relations of Governor Wilson and the Foreign Office. Part 2, the main focus of the book, concentrated on the last British Hong Kong Governor, Chris Patten, paying particular attention to his rhetoric as he tried to ensure that Britain's legacy to the last of its major colonies would go down in history as an honourable one.

In a way, the book has come full circle; the imposition of British rule in Hong Kong, in the name of free trade, the rule of law, and individual freedom, as described in Chapter 1, was repeated in Patten's attempt to promote Western values in the colony during the lead-up to its reversion to China, again with the emphasis on free trade, the rule of law, and individual freedom, but this time with the additional dimension of democracy. The difference is that Britain's early position was backed by a powerful navy, while Patten's only weapon was rhetoric – his discourse of confrontation with China, as documented in Chapters 6–10, and his discourse of Western liberal values, as described in Chapter 11.

Considering Patten's discourse of liberalism to what extent are the values attaching to free trade, the rule of law, individual freedom, and democracy likely to prevail as a lasting legacy beyond 30 June 1997? First, the market economy is the concept most likely to continue. China itself has already embraced free-market economics, under the slogan, 'socialism with Chinese characteristics', and it is generally agreed that Hong Kong's main value to China is its economy.[1] Positioned as China's gateway to the world, Hong Kong's place as a centre for trade, finance, manufacturing headquarters, information and other services for China and the region, and as a regional business hub, seems assured. With China's economy growing at a rate which regularly exceeds 10 per cent per year there is every reason to expect Hong Kong's position to grow even stronger, especially with a business-oriented, executive-led administration running the SAR. It is true that Shanghai is also making rapid strides as a business and manufacturing centre, but it is unlikely to pose any real threat to Hong Kong for many years to come. To what extent this economic success is a legacy of the British is another matter. It is true that it has depended upon the rule of law and has been based on a philosophy of free trade, concepts historically associated with the British (although, as noted in Chapter 11, the extent to which a free market can be said to apply in Hong Kong is limited). On the other hand, the main impetus for Hong Kong's economic development in the last 50 years came, first, from the influx of entrepreneurs and capital from the Mainland, following the rise to power of the communists in 1949, and, second, from China's 'open door' policy, starting in the 1970s. With the support of these impetuses the high achievement motivation of Hong Kong's working population, based upon Confucian principles of hard work and filial piety, has ensured Hong Kong's development.

Second, individual freedom and help for the disadvantaged: it is very difficult to predict what post-1997 Hong Kong will be like in this regard. In spite of the guarantees in the Joint Declaration and the Basic Law, there are already signs that China envisages greater control on personal freedom. China has already stated that it will reinstate some of those laws relating to personal freedom which were repealed by the British in the lead-up to the handover, a signal that it envisages powers at least as great as the British had in the pre-1984 colonial period. The main fear, from Beijing's point of view, is that pro-democracy groups will try to promote democracy on the Mainland, something which it will not tolerate. It is unclear whether street demonstrations, such as the 4 June commemorations, will be allowed. Tung Chee-hwa has said that demonstrations are a part of Hong Kong's way of life and that they will be allowed, but only so long as they are within the law. Until the future SAR Government introduces laws on subversion, as it is required to, according to the Basic Law, nobody can say if mass demonstrations will be lawful or not. As far as freedom of speech is concerned, already, before the handover, it is clear that the emphasis will change, although to what extent it is difficult to predict. The signs are ambivalent. The Deputy Secretary General of the PC has said that the existence of various political parties in the community was healthy, but, at the same time, committees set up in Hong Kong by China to prepare for the handover, including the PC, insisted on unanimity from their members and did not tolerate dissenting voices.[2] While the pronouncements of Chinese officials claim that journalists are free to write what they want, these same officials also stress that journalists must be 'patriotic' and 'love the Motherland' and that they should not criticise Chinese leaders individually or engage in 'advocacy'. The future Chief Executive has entered into dialogue with the Democrats, but, on the other hand, he has criticised them for rejecting everything 'Chinese' (an accusation which they deny). He has also said that he wants to make Hong Kong 'less political' and has stressed the importance of 'obligations' as well as 'rights'.

Regarding help for the disadvantaged, China has already made it clear that it is not happy with the modest increases in social welfare introduced under Patten, arguing that he is spending beyond Hong Kong's means.[3] Less emphasis on social welfare and more on business is thus likely to be the pattern for the future. On the other hand, the future Chief Executive has said that he will increase spending in education, do more to improve the housing situation and do more for the elderly.

Third, the rule of law: it is likely that those laws relating to property and contracts will be maintained, given the pro-business stance of the future SAR leadership and Beijing. There is, however, a fear that corruption will increase. It is widespread in Mainland China and the fear is that, with the increasing participation of Mainland firms in the Hong Kong economy, it will be difficult to stop it seeping into Hong Kong. During the transitional period, Hong Kong businessmen have developed networks of links with Mainland business interests, often held together by personal relations of mutual interest and trust, or *guanxi,* rather than legal contracts. The expectation on the part of many is that such arrangements will become the norm in Hong Kong, as they are in China. Already, significant stakes have been taken by Mainland interests in some of Hong Kong's listed companies which make more sense in political, rather than strictly business, terms.

As regards the separation of the executive and the judicial branches of government, there are again grounds for expecting change. Initially, judges were to be allowed to ride the 'through train', but subsequently the PWC indicated that they would have to be re-appointed upon the establishment of the SAR, suggesting to some that the future Chief Executive will want to feel comfortable that judges will not diverge from the Government line. Such a move is easily understood, given that there are likely to be legal challenges to the first SAR Government.

Fourth, democracy: China has replaced the legislature created by Patten with an appointed, 'provisional' legislature of its own, from which dissenting voices will be excluded. The permanent legislature which will follow the 'provisional' one is more likely to resemble the earlier colonial model than the new-look Patten version, based as it will be on the formula provided by the Basic Law. There is no reason, however, to doubt that China will fulfil its commitments, according to the constitutional model laid out, conservative as it is. However, the Basic Law, and, indeed, the Joint Declaration, never offered what would be considered a democracy in the West.

\* \* \*

Patten began his key 1992 policy speech, *Our Next Five Years: The Agenda for Hong Kong* as follows: 'My goal is simply this – to safeguard Hong Kong's way of life. This way of life not only produces impressive material and cultural benefits; it also incorporates values that we all cherish.'

As the previous chapter of this book has shown, the values projected by Patten onto the Hong Kong people here are essentially the values of Western liberalism. Various commentators have noted how Britain's goal, with Patten as architect and animator, in the last five years of Hong Kong under British rule, was not only to promote these values within Hong Kong but to demonstrate to the world at large and to history how hard Britain had tried to do its best for what was the last of its significant colonies. In demonstrating the fulfilment of its 'moral obligation' in this way, Britain tried to ensure that its exit from its last major colony was an honourable one. In separate interviews with the author, both Patten and his personal advisor, Edward Llewelyn, stated that they were well aware that Britain's departure from Hong Kong would be, as they both put it, 'the prism' through which British colonial history would be viewed.[4] This historical dimension to the final years of British Hong Kong was also evoked in Chapter 9 of this book, with its account of the British preoccupation with the actual handover arrangements, and in Chapter 8, with its quotation of the stirring rhetoric at the end of the 1995 policy speech.

In terms of actual policy initiatives (as opposed to rhetoric), it is significant that Patten put most effort into democratic reform and social welfare, areas where, based on its record up to the time of Patten (and ignoring the refusal to grant passports to Hong Kong people, which was taboo)[5], Britain would be most vulnerable in any evaluation of its colonial legacy. One way of interpreting the constitutional and social reforms that Patten tried to introduce is therefore as a means by which Britain could achieve this goal of withdrawal with honour. This view was presented by a local political commentator, for example, as follows:

By the time the Union Flag is lowered, Mr Patten will probably say, with pride, that 155 years of British rule has turned Hong Kong from a barren rock into a world-class financial centre, with a governmental system that is as democratic as can be, an efficient infrastructure marked by a modern airport and port facilities and an affluent population that enjoys free education and heavily subsidised medical and housing benefits. 'The Brits go with pride,' the Western press will probably say, subject to the fact that Hong Kong is returning to a motherland that is ruled by a Communist regime which has a chequered record of managing its own affairs.[6]

Greater democracy suited Britain's purpose to allow it to leave honourably, as noted by another local commentator:

Much has been said about what really matters in the Patten scheme of things. Few really believe that he cares for us in the way he pretends. How could he, seeing as he had come to know of us little more than a year ago. His mission here is certainly due to a belated realisation that the British could not decently withdraw with history glaring at them for their decades of neglect and omissions. The democracy crusade Governor Patten has undertaken serves this purpose and beyond.[7]

The theme of honourable colonial withdrawal was indeed developed publicly on various occasions by Patten himself (although usually for non-Hong Kong audiences). Writing for a British audience in the *Sunday Times*, under the headline, 'Out of Hong Kong with honour – and a good deal for China', Patten described this historical mission as follows:

In just over 1000 days, Britain's colonial history will draw to an end. It matters that we close the book honourably and well. We are more likely to do the job competently if we try to do it honourably. Then when we do leave, we will do so with self-respect, and in the knowledge that by playing fair by Hong Kong, we helped to give Hong Kong a chance of contributing its uniqueness to China.[8]

During a press conference, Patten conceptualised what Britain was trying to do in Hong Kong as the end of a long process of British decolonisation, a process which, he claimed, had been an honourable one:

Everywhere else, from India to Zimbabwe, Britain in the 20 or 30 years of decolonisation from the 40s onwards, saw its role as preparing a dependent territory acquired during the height of imperial power in the 19th century – preparing a dependent territory for independence. As we put in place, in all those communities, basically the same constitutional kit: bicameral legislature, democratic model, independent judiciary, judges in wigs – even in Africa – a pretty clean civil service trained at St Anthony's, Oxford, and the Institute of Local Government Studies at Birmingham. And sometimes that worked – you blasted the satellite off into orbit. And sometimes it didn't work; it came crashing to the ground. But it was an honourable endeavour.[9]

To what extent the six and a half million people of Hong Kong might be happy about being 'blasted off' into orbit like this was perhaps secondary to Patten's pursuit of honourable withdrawal.

* * *

In any evaluation of Britain's role and that of its last Governor, Chris Patten, during the final years of British Hong Kong, one must take into account the fact that, as sinologists such as Percy Cradock and David Wilson would be the first to point out, once Britain had agreed, in 1984, to pass sovereignty to China, Britain had very little real power to affect the outcome of the transition. Effectively, the limited power that Britain had lay in its ability to persuade China that it would be in its own best interests to allow Hong Kong to maintain and, indeed, augment the democratic aspects of its way of life under British rule. Persuading China – a country which is seeking to redeem itself from a history of colonial subjugation, has deep feelings of national shame, is strongly nationalistic, is growing in international influence and power (both economic and political), and to which Western ideas of democracy and capitalism are alien – was always going to be a task of monumental proportions.

Perhaps, if Britain had seriously gone about democratic development following World War II, according to the Young Plan, then by the time China came to take over Britain would have been able to demonstrate that Hong Kong was capable of operating within a democratic framework in a way which posed no threat to stability and prosperity. Democracy would have been up and running and China would have incurred less risk in taking it over. This, however, was not the case. Britain always took the short-term view and democracy was only seriously thought about once Britain had decided to give up sovereignty. From this perspective, the high degree of autonomy agreed for

Hong Kong under the terms of the Joint Declaration represented a considerable achievement on the part of British negotiators.

Following the signing of the Joint Declaration, Britain adopted two opposing strategies in persuading China to its conception of what was best for Hong Kong: first, the strategy of convergence, as espoused by Cradock and Wilson, and second, the more confrontational strategy employed by Patten. If the path of convergence had been followed through to the end, it is likely that Hong Kong would have had a through train, but that the degree of democratic government allowed would have been considerably less than Britain might have preferred. As it is, the through train was derailed by Patten and the way was left open for China to set up the sort of constitutional system it had all along foreseen, as set out in the Basic Law. Patten used the argument that if he had not aligned himself with the pro-democracy forces, then there would have been more civil disturbances in Hong Kong. 'If we'd made the accommodations that some old Sinologists had wanted,' he said in a 1995 interview, 'we would now have in place less freedom, less democracy, less protection of human rights. All that would have happened is that we would have had those things before 1997, with Britain's connivance and Britain's imprimatur, Britain's chop. Who do you think the demonstrations would have been against?'[10] Similarly, at the time of the demonstrations against Lu Ping's visit, in the spring of 1996, Patten said that there would have been 'pretty good chaos' if he had not spoken out in defence of Hong Kong's freedoms, and suggested that people would have been 'chaining themselves to the railings.'[11]

From the British perspective, nevertheless, thanks to Patten's rhetoric, the change in policy meant that the final years of British Hong Kong are likely to be recorded by Western historians as a struggle to preserve Hong Kong's freedoms and win greater democracy, in contrast to a more demeaning historical account which would likely have been the result of a continuation of the more conciliatory policy of convergence, which might have been recorded as appeasement. At the same time, in aligning himself with the pro-democracy group, Patten avoided civil disturbances directed at him and the British Government and deflected opposition towards China. This is the result of choosing a politician to run Hong Kong in its final years, rather than a diplomat.

From Hong Kong's point of view, perhaps the end result would not have been that different, whether or not Britain had switched from the policy of convergence to that of confrontation. China all along envisaged a very conservative introduction of limited democracy to Hong

Kong and this is what Hong Kong will get. The extent to which any further democratic development is allowed to take place, as is possible, according to the Basic Law, will probably depend upon events in China, rather than Hong Kong. No doubt the proponents of greater democracy in Hong Kong will continue to argue their case, although their opportunities will be diminished.[12] Whether or not demands for more representative democracy are accepted by the Mainland Government will depend on the climate prevailing in Beijing. Some political scientists and democratic politicians, including Chris Patten, as mentioned in Chapter 11, argue that economic development is inevitably followed by democratic reform. The historical precedents for such a process, in the Southeast Asian context, are at best mixed. There are more cases of movement away from Western-style democracy in the post-colonial situation (Burma, Indonesia, Malaysia and Singapore) than of democratic strengthening (the Philippines is probably the only clear example).[13] There is a considerable level of agreement among the leaders of these Southeast Asian countries that democracy, where adopted, should be adapted to fit in with local traditional cultural values, which are often paternalistic and authoritarian in nature. Governments in countries such as Malaysia, Singapore and Indonesia, operating in concert with the economic elite, have sought to build legitimacy for their regimes by creating conditions for rapid material progress rather than Western-style democracy. The development of a model like this in Hong Kong seems quite possible. Tung Chee-hwa, the first Chief Executive, for example, has expressed his admiration for Lee Kuan Yew, the former Singaporean leader, and, as mentioned in Chapter 11, puts emphasis on Chinese values; but only time will really tell.

# Notes

## INTRODUCTION

1.  Most of the information in this paragraph is to be found in Bob Howlett (ed.), *Hong Kong 1996: A Review of 1995 and a Pictorial Review of the Past Fifty Years* (Hong Kong Government Printer, 1996).
2.  Michael Foucault, *Madness and Civilisation* (London: Tavistock, 1971).
3.  Indeed, English serves a 'gate-keeping' function in Hong Kong, controlling access to positions of power and influence in all sectors of society.
4.  Interview with the author, Government House, 16 September 1996. Patten would also have been aware that a BBC television crew were regularly filming him for a television series, 'The Last Governor', and that a number of books on his governorship were in preparation.
5.  *Ibid.*

## CHAPTER 1

1.  The historical account of the early chapters of this book draws on the following standard works, among others: Nigel Cameron, *An Illustrated History of Hong Kong* (Hong Kong: Oxford University Press, 1991); G.B. Endacott, *Government and People in Hong Kong 1841–1962* (Hong Kong: Hong Kong University Press, 1964); G.B. Endacott, *A History of Hong Kong,* (Oxford: Oxford University Press, 2nd Edition, 1973); Lawrence James, *The Rise and Fall of the British Empire* (London: Little Brown and Company, 1994); Frank Welsh, *A History of Hong Kong* (London: HarperCollins, 1994).
2.  John King Fairbank, *China: Tradition and Transformation* (Boston: Houghton Mifflin, 1989, revised edition) p. 34.
3   For a detailed account of the Macartney mission, see Alain Peyrefitte, *The Collision of Two Civilizations: The British Expedition to China 1792–4* (London: Harvill, 1993).
4.  Welsh (*op. cit.*) p. 33.
5.  *Ibid.*, p. 41.
6.  *Ibid.*, p. 58.
7.  *Ibid.*, p. 61.
8.  *Ibid.*, p. 63.
9.  *Ibid.*, p. 68.
10. *Ibid.*, pp. 69–70.
11. Cameron (*op. cit.*) p. 20.
12. Cameron (*op. cit.*) p. 28.
13. The indigenous population has been estimated to have been about 3650, scattered over 20 villages and hamlets, together with some 2000 fishermen

who lived on board their boats in the harbour (Bob. Howlett (ed.), *Hong Kong 1996: A Review of 1995 and a Pictorial Review of the Past Fifty Years,* Hong Kong Government Printer, 1996) p. 404.

14. The agreement is referred to as the Second Convention of Beijing, the first being the cession of Kowloon, signed in 1860.
15. *Hong Kong Standard,* 21 March 1995.

## CHAPTER 2

1. G. B. Endacott, *A History of Hong Kong* (Hong Kong: Oxford University Press, 1983, second edition) pp. 74, 126.
2. *Ibid.,* p. 194. Opium was only made illegal in 1945, by the post-war military government.
3. Frank Welsh, *A History of Hong Kong* (London: HarperCollins, 1994) pp. 137, 253.
4. The British and other foreign residents also only stayed for short periods. Welsh *(op. cit.)* p. 217 cites a dispatch from the Colonial Secretary Labouchere, in 1856: 'Few if any of the British residents in Hong Kong are persons who go to establish themselves and their descendants permanently in that place; they merely sojourn there during a limited time, engaged in commercial or professional pursuits, but intending to quit the colony as soon as circumstances will permit.'
5. Elliot had been an Administrator, not officially a Governor.
6. As Welsh *(op. cit.)* p. 216, points out, it is worth bearing in mind that in Britain, at the time of Bowring's proposals, parliamentary democracy was still far from fully developed, with less than one in five of the male population having the vote. Lord Palmerston's constituency had an electorate of only 508, for example.
7. *Ibid.,* pp. 217–8.
8. *Ibid.,* p. 153.
9. The ordinance did not specifically exclude non-Europeans; it reserved the higher part of the town 'not for exclusive European occupation, but for houses built according to European models.'
10. Welsh *(op. cit.)* p. 278.
11. Welsh *(op. cit.)* p. 304.
12. Endacott *(op. cit.)* pp. 289–90.
13. The figures are taken from Endacott *(op. cit.)* pp. 274–5.
14. Endacott *(op. cit.)* p. 275.
15. Welsh *(op. cit.)* p. 415.
16. Michael Yahuda, *Hong Kong: China's Challenge* (London: Routledge, 1996) pp. 45–6.
17. Britain had also sent reinforcements and this may have deterred the People's Liberation Army. The British Foreign Secretary, Bevin, described Hong Kong as 'the Berlin of the Middle (sic) East'.
18. Cited in Endacott *(op. cit.)* p. 308.
19. Nigel Cameron, *An Illustrated History of Hong Kong* (Hong Kong: Oxford University Press, 1991) p. 274.

20.   Cited in Welsh (*op. cit.*) p. 440.
21.   Cited in Shiu-hing Lo, 'The Problem of Perception and Sino-British Relations over Hong Kong', *Contemporary Southeast Asia* (vol. 13, no. 2, 1991) p. 201.
22.   Ambrose Yeo-chi King, 'The Administrative Absorption of Politics in Hong Kong: Emphasis on the grass roots level', *Asian Survey* (Vol. 15, No. 5, May 1975) pp. 422–39.
23.   By now, however, the Hong Kong economy has been transformed from being manufacturing-based to being largely service-based. Manufacturing has been transferred over the border to Mainland China, with management functions being carried out in Hong Kong.
24.   Felix Patrikeef, *Mouldering Pearl: Hong Kong at the Crossroads* (London, 1989) pp. 66–7, cited in Welsh (*op. cit.*) p. 476.
25.   Ian Scott, *Political Change and the Crisis of Legitimacy in Hong Kong* (Hong Kong: Oxford University Press, 1989) p. 163.
26.   *Ibid.*, p. 128.
27.   The Hong Kong Government's budget was also helped by revenues from sales of crown land.
28.   Cited in Scott (*op. cit.*) p. 152. Again, there are echoes of Patten here. Scott (*op. cit.*) p. 153, describes Maclehose's policy speech as having 'a strong moral flavour and considerable popular appeal. It enlarged the role of government, committed it to the primary goal of improving the quality of life, and offered a yardstick of accountability.'
29.   See Scott (*op. cit.*) Chapter 4.
30.   In evaluating MacLehose's achievement, it should be borne in mind that Hong Kong was starting from a very low base and that spending on social provision under MacLehose still represented a tiny proportion of Gross Domestic Product (GDP), compared to developed Western countries.
31.   For an insider's view, see Jimmy McGregor, 'Fighting the "Vermin of Society"', in Sally Blyth and Ian Wotherspoon, *Hong Kong Remembers* (Hong Kong: Oxford University Press, 1996) pp. 148–66. McGregor argues that MacLehose should have taken a stronger line and not granted an amnesty. Describing the extent of corruption, McGregor, who was a government official, recounts how he asked one officer how many in a particular unit were corrupt. The response was: 'How many are not? You should be asking that question.' The answer to 'that question' was that none were, according to McGregor (*ibid.*, pp. 152–3).
32.   As a small caveat, in 1981 there was some reform of local administration, with the introduction of elected members to District Boards. According to a government official at the time, John Walden, in a letter to the *South China Morning Post* of 9 April 1997, the initiative for direct elections followed a vist to the territory in late 1979 of two British MPs, Ted Rowlands (Labour) and Chris Patten (Conservative), who persuaded the Foreign Secretary that direct elections to District Boards would be a good idea, as a first step on the road to democrative participation. However, the measure was "neutered politically", in the words of Walden, as the District Boards were given neither executive powers nor significant funds. (Ironically, this was not to be the first time

that Patten's democratic ideas for Hong Kong were to be thwarted, as Part 2 of this book will make clear.)

33. *South China Morning Post,* 13 March 1972.
34. *Ibid.*
35. Dick Wilson, *Hong Kong! Hong Kong!* (London: Unwin Hyman, 1990) p. 196.
36. David Bonavia, *Hong Kong 1997: The Final Settlement* (Hong Kong: South China Morning Post Ltd., 1985) p. 143.
37. Percy Cradock, *Experiences of China* (London: John Murray, 1994) p. 162.
38. *Sunday Morning Post,* 7 May 1995.
39. *Hong Kong Standard,* 29 April 1976, referred to in James T.H. Tang and Frank Ching (pp. 144–5) in Ming K. Chan (ed.), *Precarious Balance: Hong Kong Between China and Britain 1842–1992* (New York: M. E. Sharpe, 1994) pp. 149–171.
40. Reported in Geoffrey Howe, *Conflict of Loyalty* (London: Macmillan, 1994) p. 366.

## CHAPTER 3

1. This chapter deals with the negotiations leading to the Joint Declaration. It draws on accounts in the following sources, some of whom are commentators and others participants in the negotiations themselves: David Bonavia, *Hong Kong 1997: The Final Settlement* (Hong Kong: South China Morning Post Ltd., 1985); Robert Cottrell, *The End of Hong Kong: The Secret Diplomacy of Imperial Retreat* (London: John Murray, 1993); Percy Cradock, *Experiences of China* (London: John Murray, 1994); Geoffrey Howe, *Conflict of Loyalty* (London: Macmillan, 1994), Mark Roberti, *The Fall of Hong Kong: China's Triumph and Britain's Betrayal* (New York: John Wiley and Sons, 1994); Ian Scott, *Political Change and the Crisis of Legitimacy in Hong Kong* (Hong Kong: Oxford University Press, 1989); Gerald Segal, *The Fate of Hong Kong* (London: Simon & Schuster, 1993); Margaret Thatcher, *The Downing Street Years* (London: HarperCollins, 1995); Dick Wilson, *Hong Kong! Hong Kong!* (London: Unwin Hyman, 1990).
2. Thatcher (*op. cit.*) p. 261.
3. *Ibid.,* pp. 261–2.
4. *Ibid.,* p. 261.
5. *Ibid.,* p. 261.
6. *Ibid.,* p. 262.
7. Xinhua, or the New China News Agency, is the *de facto* Chinese embassy in Hong Kong. Its statements, therefore, have official authority.
8. Bonavia (*op. cit.*).
9. Thatcher (*op. cit.*) p. 488.
10. In October 1984, Cradock reached retirement age, but remained in post until December of that year. Thatcher then made him her special

adviser on foreign affairs and Under-Secretary of State at the Foreign Office, with special responsibility for overseeing the negotiations. He remained in this position right up until 1992, when the decision was taken by newly-elected Prime Minister John Major to appoint Chris Patten as Governor.

11. Thatcher (*op. cit.*) p. 489, refers to Sir Geoffrey Howe, as Foreign Secretary, leading the Foreign Office view. However, as Howe points out in his memoirs (*op. cit.*) p. 366, he did not take up that position until 11 June.

12. See Cottrell (*op. cit.*) p. 117 for a personal account from one of those present.

13. *South China Morning Post*, 8 and 9 July, and 18 August 1983.

14. Scott (*op. cit.*) pp. 131–2. Scott cites six public opinion polls. *South China Morning Post*, 11 April 1982; *South China Morning Post*, 13 August 1982; *Far Eastern Economic Review*, 21 July 1983; *Hong Kong Standard*, 22 September 1983; *South China Morning Post*, 21 October 1983; *South China Morning Post*, 19 November 1983.

15. *South China Morning Post*, 14 August 1983.

16. *Hong Kong Standard*, 21 August 1983.

17. Thatcher (*op. cit.*) p. 490.

18. *Ibid.*, p. 491.

19. *Ibid.*, p. 491.

20. En route for his posting as Hong Kong Governor, Patten stopped off in Singapore for discussions with Lee, no doubt to seek advice on how to deal with the Chinese. Lee was subsequently a strong critic of Patten's approach.

21. This deadline had already been set by Deng, in his meeting with Thatcher. The Chinese leader had said that the time-frame for negotiations would be 'one or two years', from September 1982. In Howe (*op. cit.*) p. 365.

22. Details of Howe's visit are drawn from Cottrell (*op. cit.*) pp. 148–9 and Howe himself (*op. cit.*) pp. 375–8.

23. These issues all remained bones of contention in Sino-British relations right up to the handover.

24. *South China Morning Post*, 29 March 1984.

25. Cited in Cottrell (*op. cit.*) p. 149.

26. Cradock (*op. cit.*) p. 197.

27. Howe (*op. cit.*) p. 379; also see Roberti (*op. cit.*) p. 113.

28. Cradock (*op. cit.*) p. 277, the chief British negotiator, describes the agreement to include the reference to elections as one of Britain's 'last shots' and that there was no way the Chinese would have agreed to the term 'direct elections'. Howe (*op. cit.*) p. 379, who achieved the agreement by correspondence with his counterpart, Wu Xueqian, simply states in his memoirs that the Chinese agreed in two days to his proposal that the legislature would be 'constituted by elections' and that the executive would be 'accountable to the legislature.' He makes no mention of trying to obtain agreement to anything more detailed or specific. See Chapter 8 for further discussion of this point.

29. Cited in Cradock (*op. cit.*) p. 214.

30. *South China Morning Post*, 11 December 1982.
31. This point is made in many places by Cradock (*op. cit.*) in his memoirs.
32. Cited in Cottrell (*op. cit.*) p. 153.
33. Cited in Roberti (*op. cit.*) p. 91.
34. Cited in Cottrell (*op. cit.*) p. 138.
35. Roberti (*op. cit.*) p. 82.
36. James T.H.Tang and Frank Ching, 'The MacLehose–Youde Years: Balancing the "Three-Legged Stool," 1971–86', in Ming K. Chan (ed), *Hong Kong Becoming China: The Transition to 1997: Precarious Balance: Hong Kong Between China and Britain* (New York: M. E. Sharpe, 1994) pp. 144–5, 159.
37. *Ibid.*, p. 160.
38. Martin Lee, 'The Fight For Democracy', in Sally Blyth and Ian Wotherspoon (eds.), *Hong Kong Remembers* (Hong Kong: Oxford University Press, 1996) pp. 233–43. Interestingly, Lee expresses himself as very satisfied with the Joint Declaration. It is subsequent negotiations conducted by Cradock that he is critical of.
39. Cradock (*op. cit.*) p. 211.
40. See Michael Yahuda, *Hong Kong: China's Challenge* (London: Routledge, 1996) p. 72.
41. One senses that this insensitivity noted in Thatcher's insistence on the validity of the treaties was perhaps not shared by her officials, who would have been more willing to accept from the outset that sovereignty should pass to China.
42. The quotation from Chinese official, Li Ruihan, at the end of Chapter 1, is a good example of an expression of this Chinese attitude.
43. Demonstrating an ignorance of Britain's imperialist intervention in China, Thatcher went so far as to state that, through the 19th and early 20th centuries, Sino-British 'cultural and scientific contact went from strength to strength'. Cited in Chalmers Johnson, 'The Mousetrapping of Hong Kong: a Game in Which Nobody Wins' *Asian Survey* (vol. 24, no. 9, 1984) p. 895.
44. See for example, Richard Solomon, 'Friendship and Obligation in Chinese Negotiating Style' in Hans Binnendijk, (ed.) *National Negotiating Styles* (Washington, D.C.: Foreign Service Institute, US Department of State, 1987), and Lucien Pye, *Chinese Commercial Negotiating Style* (Cambridge: Oelgescher, Bunn and Hain, 1982).
45. Time may not always have been on the side of the Chinese negotiators, however. It seems that the Chinese were under some sort of time pressure at the end of the negotiations and offered considerable concessions to wrap up the agreement. On the other hand, by this stage, the British were pressing for as much detail in the agreement as possible. By introducing a time limit, the Chinese curtailed British attempts to negotiate, for example, detailed constitutional arrangements, which were not set out in the final agreement.
46. In accordance with this objective, the Chinese created visa problems for Governor Youde's press secretary. See *Far Eastern Economic Review*, 25 August 1983.

47. The economic blockade would have been very easy. Not only did Hong Kong depend on China for a significant part of its trade, but most of its water was supplied by the Mainland.
48. Cradock (*op. cit.*) p. 212, writes: 'The Chinese approach, as in many other negotiations, was to set up principles and make acceptance of them the precondition for further discussion. Since the principle invariably involved the whole point at issue, finesses had to be devised permitting continued discussion and exploration without irrevocable concessions.'
49. Thatcher (*op. cit.*) p. 259.
50. Interview with the author, Government House, 16 September 1996.
51. Reported in Chalmers Johnson (op. cit) p. 895.
52. The extreme language tactic was to reach its height in the campaign waged against Patten in response to his 1992 reform proposals.
53. Scott (*op. cit.*) p. 198.
54. *South China Morning Post,* 26 September 1984.
55. International Commission of Jurists, *Countdown to 1997: Report of a Mission to Hong Kong* (Geneva: International Commission of Jurists, 1992).
56. *Ibid.,* p. 52.
57. Scott (*op. cit.*) p. 190; Chalmers Johnson, 'The Mousetrapping of Hong Kong: A Game which Nobody Wins', *Asian Survey* (vol. 24, no. 9) pp. 897–904, pp. 901–2.
58. Scott (*op. cit.*) pp. 190–1.
59. *Ibid.,* p. 192.
60. *Ibid.,* p. 178, cites British MP, Robert Adley, who, in December 1982, asked the Foreign Secretary 'to give an assurance that nothing will be done that will cause detriment or harm to our relations with Hong Kong.'
61. *The Times,* 27 September 1984.

CHAPTER 4

1. Green Paper: The Further Development of Representative Government in Hong Kong (Hong Kong Government Printer, 1984) p. 4.
2. White Paper: The Further Development of Representative Government in Hong Kong (Hong Kong Government Printer, 1985).
3. Frank Welsh, *A History of Hong Kong* (London: HarperCollins, 1994) p. 516.
4. There is the possibility that the Governor can appoint members from the Legco to simultaneously sit on the Exco. Indeed, after the 1991 elections, Governor Wilson appointed four Legislative Councillors to the higher body, although only one had been directly elected and he did not represent the most popular party, the United Democrats. This policy was later reversed by Chris Patten, who decided to keep the two Councils separate (see Chapter 5).
5. White Paper (*op. cit.*) p. 8.

6. Robert Cottrell, *The End of Hong Kong: The Secret Diplomacy of Imperial Retreat* (London: John Murray, 1993) p. 182.
7. Percy Cradock, *Experiences of China* (London: John Murray, 1994) p. 227. In an article in the *South China Morning Post* of 30 September 1996, Cradock went so far as to say that: 'The facts are that there is no reference to democratisation in the Joint Declaration.'
8. Margaret Thatcher, *The Downing Street Years* (London: HarperCollins, 1995) p. 493.
9. Mark Roberti, *The Fall of Hong Kong: China's Triumph and Britain's Betrayal* (John Wiley & Sons, 1994) p. 140.
10. *South China Morning Post*, 10 November 1985.
11. The pro-democracy activist and BLDC member, Martin Lee, has written that he was told by Chinese officials that Britain wanted the Basic Law to be prepared at the end of the transitional period. Lee, because he thought the Joint Declaration a good one, recommended that the Chinese side start on it early. He was afraid that if they waited, Chinese leaders might change their minds and regret having written so many freedoms into the Joint Declaration. ('The Fight for Democracy' in *Hong Kong Remembers* by Sally Blyth and Ian Wotherspoon (eds), Hong Kong: Oxford University Press, 1996, pp. 233–43, 236.)
12. Frank Ching, 'Toward Colonial Sunset: The Wilson Regime, 1987–92' in Ming K. Chan (ed.) *Precarious Balance: Hong Kong Between China and Britain: 1842–92.* (New York: M. E. Sharpe, 1994) pp. 173–197, p. 174.
13. See Ching (*op. cit.*) p. 174; Norman Miners, *The Government and Politics of Hong Kong* (Hong Kong: Oxford University Press, 1995) pp. 26–7; Roberti (*op. cit.*) pp. 205–8; Ian Scott, *Political Change and the Crisis of Legitimacy in Hong Kong* (Hong Kong: Oxford University Press, 1989) pp. 293-298; and Welsh. (*op. cit.*) pp. 517–8.
14. Roberti (*op. cit.*) p. 159.
15. Whether or not Wilson, who was shortly to become Governor, was responsible for inventing the idea, his future performance was to demonstrate his close attachment to it.
16. Cottrell (*op. cit.*) pp. 182–3.
17. Cited in Roberti (*op. cit.*) p. 163.
18. China's 'united front policy' refers to the mobilization of all possible forces in the pursuit of a political or diplomatic goal. It may include the following: the creation and use of front organizations and personalities in the target area, including 'old friends of China'; the use of media propaganda and threats; the ostracisation and abuse of key opponents; and the exertion of pressure on negotiations by staking out positions in public in advance or revealing the contents of supposedly secret negotiations as they are proceeding.
19. Cited in Roberti (*op. cit.*) p. 137.
20. In a feature article in the *South China Morning Post* of 8 March 1987, Ann Quon refers to 'The Group of 71'. Roberti, rather confusingly, refers to 'The Group of 89'.
21. Scott (*op. cit.*) p. 282.
22. Deng Xiaoping, 'Speech at a meeting with the members of the committee for drafting the Basic Law of the Hong Kong Special Administrative

Region', April 1987. In *Selected Works of Deng Xiaoping* (vol. 3, Beijing: Foreign Languages Press) pp. 214-220, pp. 218-9.

23. The Committee contained about 190 organizations, including groups representing religious interests, students, teachers and civil servants, as well as strictly political groups.
24. *South China Morning Post*, 3 November 1986.
25. Peter Hennessy, 'Cradock's People', *New Society*, 11 October 1984.
26. Roberti (*op. cit.*) pp. 184–5.
27. *Ibid.*, p. 186,
28. The following account is based on Roberti (*op. cit.*).
29. *Ibid.*, p. 220.
30. Albert H.Y. Chen, *An Introduction to the Legal System of the People's Republic of China* (Singapore: Butterworths Asia, 1992) pp. 39–41.
31. This account of events is based on Roberti (*op. cit.*) pp. 202–10.
32. Cited in Roberti (*op. cit.*) pp. 232–4.

CHAPTER 5

1. *South China Morning Post*, 16 April 1989.
2. The May Fourth Movement was a student-initiated grouping which sprang up in protest at the 1919 Versailles peace conference decision to confirm Japanese rights over the Shandong peninsula. It led to an intellectual revolution, the New Culture Movement, which eventually, in turn, led to the creation of the Chinese Communist Party.
3. Szeto and Lee were later voted off the Committee, anyway, by the NPC, for their behaviour over Tiananmen.
4. *Xinhua*, 9 July 1989.
5. *People's Daily*, 21 July 1989.
6. The Bill of Rights would make Hong Kong a signatory of the International Agreement on Civil and Political Rights. Hong Kong's laws would therefore have to comply with the International Agreement. China, however, is not a signatory, casting doubt on the validity of the Bill after 1997.
7. United Kingdom, House of Commons Hansard. Debates: 'China and Hong Kong', 13 July 1989.
8. United Kingdom, House of Commons Hansard. Debates: 'Hong Kong', 20 December 1989.
9. Frank Welsh, *A History of Hong Kong* (London: HarperCollins, 1994) p. 181.
10. *People's Daily*, 1 September and 21 November 1989; cited in Welsh (*op. cit.*) p. 181.
11. Evidence of these diplomatic negotiations came to light in 1993, when Britain and China made public an exchange of seven letters from January and February 1990 between the two Foreign Ministers. In one of the letters, Douglas Hurd, for the British, confirmed the agreement for two extra seats by 1997. He stated that: 'If the final version of the Basic Law provides for 20 directly elected seats in the SAR legislature in

Notes

1997, 24 in 1999, and 30 in 2003, the British Government would be
prepared to limit to 18 the number of directly elected seats to be
introduced in 1991.' Hurd's confirmation was cited in a signed article
by Zhou Nan, Head of Xinhua in Hong Kong, in the *South China
Morning Post* of 11 April 1993. See Chapter 7, for further discussion.
12. Cited in Brian Hook, 'Political change in Hong Kong' in David Shambaugh (ed.) *'Greater China: The Next Superpower?'* (Oxford: Oxford
University Press, 1995) p. 196.
13. 'Learning to live with China' p. 183, in *Hong Kong Remembers* by Sally
Blyth and Ian Wotherspoon (eds.) (Hong Kong: Oxford University
Press, 1996) pp. 175–184.
14. *South China Morning Post*, 28 April 1990.
15. *South China Morning Post*, 14 September 1990.
16. *South China Morning Post*, 21 September 1990.
17. *South China Morning Post*, 4 December 1991.
18. Figures provided by the Headquarters of the Electoral Office, 29 January 1997.
19. Hong Kong 1991 Population Census: Summary Results (Census and
Statistics Department, Hong Kong Government Printer) p. 40.
20. Reported in Lau Siu-kai, *Society and Politics in Hong Kong* (Hong
Kong: Chinese University Press, 1987). Also referred to by Hook (*op.
cit.*) pp. 191–2.
21. As Anna Wu notes, the group was monitored by a high-level, secret
government committee, with members from the Special Branch and the
British Military Representative in Hong Kong. In 'Government by
whom?' by Blyth and Wotherspoon (*op. cit.*) pp. 158–66, 162.
22. *Ibid.*, pp. 160–1.
23. Hook (*op. cit.*) p. 191.
24. In spite of this Chinese representation, it should be noted that the top
Government officials were all British. As late as 1990, Welsh (*op. cit.*)
reports that all the most senior posts – Governor, Chief Secretary,
Financial Secretary, Attorney-General, and Commander British Forces,
all the ex-officio members of the Exco, and 40 per cent of the 1220
directorate officers – were still held by expatriates. By 1996, however,
the only remaining expatriate senior official was the Attorney General.
25. *Ibid.*, p. 191.
26. *Hong Kong 1996* (Hong Kong Government Printer, 1996) pp. 396–7.
27. *Ibid.*, p. 396. These figures are probably on the low side, as many people
leave without notifying the authorities they are emigrating. In addition,
those going abroad to study who do not return are not included.
28. Norman J. Miners, *The Government and Politics of Hong Kong* (Hong
Kong: Oxford University Press, 5th ed., 1991) p. 24.
29. Both Wilson and his mentor, Percy Cradock, have tried to refute this
view. Referring to the popular belief that Wilson was replaced because
John Major was angry at being compelled to make the visit to Beijing,
Cradock says that: 'Travelling with him [Major], I saw no evidence of
this' (Cradock, *op. cit.*, p. 243.). Wilson has written: 'In no way do I
believe that the decision [to replace me] was connected simply to the
airport.' (Wilson, *op. cit.*, p. 183). Neither of these statements, however,

negates the possibility that Wilson was replaced, at least partly, for his handling of the airport issue.

30. China wanted Lee and Szeto excluded because of their participation in the Alliance in Support of the Patriotic Democratic Movement in China, a group they held to be subversive. In 1991, Wilson, for the first time, appointed four Legislative Councillors to the Executive Council. However, only one of them, Andrew Wong, was directly elected and he was not a member of the most popular party, the United Democrats. He was not even the more popular of the two Legislative Councillors in his constituency. This was Emily Lau, an outspoken liberal.

31. The government claimed the corporatization plan was dropped because Radio Television Hong Kong (RTHK) had increased its efficiency to such an extent that it was no longer necessary.

32. Agence France-Presse, 1 July 1992.

33. Percy Cradock also retired at about this time.

## CHAPTER 6

1. The title for this chapter is borrowed from a section heading of an article by Brian Hook, 'Political Change in Hong Kong' in David Shambaugh, (ed.) *Greater China: The Next Superpower?* (Oxford: Oxford University Press, 1995) pp. 188–211, 202. It seems to capture the dramatic nature of Patten's arrival in Hong Kong.

2. Margaret Thatcher, *The Downing Street Years* (HarperCollins, 1995) p. 853.

3. Alan Clark, in his notorious *Diaries* (Phoenix, 1994), reports Thatcher as claiming that, 'Patten had plotted the whole thing.' (London: Weidenfield and Nicolson, 1st ed., 1993) p. 384. In her memoirs, Thatcher (*op. cit.*) p. 853, merely reports that Patten told her that he would support her in a second round of leadership elections, but that she would not be able to win. See Alan Watkins, *A Conservative Coup: The Fall of Margaret Thatcher* (London: Duckworth, 1991) for a detailed account.

4. Thatcher (*op. cit.*) p. 853. Patten worked on these speeches from 1975–9 and from 1985–9, with a playwright called Ronnie Miller. Patten described the job as 'an onerous task' and Thatcher as 'a very tough task mistress' (interview with the author, Government House, 16 September 1996). The political commentator, John Cole, refers to Patten as 'one of the sharpest pens in the Conservative Party.' (*As It Seemed to Me: Political Memoirs*, revised and updated edition, Pheonix Books, 1996. First published by Weidenfield and Nicolson in 1995, p. 322.

5. Kevin Sinclair in *South China Morning Post*, 3 October 1992.

6. Bruce Anderson, *John Major: The Making of the Prime Minister* (London: Fourth Estate, 1991).

7. *Sunday Morning Post*, 21 May 1992.

8. Alan Clark (*op. cit.*) p. 120.

9.  *Ibid.*, p. 397.
10. *South China Morning Post*, 7 March 1993. See also the leading article of *The Times*, 9 March 1996. Major stated as follows: 'I believe British politics would be the stronger and more effective if Chris Patten were to come back and take his proper place in it and I personally hope that he will. He is a man of outstanding ability. When the time comes for me to step down, there are a number of colleagues with outstanding ability who would have a legitimate claim to be leader of the Conservative Party and Prime Minister. Were Chris Patten back he would certainly be among that number.'
11. *South China Morning Post*, 3 October 1992.
12. See Patten's review of the biography of MacLeod, 'Playing to Win', in *The Times Literary Supplement*, 9 December 1994, for an account of Patten's admiration for MacLeod.
13. Lawrence James, *The Rise and Fall of the British Empire* (London: Little, Brown and Company, 1994) p. 614.
14. Interview with the author, Government House, 16 September 1996. Patten did, however, qualify this statement, by saying that he was not conscious of the historical dimension 'every time I put pen to the paper or I open my mouth.'
15. *Hong Kong Standard*, 5 July 1992.
16. *South China Morning Post*, 10 July 1992.
17. *Hong Kong Standard*, 10 July 1992.
18. *Ming Pao*, 10 July 1996. Patten's Chinese name is pronounced 'Pang Ding Hong'.
19. S. K. Tsang, 'Income distribution' in P. K. Choi and L. S. Ho (eds.) *The Other Hong Kong Report 1993* (Hong Kong: Chinese University Press, 1994) pp. 361–8.
20. In later statements, addressed to a British audience, Patten was to emphasis the momentousness of the transition in terms of a fitting ending to Britain's long history of empire. Such a formulation was not appropriate of course in the context of Patten's maiden speech addressed to the people of Hong Kong.
21. As noted in Chapter 3, during the negotiations leading up to the Joint Declaration this tri-partite relationship was referred to by Lord Belstead, the British Minister of State with Responsibility for Hong Kong, as a 'three-legged stool'. Britain always emphasised that the views of Hong Kong should be paramount in any negotiations over Hong Kong's future and that each of the three parties should be represented. China, however, always rejected the 'three-legged stool' formulation, on the grounds that Hong Kong is a part of its territory and so could not be put on the same level as the two sovereign powers. See James T. H. Tang and Frank Ching, ' The MacLehose–Youde Years: Balancing the "Three-legged Stool" ', 1971–86' in Ming K. Chan (ed.) *Precarious Balance: Hong Kong Between China and Britain 1842–1992* (New York: M. E. Sharpe, 1994) pp. 149–71.
22. About 8 per cent of Hong Kong citizens are Christians.
23. The two daughters, Laura and Alice, excited a lot of press interest, especially the elder one, Laura, who was dressed in a mini skirt. This

daughter did not stay in the territory for long, soon returning to Britain for study.

24. Most notably Max Atkinson, in *Our Masters' Voices*, (Harmondsworth: Penguin, 1984).
25. Most of Patten's audience, as Hong Kong Chinese, it needs to be borne in mind, would not have been native-speakers of English. However, see the comments on this in the Introduction.
26. The 'I have a dream' speech of Martin Luther King is a very good example of the use of parallelism. See Deborah Tannen *Talking Voices: Repetition, Dialogue, and Imagery in Conversational Discourse* (Cambridge: Cambridge University Press, 1989), for an analysis of this speech.
27. Robert Cockroft and Susan Cockroft, *Persuading People: An Introduction to Rhetoric* (Basingstoke: Macmillan, 1992).
28. *South China Morning Post*, 11 July 1992.
29. *Ibid.*
30. *Wen Wei Po*, 11 July 1992.
31. *South China Morning Post*, 9 July 1992.
32. *Hong Kong Standard*, 11 July 1992.
33. *Hong Kong Standard*, 14 September 1992.
34. *South China Morning Post*, 15 September 1992.
35. *South China Morning Post*, 9 August 1992.
36. Regular polls, conducted weekly by the Social Sciences Research Center (SSRC) of the University of Hong Kong, show that Patten's popularity consistently increased from the day of the announcement of his appointment right up to the day of his policy speech. His popularity fluctuated at that level for five weeks, before plunging to a record low in mid-December, following severe attacks by China. Robert Chung, the research officer of the SSRC, attributes Patten's early popularity to 'the tremendous effort he [Patten] spent in meeting the media and the public'. See Robert T. Y. Chung 'Public Opinion' in L. W. Poon (ed.), *The Other Hong Kong Report: 1993* (Hong Kong: Chinese University Press, 1993) pp. 401–232 p. 408.
37. *South China Morning Post*, 28 July 1992.
38. Irene Yau, Director of Information Services, was an exception.
39. Interview with the author, Government House, 16 September 1996. The interview question and answer were as follows:

> Author: 'You mentioned yourself earlier the difficulty of addressing an audience which is from a different culture and language from your own. Do you have people to advise you on these issues?'
> Patten: 'I could get advice on these issues. How useful it would be and how much that would certainly affect what I say is another matter.'

40. *Hong Kong Standard*, 29 September 1992.
41. The United Democrats of Hong Kong (UDHK), under their leader, Martin Lee, did not accept the Basic Law, as they felt it compromised some of the democratic provisions in the Joint Declaration.
42. *Bauhinia*, 3 August 1992.
43. *Far Eastern Economic Review*, 19 September 1992.

44. *Hong Kong Standard*, 4 October 1992.
45. *South China Morning Post*, 12 July 1992.
46. *South China Morning Post*, 23 September 1992.
47. *New Evening News*, 23 September 1992.
48. *Ta Kung Pao*, 23 September 1992.
49. *Bauhinia*, 29 September 1992.
50. *Hong Kong Standard*, 29 September 1992.
51. *Far Eastern Economic Review*, 10 September 1992.
52. *Sunday Hong Kong Standard*, 13 September 1992.
53. *Hong Kong Standard*, 6 October 1992.
54. *Hong Kong Standard*, 7 October 1992.
55. *South China Morning Post*, 3 October 1992.
56. *Hong Kong Standard*, 24 September 1992.
57. *Hong Kong Standard*, 24 September 1992.

## CHAPTER 7

1.  *Hong Kong Standard*, 8 October 1992.
2.  The farewell visit by Cradock followed in the footsteps of that of Wilson, suggesting it was a tactic by the Chinese side to create 'old friends of China' who they might later call upon to intercede on their behalf. Martin Lee, the pro-democracy activist, refers scathingly to Cradock's visit, quoting the British diplomat as saying to him that the purpose of the trip was, 'to say good-bye to his Chinese friends'. Martin Lee' 'The Fight for Democracy'. In *Hong Kong Remembers* by Sally Blyth and Ian Wotherspoon (eds.) (Hong Kong: Oxford University Press, 1996) pp. 233–43, 238.
3.  This idea seems to be based on the British Prime Minister, John Major's, 'citizen's charter'.
4.  Patten revealed that the British Foreign Minister, Douglas Hurd, in his meeting with his Chinese counterpart, Qian Qichen, had tried to have the Chinese agree to an increase in the number of directly elected seats, but without success, the Chinese arguing that they should stand by what was already in the Basic Law.
5.  Opinion survey conducted by Robert Chung of the Social Sciences Research Centre, University of Hong Kong.
6.  *Hong Kong Standard*, 8 October 1992.
7.  *Ming Pao*, 8 July 1992.
8.  *Hong Kong Standard*, 9 October 1992.
9.  *Hong Kong Standard*, 24 October 1992.
10. *Ibid.*
11. *Ibid.*
12. *South China Morning Post*, 8 October 1992.
13. *Wen Wei Po*, 8 October 1992.
14. *Hong Kong Standard*, 8 October 1992. The paradoxical nature of this statement is explained by the concern on the part of the Chinese that the British would drain Hong Kong's financial reserves before the handover.

15. *Sing Tao Jih Pao*, October 8 1992.
16. *South China Morning Post*, 13 October 1992.
17. For example, Emily Lau, in a BBC 'Any Questions' radio programme broadcast from the governor's residence in Hong Kong (Hong Kong Government, 1995).
18. In the above statement, of course, there is an irony that Patten would not have wanted to be picked up on by his audience. The 'free and open meetings like these' were, of course, only occurring for the first time. During 150 years of colonial rule no British Governor had ever deigned to organise one before. This question of Patten's ability to conveniently gloss over the reality of British colonial history in Hong Kong is a theme which will be returned to, especially in Chapter 11.
19. Eric Hobsbawm, 'Introduction: Inventing Traditions', in Eric Hobsbawm and Terence Ranger (eds) *The Invention of Tradition* (Cambridge: Cambridge University Press, 1983) pp. 1–14.
20. Patten was one of the very few people involved in dealings with China to refer to the Chinese capital as Peking, in preference to the official name Beijing, adopted by the PRC. It is a further sign of his refusal to accommodate to China.
21. Interview with the author, Government House, 16 September 1996. Patten's admission came as part of a characteristically humorous exchange:
    The Author: Can you think of any situations where cultural issues have led to misunderstandings, either in Hong Kong or with the Chinese Government, for example?
    Patten: I am told that irony can sound like sarcasm and that humour is open to misunderstanding but when you've been called a whore and a serpent, you start to scratch your head about what precisely the subtleties are that you haven't quite managed to learn about. ('Whore' and 'serpent' were epithets which were used to refer to Patten, in the months following the 1992 policy speech.)
22. The level at which foreign representatives are received depends first on the level of the visitor himself or herself. But it also depends on how successful China considers the visit to have been. If the visitor is co-operative, and amenable to China's point of view, then a higher level audience will be arranged. If the visitor is not co-operative, then s/he will not progress very high up the hierarchy.
23. The following account of the meeting is based on Crothall's article, 'The Wall Patten could not Climb', *South China Morning Post*, 24 October 1992.
24. See for example, 'The Fight for Democracy' by Martin Lee in Sally Blyth and Ian Wotherspoon (eds.) (*op. cit.*) pp. 233–43.
25. The contrasting approaches of Cradock and Patten led to bitter exchanges through the columns of the press. For Cradock's position, see, for example, his article in the *South China Morning Post* of 30 September 1996. In response, see the letter from the governor's information co-ordinator, Kerry McGlynn, in the 1 October edition of the same newspaper.
26. Intellectuals and teachers were labelled by Mao Zedong as the 'stinking ninth category'. Ironically, of the nine new functional constituencies

created by Patten's reforms, the ninth included teachers and intellectuals.

27. Reported in *Hong Kong Standard*, 18 October 1992.
28. Brian Hook 'Political Change in Hong Kong' in David Shambaugh (ed.), *Greater China: The Next Superpower?* (Oxford: Oxford University Press, 1995) pp. 188–11.
29. *South China Morning Post*, 13 October 1992.
30. *South China Morning Post*, 25 October 1992.
31. Interesting in this intervention, also, is Patten's indirect refutation of Lau's use of the word 'colony', by using, as his last words, the phrase 'dependent territory', the term preferred by the British Government to refer to Hong Kong.
32. *Far Eastern Economic Review*, 12 November 1992.
33. *Far Eastern Economic Review*, 12 November 1992.
34. *Far Eastern Economic Review*, 26 November 1992.
35. Sum, Ngai-Ling, 'More than a "War of Words": Identity, Politics and the Struggle for Dominance During the Recent "Political Reform" Period in Hong Kong', *Economy and Society* (vol. 24, no. 1, 1995) pp. 67–100.
36. Hook (*op. cit.*) p. 191.
37. As it was, Patten still came under a lot of pressure from the UDHK (later Democratic Party) for denying them a place on the Exco.
38. *Far Eastern Economic Review*, 26 January 1992.
39. Most Favoured Trading status is something of a misnomer. MFN simply means that a country will not be subject to any special tariffs. It is, in fact, the norm, not the exception.
40. *Far Eastern Economic Review*, 3 December, 1992.
41. See for example, Hook (*op. cit.*).
42. Interviewed in the *Sunday Morning Post* , 23 January 1994.
43. Hook (*op. cit.*) pp. 203–4.
44. Ron Scollon and Suzanne Scollon, 'Face in Interethnic Communication', in Jack C. Richards and Richard W. Schmidt (eds) *Language and Communication* (London: Longman, 1983) pp. 156–88.
45. Interview with the author, Government House, 16 September 1996.
46. Public Opinion Programme of Social Science Research Centre, University of Hong Kong. Cited in Hook (*op. cit.*) p. 208.
47. *Sunday Morning Post*, 1 November 1992.

CHAPTER 8

1. *South China Morning Post*, 28 November 1992.
2. *South China Morning Post,* 10 December 1992.
3. *South China Morning Post*, 17 November 1992.
4. *South China Morning Post*, 17 March 1993.
5. On 13 April 1993, on the other hand, when Sino-British discussions were announced, it recorded a record one-day rise of 371 points. *Monthly Market Statistics, Stock Exchange of Hong Kong*, December 1991.

6.  *South China Morning Post*, 19 March 1993.
7.  This list of epithets was recited to the author in an interview with Patten's information co-ordinator, Kerry McGlynn, 25 January, 1996.
8.  *Wen Wei Po*, 1 April 1993.
9.  *Wen Wei Po*, 2 April 1993.
10. *Hong Kong Standard*, 20 March 1993.
11. *Hong Kong Standard*, 8 April 1993.
12. *Wen Wei Po*, 23 April 1993.
13. *The Times*, 1 December 1992; BBC Television, 3 December 1992.
14. *South China Morning Post*, 10 January 1993.
15. *South China Morning Post*, 31 January 1993.
16. *South China Morning Post*, 19 March 1993.
17. Mark Roberti, *The Fall of Hong Kong: China's Triumph and Britain's Betrayal* (John Wiley and Sons, 1994).
18. *South China Morning Post*, 13 March 1993.
19. In a reiteration of China's policy on sovereignty, on 1 February, Zhang Junsheng refuted a statement by British Foreign Minister, Douglas Hurd, that Hong Kong people had to be involved in discussions on their future. This view was reiterated by Zhang, on 26 February, when he said that, as mere advisory bodies to the Hong Kong Governor, neither Exco nor Legco had any right to a say in the electoral arrangements for 1995.
20. *South China Morning Post*, 2 March 1993.
21. Geoffrey Howe on numerous occasions referred to the predatory nature of the Hong Kong press corps.
22. *Hong Kong Standard*, 12 October 1993.
23. See *South China Morning Post*, 15 February 1994, for the text of the British White Paper. The Chinese account was disseminated by Xinhua, 28 February 1994.
24. Although they proposed that whereas the Basic Law provides for a Committee of 800 members for election of the Chief Executive (see Annex 1), this should be reduced to 600 for the Election Committee for legislators.
25. Legco Question Time session, 2 December 1993.
26. Interview in the *Sunday Morning Post*, 29 February 1993.
27. The *Guardian*, 18 January 1994.
28. The most easily accessible statements on this are in the 1993, 1994, and 1995 annual policy addresses.
29. Lo Shui Hing, 'An analysis of Sino-British Negotiations over Hong Kong's Political Reform', *Contemporary Southeast Asia* (vol. 16, no. 2, 1994) pp. 178–209.
30. Interview with the author, Government House, 16 September 1996.
31. United Kingdom, House of Commons Hansard. Debates: Hong Kong, volume 164, 20 December 1989.
32. *South China Morning Post*, 7 March 1996.
33. *Far Eastern Economic Review*, 1 April 1993.
34. *Hong Kong Standard*, 21 January 1994.
35. When asked whether this was a view shared by Whitehall, however, his answer was: 'No, no.' Asked to elaborate, indicative of the difference of

opinion between Foreign Office officials and Patten, he said that Whitehall did not see beyond 30 June 1997.

36. *Hong Kong Standard*, 22 January 1994.
37. *Newsline*, Asian Television (ATV) World, 10 October 1993.
38. Reprinted in *South China Morning Post*, 14 January 1994.
39. 'Speech at a meeting with the members of the committee for drafting the
Basic Law of the Hong Kong Special Administrative Region, April 16
1987,' In *Selected Works of Deng Xiaoping: Volume III (1982-1992)*
(Beijing: Foreign Languages Press, 1993) pp. 215–23 p. 219.
40. Interview with the author, Government House, 16 September 1996.
41. Geoffrey Howe, *Conflict of Loyalty* (London, Macmillan, 1994), p.379.
42. Percy Cradock, *Experiences of China* (London, John Murray, 1994) p.
277
43. Interview Radio Television Hong Kong (RTHK), Radio Channel 3, 8
July 1995.
44. *South China Morning Post*, 23 June 1993.
45. As a precursor to the creation of the Liberal Party, members of the pro-
business lobby in Legco had met in a loose alliance called the Co-
operative Resources Centre.
46. Their influence was also reduced by Patten's decision to separate Legco
and Exco. Until then, four of those Legco members who were to
become leading figures in the Liberal party were also members of Exco.
47. Brian Hook, 'Political change in Hong Kong', in David Shambaugh
(ed.) *Greater China: The Next Superpower?* (Oxford: Oxford University
Press, 1995) pp. 188–211.
48. See Chapter 4.
49. *Hong Kong Standard*, 4 December 1993.
50. *Hong Kong Standard*, 10 December 1993.
51. *South China Morning Post*, 12 December 1993.
52. *Hong Kong Standard* 20 December 1993,
53. *South China Morning Post*, 28 December 1993.
54. Hook (*op. cit.*) p. 207.
55. *South China Morning Post*, 5 March 1994.
56. *People's Daily*, referred to in *Eastern Express*, 31 May 1995.
57. *Hong Kong Standard*, 23 August 1994.
58. Until this time, notes had been issued by the two British-controlled
banks, Hong Kong and Shanghai Bank and Standard Chartered
Bank. With the approach of the handover, it had been decided that
it would be appropriate for a Chinese-controlled bank to also issue
notes.
59. *South China Morning Post*, 31 December 1993.
60. *Hong Kong Standard*, 30 December 1993.
61. Interview, 25 January 1996.
62. Examples of parallelism and antithesis (which work together) are as
follows:
the rulers / the ruled
a high privilege of democracy / a heavy responsibility
I say all this... / I say it as well
I... love Hong Kong / you... love Hong Kong

I want.../ you want
a blazing beacon of good fortune / a dazzling example of what free men
and women . can together achieve
That is what we want.../ that is what we can achieve
the courage that has brought success in the past.../ the confidence that
success has earned
I believe / you believe
The following are examples of metaphor:
The democratic ideal is 'enshrined' in the Joint Declaration.
Hong Kong was 'created' from rock and scrub.
Hong Kong will 'enter' the next millennium.
Hong Kong will be 'a blazing beacon of good fortune'.
Hong Kong will be a 'dazzling' example of what free men and women
can achieve.
The community is 'bound' by common values.
Courage can 'bring' success.
Confidence can be 'earned' through success.

Notable also, in this extract, is how Patten integrates himself into Hong
Kong society, by the repeated use of inclusive 'we'. Finally, the extract
is notable for the extreme deference and praise for the achievements of
the people of Hong Kong, a strategy already noted in his maiden
speech, in Chapter 6.
63.   Interview, 25 January 1996.


## CHAPTER 9

1.   *Hong Kong Standard*, 30 June 1994.
2.   The exact figures were: 15 per cent were interested, 69 per cent were not
      interested and 16 per cent were not sure. *South China Morning Post*, 26
      June 1994.
3.   *Eastern Express*, 22 April 1994
4.   *Hong Kong Standard*, 3 June 1994.
5.   *Hong Kong Standard*, 18 September 1994.
6.   *Hong Kong Standard*, 18 September 1994.
7.   The exact figures were: 52 per cent felt Patten no longer had a useful
      role to play in Hong Kong, 32 per cent disagreed and 16 per cent were
      undecided. *South China Morning Post*, 26 June 1994.
8.   *South China Morning Post*, 23 September 1992.
9.   S. K. Tsang, 'The Economy', in D. H. MacMillen and S.W. Man (eds.)
      *The Other Hong Kong Report 1994* (Hong Kong: Chinese University of
      Hong Kong Press, 1994) pp. 125–48.
10.  *South China Morning Post*, 30 November 1995. An unnamed Hong
      Kong Government official pointed out the absurdity of being
      denounced by communists for socialism. However Article 5 of the Basic
      Law demonstrates the rationale of China's stance, with its statement
      that: 'The socialist system and policies shall not be practised in the

Hong Kong SAR, and the previous capitalist system and way of life shall remain unchanged for 50 years.'

11. Cited in 'Hong Kong Review 1995', *South China Morning Post*, 15 January 1996. pp. 26–7.

12. *Forbes* magazine, July 1996.

13. Much of this paragraph draws on Hung Wing-tat, 'The Environment', in S. Y. L. Cheng and S. M. H. Sze *The Other Hong Kong Report 1995* (Hong Kong: Chinese University of Hong Kong Press) pp. 343–59.

14. James Rice, 'Human rights' in *The Other Hong Kong Report: 1995* (Hong Kong: Chinese University of Hong Kong Press, 1995) pp. 103–20.

15. *Eastern Express*, 28–9 January 1995.

16. *South China Morning Post*, 26 May 1995.

17. *South China Morning Post*, 29 May 1995.

18. Interview, Radio Television Hong Kong (RTHK) Channel 3, 8 July 1985.

19. Patten described this situation, in his 1994 policy speech, as follows: 'Hong Kong has been provided by history, design and chance [he did not mention the various British colonial governments which most would have pointed to as the responsible party] with a constitution which, without good-will and common-sense on all sides, could be a recipe for political and administrative gridlock. Where else in the world is there a permanent government which does not have a party in the legislature to push through its policy proposals?'

20. *The Times*, 10 June 1996.

21. RTHK Channel 3, 8 July 1995.

22. *South China Morning Post*, 23 March, 1996.

23. *South China Morning Post*, 27 March 1996.

24. Interview with the author, Government House, 16 September 1996.

25. *South China Morning Post*, 8 September 1994.

26. *Hong Kong Standard*, 28 October 1995.

27. *Eastern Express*, 30 October 1995.

28. *Hong Kong Standard*, 15 November 1995.

29. *South China Morning Post*, 29 January 1995.

30. *South China Morning Post*, 25 May 1995.

31. Frank Ching in *Far Eastern Economic Review*, 8 December 1994.

32. She was later to be appointed President of the Provisional Legislature.

33. *South China Morning Post*, 11 April 1994.

34. Later to be appointed as the first Senior Member of the Executive Council of the SAR, under Chief Executive Tung Chee-hwa.

35. *South China Morning Post*, 7 December 1994.

36. *Eastern Express*, 18 September 1995.

37. *South China Morning Post*, 7 September 1994. Tsang had subsequently withdrawn his application, but his wife and children had gone ahead with theirs and were already settled in Canada, making it very easy for Tsang to do likewise, if things went wrong in Hong Kong.

38. In December, Patten's threat was to be carried out and the true meaning of 'executive-led' government became apparent. The government

blocked an amended bill on labour benefits by the simple expedient of withdrawing it once it became clear that it would likely not be approved without amendment. This occurrence led to the resignation from the Legco of the legislator responsible for the amendment, Lau Chin-shek, in a move calculated to embarrass the government.
39. *Eastern Express*, 13 October 1995.
40. 26 October 1996, Legislative Council.

## CHAPTER 10

1. *Eastern Express*, 23 January 1994.
2. *Hong Kong Standard*, 5 October, 1995.
3. *Eastern Express*, 4 January 1996.
4. An 'appraisal' in Chinese Communist Party parlance is the political obituary issued on politicians. It may be written and then rewritten by subsequent generations of leaders, as attitudes change. In recent years, for example, there has been a gradual reassessment of Mao and the cultural revolution. Similarly, the Tiananmen crackdown and Deng's role in it is also in the melting pot.
5. *Wen Wei Po*, 3 January 1996.
6. *South China Morning Post*, 5 January 1996.
7. *South China Morning Post*, 23 December 1995.
8. *Eastern Express*, 4 January 1996.
9. *Financial Times*, 12 June 1996.
10. *Hong Kong Standard*, 11 January 1996.
11. *Mirror*, May 1996.
12. *Hong Kong Standard*, 6 June 1996.
13. *South China Morning Post*, 8 January 1996.
14. *Wen Wei Po*, 15 January 1996.
15. *Sunday Morning Post*, 3 March 1996.
16. *Sunday Morning Post* 8 October 1995.
17. *South China Morning Post*, 1 March 1996.
18. *South China Morning Post*, 30 April 1996.
19. *South China Morning Post*, 4 March 1996.
20. *Eastern Express*, 18 January 1995.
21. *South China Morning Post*, 26 September 1995.
22. See e.g. the editorial in *The Times* of 23 January 1994.
23. *South China Morning Post*, 29 November 1995.
24. *South China Morning Post*, 2 December 1995.
25. *South China Morning Post*, 29 October 1995.
26. *Eastern Express*, 26 December 1995.
27. *South China Morning Post*, 20 March 1996.
28. *Ibid.*
29. *Hong Kong Standard*, 8 May 1996.
30. *Hong Kong Standard*, 13 June 1996.
31. *South China Morning Post*, 13 June 1996.
32. *Hong Kong Standard*, 13 June 1996.

33. These Beijing-backed newspapers had been the most outspoken in calling for ('advocating') Patten's replacement.
34. *South China Morning Post*, 19 October 1996.
35. 'Speech at a meeting with the members of the Committee for Drafting the Basic Law of the Hong Kong Special Administrative Region, 16 April 1987.' In *Selected Works of Deng Xiaoping , Volume 111* (Beijing: Foreign Languages Press, 1994) vol. 111, pp. 214–20. Deng distinguished between 'words' and 'action', as opposed to 'words' and 'advocacy'. He stated as follows: '... after 1997 we shall still allow people in Hong Kong to attack the Chinese Communist Party and China verbally, but what if they should turn their words into action, trying to convert Hong Kong into a base of opposition to the mainland under the pretext of "democracy"?'
36. *South China Morning Post*, 17 October 1996.
37. *Newsweek*, May 13 1996.
38. *South China Morning Post*, 21 May 1996.
39. *South China Morning Post*, 24 May 1996.
40. *Far Eastern Economic Review*, 6 June 1996.
41. They had, in fact, already said that they would have nothing to do with the provisional body.
42. *South China Morning Post*, 25 March 1996.
43. *South China Morning Post*, 26 March 1996.
44. *Hong Kong Standard*, 17 March 1996.
45. During one Governor's Question Time session in the Legco, which the author attended, a group of some 20 old people made a similar display, demanding the introduction of an old age pension scheme. A similar protest occurred during one of Patten's question time sessions with the general public. On this occasion, when the protesters stood up and uncovered their political message, Patten merely responded, 'I was waiting for that.' ('Question Time with the Governor', public forum held at the Hong Kong Convention and Exhibition Centre, 4 October 1996. Transcript from Information Services Department).
46. Mark Roberti, *The Fall of Hong Kong: China's Triumph and Britain's Betrayal* (New York, John Wiley and Sons, 1994) p. 137.
47. *South China Morning Post*, 7 December 1995.
48. *South China Morning Post*, 16 September 1996.
49. *South China Morning Post*, 25 September 1996.
50. Li also attracted little public support and was defeated in the first round of balloting.
51. A cartoon in the *South China Morning Post* on the same day depicted the candidates as school boys receiving their school reports, with Lu Ping portrayed in the background, as the headmaster. Tung is being told by one of his classmates: 'Never mind about the marks, it's what the headmaster thinks that's important.'
52. *Hong Kong Standard*, 16 November 1996.
53. *South China Morning Post*, 19 December 1996.
54. *Far Eastern Economic Review*, 26 December 1996.
55. See *Time*, 11 November 1996 for a profile of Tung and his background.

56. It has been speculated that Tung, who was simultaneously appointed to Patten's Executive Council and as one of China's 'advisers', was all along viewed as a possible first Chief Executive by Britain and China and was being groomed for this future role (*Far Eastern Economic Review*, 19 December 1996). This would explain his apparent contradictions on Patten's reforms and the provisional legislature. In addition, as a member of both Britain's and China's advisory bodies he would have been in a position to act as a go-between for the two governments.
57. See Tung Chee-hwa, *Building a 21st Century together: Election Manifesto*, 22 October, 1996, p. 10.
58. See e.g. 'The Pearl Report', Television Broadcasting (TVB), Pearl Channel, 4 November 1996.
59. *South China Morning Post*, 28 October 1996. In spite of this statement, however, Tung nevertheless accepted the PWC proposal to reinstate certain restrictions on the right to demonstrate which had been done away with by Patten's government.
60. *South China Morning Post*, 24 December 1996.
61. The Democratic Party had no candidates, as they regarded the provisional body as illegal.
62. *Hong Kong Standard*, 22 December 1996.
63. *Ibid.*
64. Press conference following the 1996 Policy Speech, 2 October 1996.
65. The international court will only deal with a case if both parties agree to participate.
66. *South China Morning Post*, 21 December 1996.
67. *South China Morning Post*, 18 December 1996.
68. *South China Morning Post*, 24 December 1996.
69. Special supplement, *Hong Kong Standard*, 3 October 1996, p. 1.

CHAPTER 11

1. Kenneth Hudson, *The Language of Modern Politics* (London: Macmillan, 1978) p. 13.
2. Gunther R. Kress, 'Ideological Structures in Discourse', in Van Dijk (ed.), *Handbook of Discourse Analysis, vol. 4: Discourse Analysis in Society*, 1985, pp. 27–42; Norman Fairclough, *Language and Power* (London: Longman, 1989).
3. Kress (*op. cit.*).
4. Fairclough (*op. cit.*) p. 185.
5. Confirmed by Patten in interview with the author, Government House, 16 September 1996.
6. Gunther R. Kress, *Linguistic Processes in Sociocultural Practice* (Oxford: Oxford University Press, 2nd ed., 1989) p. 7.
7. Hong Kong Government, 1991, cited in Lo, forthcoming.
8. Reported in *Eastern Express*, 26 December 1995.

9. Percy Cradock, *Experiences of China* (London: John Murray, 1994) p. 209.
10. *South China Morning Post*, 15 November 1993.
11. M. H. Bond, (ed.) *The Psychology of the Chinese People* (Hong Kong: Oxford University Press, 1986); M. H. Bond, *Beyond the Chinese Face: Insights from Psychology* (Hong Kong: Oxford University Press, 1991); M. H. Bond, (1997) *Handbook of Chinese Psychology* (Hong Kong: Oxford University Press); Chao-chia Liu, *The Ethos of the Hong Kong Chinese* (Hong Kong: Chinese University of Hong Kong, 1988).
12. Kress (*op. cit.*) p. 7.
13. Tsang, *The Other Hong Kong Report* (Hong Kong: Chinese University of Hong Kong, 1994).
14. See for example, Lunar New Year message, Radio Television Hong Kong, 30 January 1995.
15. *Sunday Times*, 3 July 1994.
16. BBC Television, 5 November 1995; *South China Morning Post*, 24 October 1995.
17. As Richard Margolis, assistant political adviser at the time of the Joint Declaration put it: 'Hong Kong enjoyed the fruits of democracy without cultivating the tree' (cited in Mark Roberti, *The Fall of Hong Kong: China's Triumph and Britain's Betrayal* (John Wiley and Sons, 1994) p. 139.
18. *South China Morning Post*, 20 April 1995.
19. Roland Barthes, *Mythologies* (Translated by A. Lavers) (London: Paladin, 1972) 1972 p. 129.
20. Barthes (*op. cit.*) p. 130.
21. Norman Fairclough, *Language and Power* (London: Longman, 1989); Norman Fairclough, *Discourse and Social Change* (Cambridge: Polity, 1992).
22. *The New Encyclopaedia Britannica*, 1991.
23. D. Rodrik, 'Getting Interventions Right: How South Korea and Taiwan Grew Rich', *Economic Policy*, 20, 1995, pp. 53–107.
24. *South China Morning Post, Markets Post*, 30 January 1997.
25. David Mole (ed.), *Managing the New Hong Kong Economy: Economy Policy Beyond Positive Non-Intervention* (Hong Kong: Oxford University Press, 1996).
26. Frank Welsh, *A History of Hong Kong* (London: HarperCollins, 1994).
27. Tsang (*op. cit.*).
28. Welsh (*op. cit.*) p. 532.
29. Anna Wu, Christine Lo, and Emily Lau are probably the best known, all elected or appointed by Patten as Legislative Councillors.
30. It was only in 1974 that Chinese (and Cantonese, the spoken variety of Chinese used in Hong Kong) was given any official status in Hong Kong, in spite of the fact that it was the language of over 90 per cent of the population.
31. C. M. Walker, *The Oxford Companion to Law* (Oxford: Oxford University Press, 1980) p. 1093.
32. *Hong Kong Standard*, 14 April 1994.

33. In the final months of the transitional period there have been moves to try to speed up the use of Chinese in courts, but at the time of writing most court cases are still conducted primarily in English.
34. Radio Television Hong Kong, Radio 3, 5 November 1995.
35. Michael Chugani, 'Truth seeping through Leung case cover-up', *Hong Kong Standard*, 20 January 1997.
36. *Sunday Morning Post*, 2 February 1997.
37. The Chinese interpretation of Hong Kong's history, of course, also has an important element of myth. See Ian Scott, 'Legitimacy and its Discontents: Hong Kong and the Reversion to Chinese Sovereignty', *Asian Journal of Political Science* (vol. 1, no. 1, 1993) for a critical appraisal of China's claims to Hong Kong). Another alternative discourse to that of Patten is that of the pro-democracy forces in Hong Kong, the largest grouping of which, the Democrats, has been most successful in winning the support of the Hong Kong public on the two occasions when direct elections to the Legislative Council have taken place. The pro-democracy forces criticise Patten for not doing enough in terms of electoral reform, individual freedom and help for the less-privileged, and the rule of law.
38. This view was stated by Patten, as follows: 'What makes Hong Kong special, what it is that has made Hong Kong such an astonishingly successful community, it's partly of course Shanghainese/Cantonese entrepreneurialism but it's also the rule of law and good clean honest government.' Interview, BBC Television, 28 November 1993.
39. *Hong Kong Standard*, 21 March 1995.
40. John Gastil, 'Undemocratic Discourse: A Review of Theory and Research on Political Discourse' *Discourse & Society* (vol. 3, no. 4, 1992) pp. 469–500.
41. The level of public support for Patten was measured during the whole period of his governorship, by the Hong Kong Social Science Research Centre of the University of Hong Kong, on a twice-monthly basis. Average ratings for each complete year of Patten's governorship show overall satisfaction with the governor's performance to have been as follows: 1992–3, 58.7 per cent; 1993–4, 50.4 per cent; 1994–5, 44.3 per cent; 1995–6, 44.8 per cent. During his final year his rating returned to the heights of his early popularity.
42. Edward Said, *Orientalism* (New York: Random House, 1978).
43. Of course, in recent years, China has considerably reformed its economy and embraced market reforms, although this is a fact that Patten by no means dwells upon.
44. Interview in *Far Eastern Economic Review*, 22 October 1992.
45. *Letter to Hong Kong*, Radio Television Hong Kong, Radio 3, 2 July 1995. Another proponent of this view is Margaret Thatcher. In her memoirs, she states: 'The Chinese belief that the benefits of a liberal economic system can be had without a liberal political system seems to me false in the long term . . . The crackdown after the Tiananmen Square massacre in June 1989 convinced many outside observers that in China political and economic liberty were not interdependent. . . . At some point the increasing momentum of economic change in China itself will

lead to political change.' (Margaret Thatcher, *The Downing Street Years* (London: HarperCollins, 1st ed., 1995) pp. 494–5. United States President Bill Clinton has also subscribed to this view. In a press conference in January 1997 he stated as follows: 'They [China] are going through some significant economic changes, and I believe that the impulses of the society and the nature of the economic change will work together, along with the availability of information from the outside world, to increase the spirit of liberty over time. I don't think that there's any way that anyone who disagrees with that in China can hold that back – just as, eventually, the Berlin Wall fell, I just think it's inevitable.' *South China Morning Post*, 20 January 1997.

46.  See Michael R. J. Vatikiotis, *Political Change in Southeast Asia: Trimming the Banyan Tree* (London and New York: Routledge, 1996), for a recent book-length treatment of this theme.
47.  See note 41 for public opinion figures.
48.  William H. Overholt, for example, describes Patten as 'an enormously attractive personality'. In William H. Overholt, *China: the next economic superpower* (London: Weidenfield and Nicolson, 1993) p. 193.
49.  Interview with the author, Government House, 16 September 1996.

## CHAPTER 12

1.  It is notable, however, that Chinese state-backed enterprises, even before the handover, began to take control of the major British-backed corporations, along with their monopolistic advantages.
2.  *Hong Kong Standard*, 4 December 1996.
3.  Indicative of this approach, Simon Li, one of the candidates for Chief Executive, before dropping out of the race, revealed that Chinese pressure brought about a reduction in projected growth on welfare spending in the transitional budget for March 1996 from 25 to 20 per cent (*Far Eastern Economic Review*, 19 December 1996).
4.  Interview with Chris Patten, 16 September 1996, and with Edward Llewelyn, 25 January 1996.
5.  As the finishing touches were being put to the manuscript for this book, the British Government announced, on 3 February 1997, that it would issue British passports to the approximately 5 000 people belonging to ethnic minorities who would otherwise have remained stateless on the resumption of Chinese sovereignty. The ancestors of these people had come to Hong Kong from other parts of the British Empire at the behest of the British government. The British MP who sponsored the parliamentary bill to provide passports, Sir Patrick Cormack, described the decision as 'a matter of honour'. Lobbying by Chris Patten was generally credited with persuading the British Government to reverse its earlier position of not being willing to offer passports to these people.
6.  *South China Morning Post*, 13 October 1995.
7.  Alan Castro, writing in the 'Forum' column of the *Hong Kong Standard*, 18 November 1993.

8. *Sunday Times*, 3 July 1994.
9. *Hong Kong Standard*, 28 April 1995.
10. *Hong Kong Standard*, 3 May 1995.
11. *Far Eastern Economic Review*, 30 May 1996.
12. On the one hand they will not participate in the provisional legislature; on the other, it is likely that the electoral arrangements prepared by the provisional legislature will be less in their favour; in addition press coverage is inevitably likely to become less sympathetic to their cause.
13. Michael R. J. Vatikiotis, *Political Change in Southeast Asia: Trimming the Banyan Tree* (London and New York: Routledge, 1996) p. 194.

# Index

in spite of guarantees in, 215
internationalisation HK breach
　　of, 69, 126
judges to sit from other
　　jurisdictions, 75
lack of precision in, 123
land issues separate from, 73
last minute inclusion of 'elections'
　　in, 53
Legco rejection of JLG and, 76
Lu Ping attacks Patten over, 118
no interference in HK affairs
　　in, 57
paragraph 49 on elections in, 188
Patten briefs Legco
　　regarding, 120, 122
Patten's maiden speech on, 91–93
policy speech and, 108–109, 114,
　　116
possibility of direct elections
　　and, 64, 141, 142, 143
power used benevolently and, 205
signing ceremony for, 50, 173
sold to HK on autonomy issue, 72
tenth round negotiations and, 135
the best deal?, 51
White paper with draft of, 45
12 point basis for, 37
'3 legged stool' and, 133
50 years and, 140
Joss, 137

Kempis, Thomas a, 205
Keswick, Henry, 124, 130
King, Ambrose Yeo-chi, 24
King, Larry, 126, 194
Kissinger, Henry, 27, 50
Korea, 12, 202
　　war, 22, 24, 52
Kowloon, 12, 13, 16, 29
Kow-towing, xi, 11, 32, 37, 74, 93,
　　116, 139
Kress, Gunther, 192, 194
Krushchev, Nikita, 29

Labouchere, Henry, 17
Labour Party, 22
Lam, Peggy, 167
Lancashire Cottonware, 12

Lau, Emily, 121, 150, 151, 167, 173,
　　194
Lau Siu-Kai, 165
Lee, Alan, 121, 150
Lee Kuan Yew, 36, 37, 221
Lee, Martin, 45, 63, 64, 65, 66, 67,
　　69, 71, 72, 76, 81, 89, 101, 103,
　　108, 111, 121, 124, 139, 151, 169,
　　175, 184, 188
Lee Teng-hui, 178
Legco (Legislative Council), 17, 22,
　　23, 24, 25, 30, 35, 43, 44, 53, 54,
　　59, 60, 67, 76, 79, 80, 96, 100,
　　102, 103, 108, 109, 111, 112, 114,
　　116, 119, 120, 121, 122, 125, 128,
　　132, 133, 135, 136, 137, 138, 139,
　　144, 145, 148, 150, 151, 152, 161,
　　162, 165, 166, 167, 168, 173, 175,
　　182, 183, 188, 192, 203, 205, 206
Leung, Lawrence, 206, 207
Li Chuwen, 38
Li, Eric, 150
Li, Fred, 111
Li Hou, 64
Li Lanqing, 130
Li Ka-shing, 186
Li Ruihuan, 15, 207
Li, Simon, 184
Liao, Donald, 130
Lin Zexu, 8
Lindsay, John, 85
Llewellyn, Edward, 99, 148, 217
Lo, Christine, 167
Lo, T.S., 60, 183, 184
Lo, Vincent, 124
London, 40
London, Jack, 190
Lu Ping, 64, 81, 100, 112, 116, 117,
　　118, 119, 120, 129, 131, 148, 172,
　　177, 179, 181, 182, 193, 198, 220
Luce, Richard, 45, 54
Lushun, (Port Arthur), 13

Macartney, Lord, 4
Macau, 15, 28
Macdonald, Malcolm, 29
MacLaren, Malcolm, 134
MacLehose, Lord Murray, 25, 26,
　　27, 30, 31